KU-444-470

Broken

Broken

The most shocking childhood story ever told.
An inspirational author who survived it.

SHY KEENAN

MARDLE

Published in 2022 by Mardle Books
15 Church Road
London, SW13 9HE
www.mardlebooks.com

Text © 2022 Shy Keenan

Paperback ISBN 9781914451003
eBook ISBN 9781914451652

All rights reserved. No part of this publication may be reproduced in any form or
by any means — electronic, mechanical, photocopying, recording, or otherwise —
or stored in any retrieval system of any nature without prior written permission
from the copyright holders. Shy Keenan has asserted her moral right to be
identified as the author of this work in accordance with the Copyright, Designs
and Patents Act of 1988.

A CIP catalogue record for this book is available from the British Library.

Every reasonable effort has been made to trace copyright-holders of material
reproduced in this book, but if any have been inadvertently overlooked the
publishers would be glad to hear from them.

Design and typesetting by Danny Lyle

Printed in the UK

10 9 8 7 6 5 4 3 2 1

Cover image: Shutterstock

First published in Great Britain in 2008 by Hodder & Stoughton.

I dedicate this book to all those who have
loved and supported me and my faith in good.

Publisher's Note
Names and locations have been changed throughout
in order to protect the identities of individuals.

Prologue

Hello, my name is Shy Keenan, I was born and broken in Birkenhead, and was abused from infancy by a network of every kind of pervert from 'thinks it's love' to 'show it hurts', all the way through to 'smile for the camera'. They were supported, as always, by many witting and unwitting facilitators. I entered the world unwanted and was beaten, sold, swapped, photographed, filmed, left for dead, betrayed, ignored, orphaned and booted into adulthood; at which point I was branded the problem and left completely on my own.

My childhood was stolen, as was my education. I was brought up almost entirely by dodgy authority care, a shed load of perverts and lunatics, with one or two decent people dotted about and I was educated almost entirely by the media. It would be impossible to tell you everything that has happened to me. I don't think I could re-live my whole childhood and survive it; however, I promise that aside from changing a few names and places to respect the victims' rights to privacy, I will be honest – good and bad.

It is fair to say that society in general has certain low expectations of their victims of child sexual abuse. Some seem to believe that we're all destined for a life on the dark, wild, wrong side of the benefit-claiming, drug-blurred tracks. All broken beyond help, with no place in a normal society. I've spent my whole life trying hard not to live up to those expectations.

Like many who grew up in the early 1970s, my own teenage years were also full of maxi-skirts, flared trousers, platform shoes, bird's-nest perms, Chopper bikes, Waltons' Mountain, the BBC Top 20, Motown, the Osmonds, Cagney and Lacey, Charlie's Angels (I was Kelly) and Starsky and Hutch.

Where I came from, anything that made you different made you a target. In the council estates of Birkenhead, if none of the usual differences applied – like skin colour, religion, shape or size – then you were frequently cornered by the ultimate question: "Which football team do you support?" Depending on your answer, you would either be "beaten back to childhood" or left to fight another day. People actually died if they didn't get this answer right.

You also had to be very careful about which council-house estate you openly admitted to being from – was it the Nocy, the Woody or the Ford? This struck me as very unfair – at least with the football nutters you had something to go on (you would look for a team scarf or a tattoo scratched into their foreheads and would know to say to them that you supported that team too), but it was impossible to tell by appearances alone, which estate you should tell someone you were from. I found that it was always best to answer whilst running away. I was a Nocy girl, and I can remember on several occasions attempting to put on a Scottish accent or pretending to be visiting from so far away that I couldn't possibly have done anything to annoy or offend whoever my interrogator was.

Prologue

For many of the kids who lived on the estates, school was an irritating necessity, but all too often it was also the only place they got fed. The boys were often heavy-drinking, smoking, drug-taking, sexist, racist, smack first football nuts. The girls were just as violent; they could bicker and gossip for England, and win any drama-queen award going. Those girls not quickly married off at 16, were either pregnant by 14 (required to secure that crucial council flat) or aspired to work at the Birkenhead Outdoor Market.

For some reason, I have always wanted so much more from my life. Now, all these years on, what I have come to learn is that for those of us who have been abused, whatever path we take and however well we recover our lives, most of us are made to work very hard just to prevent ourselves from becoming the stereotype of the victim of child sexual abuse. The feared social outcasts, rejected and discriminated against because someone else committed a crime upon them. I always wanted a life free from all of that and often found it very hard to find my way.

When my childhood abusers took my childhood and stole my innocence, they also condemned me to various multiple life sentences which have stolen parts of my adulthood. To make things worse, most of these life sentences don't even become apparent until later on in life.

One of the life sentences was the unwelcome insight into how paedophiles' minds actually work. Only as I grew up, did I realise the full burden of this insight; that said, I also came to learn what an incredible weapon this insight is, in the fight against paedophiles.

As for me, I'm just an ordinary, imperfect, part-broken soul, who knows what child abusers want to keep secret and why.

Using that insight, I have gone from being the child molester's most favourite sex toy, to their worst possible nightmare.

Personally, I still have a long way to go, but I'm closer to being the person I had always hoped to be, than anything like the person my childhood abusers had planned for me. They'd already corrupted my childhood, stolen my innocence and set a firm and fatal path for what was meant to be my future - no doubt selling my body and soul, living homeless on the streets of London and sticking God knows what in my arm or down my throat.

Still, I won't pretend that every decision I've made has been the intelligent, life-enhancing step forward that I had hoped it would be. I have indeed made some stupid, monumental mistakes in my life, for which I accept full responsibility and for which I have always paid twice. Nor will I pretend that all that has happened to me didn't hurt or affect me; it did and I acknowledge that because of it, I have bits of me that work and bits of me that don't, but I work hard to manage, accept and embrace them all as best I can.

I was born a fighter with a fire inside of me, a will to survive. I call it my Phoenix fire, but you will see others call it all kinds of everything throughout my life. Along with my faith, my Phoenix fire has helped me fight the total corruption of me and my dreams. As a child, I was always the first one to speak up and the last one to shut up, with an answer for everything (not always the right one, mind) and the 'last word' queen.

I don't really have a god; I'm not the religious kind, but I do believe in good, which is just one more 'o'... I believe in the good and the bad that humans can do in the here and the now. I survived (and live my life now) by putting my faith in the good that people do. Putting my faith in their collective greater good keeps me spiritually grounded. Believe me, having faith in living, breathing human beings is no easy option. My faith in good people has been tested, it has flagged and even lost its way, but it is why I'm still here and it will always be at the very heart of who I want to be.

I'm not a victim: this word only describes what happened to me; it doesn't define me. Nor am I a survivor: this almost suggests I'm over it, when this isn't true either. I am a Phoenix, rising from the ashes of a broken life, an ongoing survival in progress.

I have for many years resisted all requests for me to write a book about my life. It has always seemed just too painful and difficult to put down on paper the complicated nightmare that was my childhood, and, in parts, my adulthood, without being me, all of me and nothing but me – at my very best and worst. That said, I have always lived by the 'be frightened and do it anyway' school of thought, but I confess I am a little scared of letting you this close and worried about how we will both cope with that.

Before we start, I want you to know that I love… and am loved. My own family (as opposed to my birth family) describe me as "three times stronger than any household bleach" and claim I have sarcastic Tourette's. I do indeed have my share of obsessive compulsive disorders and at the age of 44, am still a little immature for a grown-up, but I'm stronger now than I've ever been and more able to let you in.

I feel I must warn you that since childhood I've had an external and internal monologue constantly playing. To be clear, I don't mean I hear voices: both monologues are me. For me, the internal monologue is like an irreverent, cynical, self-doubting mind clatter, that often sits just behind the unwelcome visual flashbacks. Although I hope my external monologue has a more insightful and diplomatic aspect to it, I do constantly struggle to keep myself from saying out loud what my internal monologue is thinking. Sometimes I'm not even aware I'm doing it, and other times I am, but find it literally impossible not to voice it.

I have thought long and hard about what to share, but in order for you to see my life from where I'm standing, you really need to see some of what I'm thinking and therefore it's only fair that you see the real me, so I will try to share as much of me as I can bear to and let you be the judge.

My childhood was a dark, scary, hopeless place and we are going in more or less straight at the deep end; although this journey may be very upsetting and distressing in places, I promise, it ends as well as it can.

So, now you know what's coming, if you think you can cope, I'm ready if you are… Deep breath. Let's go.

The End

8 October 2000

My instructions were simple: remember the secret codeword for "help"; if I feel in danger, use that secret codeword; don't eat or drink anything from him; remember the questions; be friendly, smile, agree with everything he says and try not to interrupt him; and under no circumstances, no matter what he says, am I to physically attack or kill him. Oh, yes, and something about "press record". All understood and agreed.

So, there I was, on the night before the big day, in a hotel room just 20 minutes from Stanley's bungalow. I was in my late thirties, but believe me, I had waited several lifetimes for this day. I was finally big enough to stand up for myself. I had all the support I needed and was ready to face my childhood abusers, chiefly the manipulative 'Beast of Birkenhead', my stepfather, Stanley Sidney Claridge. This was the cunning, steely, tower of a man who had wielded such perverted and corrupt power over so many… for so long. The team from Newsnight and I had been planning our strategy for months. Knowing my stepfather for the selfish bastard he was, and suspecting that after everything, simply walking up to his front door and knocking might just trigger his suspicions, I had decided to turn one of his own old tricks back on himself. If Stanley was getting something for nothing, he was prepared to overlook any amount of odd behaviour, so having found out what brand of cigarettes he currently smoked, the plan was now in place. Tomorrow, when the undercover surveillance team that was monitoring him told us he was in, I would go up to his door and attempt to discreetly post his favourite brand of cigarettes through the letterbox, apparently trying not to get caught, only purposely making far too much noise. This would hopefully prompt him to open the door to see who was there. He would, of course, catch me. Though confused (and delighted), Stanley would interpret my reappearance and attempt to secretly give him cigarettes as a sign that I wanted to be mates again – that all was forgiven. The conversation would then go from there.

I would ask questions about my childhood, Stanley would incriminate himself, and every single sordid detail would be recorded by cameras concealed in my clothing and then shown as part of a special edition of Newsnight to millions of viewers. It was all planned to the last detail, and I was sure it would work.

Despite my confidence, my emotions were all over the place. I stood up and paced around my hotel room. I had not knowingly been so close to Stanley in decades and I could feel that it was already too close. My stomach felt churned up, knotty. I worried myself into a tight ball as I sat thinking about all that had happened and was about to happen. I thought of everything he'd done to me, my little sister and all those others. Then I thought about the pain and grief all this would cause everyone; but when I thought about the little ones who were involved now, nothing else mattered. I stopped wearing a hole in the carpet and sat down on the bed. I felt numb and empty. I had fought and failed to stop them for so many years. I was coming into this battle as the underdog, the outcast, with my reputation in tatters and having long been branded by those from my old life as an attention-seeking liar. Now, all these years on, in order to prevent anyone from shedding doubt on my claims, I was going to record the words from the abusers' own mouths. I was going to record interviews with not just Stanley but also Reg and others who had abused me and others as children, hopefully leaving the authorities in no doubt about what they must do to stop these monsters once and for all.

I checked the digital clock on my bedside table: 10.15pm. In just under 12 hours, I would be face to face with my childhood abuser. The time had finally come – after everything, after everyone, after all these years. Suddenly it dawned on me: Oh, my God! I'm really going to do this.

I knew that nobody from my old life was going to set up a fan club in my name for what I was about to do, but the choice had always been clear to me. I believed that children were currently at serious risk from Stanley and his perverted friends. I could, like so many before me, leave the current little ones to their fate, walk away and continue to live my own life, or I could stand up for them. Making the decision was easy, but I certainly wasn't taking the easy option.

I can find no words to fully explain what it is like to face up to your abuser. It is like walking into a wall of flames and knowing just how much it is going to hurt, but knowing you have no choice: I had tried everything else to get Stanley and the others stopped – this was the only way.

All this time on from the abuse, I now had my own wonderful family. There were good decent members of my birth family who weren't abused or abusive and didn't know anything was happening but we didn't get to see them very much. That said, my own broken and dysfunctional birth family were strangers to me, but I had always felt I had a responsibility to help them. Even so, I feared that what I was about to reveal on television could be very damaging to my own family. Their lives could be put in danger. Paedophiles are a notoriously close-knit network and they operate on fear. With a sickening lurch, having remembered all that had happened in the past, I knew that tomorrow's interview would mean I could lose my family, my career and even my mind. I checked the digital clock again. It was now 11pm and getting late, but I needed to double-check that my family would be safe once the programme was aired, so I picked up the phone and through my tears called home and went over the plans for them to be flown abroad to safety if it was needed, once the programme went out.

That night in the hotel room, my fears were deafening. I felt a familiar sense of foreboding as I tried to ignore the persistent mind clatter. All my old worries came flooding back to haunt me: 'Nobody wants your help. They won't thank you for digging all this up again!'; 'You are about to destroy your life, your future and everything you hold dear. They will never believe you and you will never stop them!'; 'How many times must certain people stab you in the back before you register enough pain to run, you idiot!'

My very worst fear was that I would kill Stanley the moment I set eyes on him. As an adult, I had moved on well past my smacky days, but I still knew it would take a monumental effort on my part not to attack him. This was the man who hurt me, my sister and all those others. He was like some insidious cancer that destroyed his family and screwed the life out of everyone he touched. He certainly deserved to be punished, but I'm no killer. I wanted him and his friends stopped, and I wanted justice for the victims, but the thought of spending the rest of my life in jail because of that sorry excuse for a human, was never a real option for me.

You might think it strange that I wasn't worried about him doing anything to me. Stanley abused children and so I didn't consider that he would dare to sexually abuse the grown-up me, plus I was big enough to stand up for myself if I needed to. Just then, another thought came into my head; a thought so terrifying that it made me feel physically sick. It was not until that moment that I truly understood what I had agreed to do. In order to encourage Stanley to talk to me, I was going to have to meet him not as my current self, but pretending to be the confused and messed-up child he used to sexually abuse and exploit, someone who had never really posed any effective threat to him. I could not stop this pretence until the evidence needed was absolutely secure. In order to stop him, I would have to be that child again. This realisation terrified and repulsed me.

My childhood was now playing back like a film inside my head, more vividly than ever before. I had spent years trying not to think about all of this, separating and blocking painful memories, avoiding anything that would trigger them, but the knowledge that I would have to face Stanley and show my old vulnerabilities to him brought it all flooding back. When

Broken

I couldn't stop the memories from coming, I started to feel overwhelmed and panicky. What was happening? I have to be at my most calm and focused tomorrow! Do I drink myself stupid and block it out, or do I play the scary movie? If I play the scary movie, will it frighten me away, or will it just strengthen my resolve?

Skip or play movie?

Play Movie

I am the second child of Jennifer and only child of Frederick Wootton. My mother, Jennifer Anne Scott, was born in Moreton, Merseyside, in 1945, at the end of World War II. She was born to poor northern parents and had three elder sisters and, later, a younger brother.

Merseyside was a frequent target for the German bombing raids during the war, not least because of the crucial Liverpool docks and ports, which were thriving just next door. Despite the air raids, the devastated landscape and all the hardships that the war brought, a very basic local infrastructure survived and things like schools, hospitals, transport and utilities were limited but operational.

Jennifer's mother, Nanny Scott, was a popular local barmaid and bus clippie, and she worked very long hours. She married young but was still a particular favourite at the local GI camp at Upton and was, by all accounts, the envy of many, with her well-stocked cupboard of cocoa powder, nylons, chewing gum, tinned fruit and Spam. Despite her highly friendly disposition (i.e. promiscuity) towards the opposite sex, she was reportedly an emotionally unavailable and physically distant parent, who seemed unable to nurture her children.

Grandpa Scott spent many of his young family's early years abroad, fighting with the Desert Rats in Egypt. He was known as a fairly amiable, friendly chap, but was prone to violent outbursts. When he returned home from the war, he took up many jobs, including working for the local council and as an ambulance man's assistant.

Despite being a mostly absent parent, it appears that Grandpa Scott was more loving than his wife and seemed content to accept the sudden and mysterious growth of his family during his many lengthy military tours of duty. Upon viewing old pictures of the whole family, it's fair to say that of their five children, the only one who actually looked like Grandpa Scott was the first one. Still, they seemed happy with their marriage and in the end were only separated by death. They had a small, modest three-bedroom home in Willaston Road, Moreton. Their daily work shifts regularly overlapped, which invariably resulted in their five small children being left home alone to fend for themselves. Thankfully, things have now changed, but this practice was not considered neglect in the 1940s and 1950s.

By the time she was seven, the eldest daughter, Violet, was being fully utilised as a by-proxy mother and was full-time housekeeper and carer to her siblings. It was no easy task for such a young child to look after, or keep silent, four hungry, lively, bored children, as well as two mostly absent 'working or sleeping' parents, at the same time as balancing the food and clothing ration books whilst enduring the regular parental beatings for any trouble (real or imagined) from her or any of the other children.

To make matters worse, one of those siblings was the fiercely independent hurricane, Jennifer, who though the youngest of the girls, was fast becoming the Scott family wild child. Determined to do everything her own way, she was a selfish, lazy, incorrigible liar. She was also a habitual shoplifter, but wasn't particularly street-smart or intelligent. By the age of just 10 or 11, her education may have been sorely lacking, but she knew one thing for certain: she was fully aware that boys liked having sex with girls.

At 12, Jennifer was so far off the rails that the local Social Services advised my despairing grandparents to send Jennifer away to a mixed 'special' boarding school for maladjusted children called Farney Close, in Haywards Heath. It was headed by a Quaker couple called the Reverend and Mrs Wallbridge, and it was here that Jennifer first met my birth father, the shy but far from retiring Robert Frederick Wootton. Robert Wootton was a dark-haired London lad, who was mad on motorbikes (anybody's motorbikes). He was considered by some to be a lovable but very criminal rogue. He was undoubtedly more streetwise than Jennifer, but was easily led, so she soon had him wrapped round her little finger. He was apparently quick-tempered and flighty, with an endearing Robin Hood complex.

Little is known about my father's family or his life before he went to Farney Close. What is known is that he was from a working-class family who could no longer deal with his criminal behaviour and who hoped he would settle down at boarding school and focus on his education.

Needless to say, Fred, as he was also known, was having none of that. He was girl-shy and desperate to lose his virginity. At Farney Close School, he was far away from his parents' strict rules about girls and was living in an impressive stately home in the beautiful Sussex countryside. The grounds were big enough to hide whatever the girls and boys who attended the school were doing.

He hoped that one day soon one of those girls might help him through his shyness and on to the other side of his virginity. Along comes Jennifer, the girl who did, by all accounts, oblige many such rides through the Sussex country lanes.

From then on, my parents were a tempestuous on-again-off-again couple. They were only about 13 or 14 when they first met, but theirs was an explosive relationship, and they fought often and openly. At best, their relationship was fragile, at worst, toxic and abusive. They seemed at their strongest when they worked together at what they both had in common and enjoyed: stealing.

Much of their arguing was about money and the acquisition of it, particularly Jennifer's spending, as well as her latest clumsy tangle with the law or her flirtatious promiscuity. They were both habitual liars, both as bad as each other; however, from what I've been told, it seems Fred loved Jennifer far more than she ever loved him, and their crimes, and more importantly the proceeds, were all that kept them together.

When she turned 16, Jennifer left school and returned home to live with her parents, but her link to Farney Close School was not completely severed: the kindly headmaster, Reverend Wallbridge, and his wife felt a responsibility to this clearly troubled young girl and so stayed in touch with her, helping out when they could.

Jennifer took full advantage of the charity of this couple and would return to the school to see them whenever the fancy took her, or whenever she wanted something. Fred remained at Farney Close. Very soon after Jennifer left school, in late 1961, she had her first child to a bus conductor she had met only briefly. Before Jennifer could finish saying, "I'm pregnant and it's yours," the baby's father had run as far and as fast as he possibly could, and was never to be seen or heard of again. For a while, Jennifer's relationship with Fred was over.

Jennifer's care of her baby was so appalling that her parents intervened and the help of Reverend and Mrs Wallbridge was once again called upon. They took the baby away to live with another family.

Over the following months, Jennifer took endless jobs for short periods of time, but only took work that gave her access to money she could steal. Her CV reads more like a list of businesses she stole from (and for how long) than an actual 'resume'.

My mother didn't just steal from strangers; she would steal from her own family, and would invariably cause further family upheaval and upset by lying when caught. She was also becoming more and more known to the local police.

In between undermining and exploiting her family, stealing, sowing her wild oats and dumping off her first-born without missing a beat, Jennifer hooked up with Fred again when she went to visit the Wallbridges at Farney Close School. In no time at all she was pregnant by him. After a shotgun wedding and just 14 months after her first child, Jennifer gave birth to me, her second daughter, Karen, in 1963.

At first Fred and Jennifer carted me around to various friends and family members, living wherever someone would put us all up. This soon wore very thin and my parents finally got a place in Conway Road, Birkenhead, in the flat below Jennifer's eldest sister, Violet.

Though I was just a tiny baby, Jennifer and Fred would often leave me alone (day or night) for hours on end, while they went out stealing, or trying to steal, or enjoying the proceeds of stealing. The flat was small, basic and started out clean, but in no time at all the piles of dirty dishes, laundry and rubbish had grown and the flat seemed smaller still. Added to this, it had developed a very unpleasant, pungent, eye-watering smell and was crawling with bugs, especially cockroaches.

When my parents left the flat, they would leave a light on and sometimes the radio, turned up a little too loud for the neighbours' liking. The neighbours didn't have to endure it for very long, though: the electric was on a coin-operated meter and would soon run out, turning off the radio and plunging the flat into darkness. The smell from food rotting in the now warmer fridge would bring even more tears to your eyes.

When I was a baby, the sixties were in full swing. Liverpool and Merseyside swung with the hardcore, drug- and drink-fuelled best, and Fred and Jennifer were no exception. They would return home at all hours, often drunk, often arguing or fighting, and always loud enough for the whole street to hear. They continued to leave me alone in the flat, returning only when it suited them.

Other family members have told me I was a sweet, loving infant who liked being cuddled, even though it must have hurt, because I had a very painful skin condition. I was red all over, with patches of bleeding sores covering about 60 per cent of my body. I was very underweight and initially cried a lot. After a while, though, I'm told I became an unusually silent child. I was rarely seen or heard by anyone for long periods of time. Fred and Jennifer never let anyone into the flat, always choosing to visit friends and relatives, so nobody saw the many part-healed injuries or the bug-infested, urine-soaked cot that I was all but chained – half naked – to 24 hours a day. Nobody saw the festering dirty nappies or sucked-dry baby bottles. Nobody saw, that is, until one day when, unusually, Violet, Jennifer's eldest sister, was home during the day and heard the most heartbreaking crying, seemingly coming from a child in the same building. Upon investigation, she traced the cries to her sister's flat below. She knew that Fred and Jennifer were out, so forced entry and discovered a red-raw and emaciated baby in a rancid cot.

Jennifer's family intervened as best they could and we were moved out of the flat. I was finally seen by a doctor for the first time since birth and my skin condition was healed.

The Wallbridges helped out by monitoring Fred and Jennifer on and off for the duration of my childhood. They stayed in touch with Jennifer and Fred throughout their lives, doing their best to help them by taking me off their hands for short periods of time.

During these early 'Karen-free' periods, Fred and Jennifer planned their biggest theft ever – they were going to rob a petrol station. The plan was as follows: Jennifer would apply to work for the local garage and, while alone on duty, this poor young woman would be robbed at knifepoint and the cash in the till would be taken by a masked armed robber. Following this terrible, shocking crime, the victim, Jennifer, would resign due to post-traumatic stress.

The scene was set, the robbery went according to plan, but it all went horribly wrong when Jennifer, by now well-known to the police, was immediately suspected as having been involved in the crime.

An investigating police officer went speeding round to Jennifer's home to arrest and interview her. Jennifer played her get-out-of-jail-free card and in no time was having passionate, unbridled sex with said police officer. Needless to say, the cash was returned and the investigation into Jennifer's part in the crime was soon dropped.

Shortly after, Jennifer discovered that she was pregnant, and in 1964, her third child, Denise, was born, just 12 months after me. The police officer, who was married with children, now found himself at the sharp end of Jennifer's other skill: manipulation. The pregnancy and resulting child were used to blackmail cash from the errant police officer; Jennifer threatened his reputation, his job, his marriage and his life as he knew it. In the end, he left his job and moved his family abroad; he kept in very brief and intermittent touch, but eventually this stopped altogether.

My mother then decided that she no longer wanted or needed Fred; but what she did want was a decent house. She decided not to break the news to Fred about their broken relationship just yet. With her growing family, Jennifer was moved to the top of the council's waiting list for housing. Even so, she wanted to make absolutely certain that she would get the house she longed for.

So, she approached the Wallbridges, claiming to have settled down, and with their wonderful help, found religion and saw the error of her ways. She appealed to the Wallbridges' good nature to help support her housing application.

Once again, her artful manipulation worked and before long we were all living in a very nice, bright, mid-terrace house in Cherrytree Road, Moreton. Fred was working, Jennifer was stealing, and they were both ignoring their children.

Jennifer may not have told Fred how she really felt about him, but she seemed unable to stop herself from showing it. This sent the fighting and arguing through the roof. In one of these rows, Jennifer finally told Fred that she didn't love him, never had and wanted him gone, and he was then unceremoniously booted out. On leaving, my father then apparently accidentally set fire to the house. When the fire crew arrived, one child was still missing. The fireman entered the house and found me in a locked wardrobe, frightened and in shock, but otherwise fine.

The house was mainly smoke-damaged and easily repaired. With the only breadwinner gone, Jennifer found herself on benefits and on her own, with very small children. She had only ever wanted the house so now needed to offload the children.

She once again went cap-in-hand to the Wallbridges, pleading poverty, abandonment and being completely unable to cope with the children alone; exasperated, they bluntly insisted that she stick at it and just learn to cope.

Jennifer returned enraged and took to visiting friends and relatives with her children, all day, every day and simply let them run wild; suffice to say, wherever she went, she always stayed long enough for mealtimes. We were bundled from one house to the next.

It was an inauspicious start to my life, but no one could have anticipated just how bad things were about to get. Jennifer was about to meet my stepfather, Stanley Sidney Claridge.

Stanley Claridge came from a very large family. His mother died young, and as his father was overseas with the military, young Stanley and his siblings were placed into the care of a Barnardo's children's home until they were all eventually adopted and fostered by various members of the extended Claridge family. All, that is, except for Stanley: nobody wanted strange, weird Stanley. In the end, Stanley's aunt and uncle took pity on him and took him in and at around the age of 10, he started calling them Mum and Dad.

Stanley's version of his time at the Barnardo's home changes almost every time you ask him, but the underlying themes tend to remain the same: his sisters and brothers hated him, as did everyone else; he had no friends; he was sexually abused at the home, but claims he enjoyed this attention. He occasionally admits that the abuse was perpetrated by a male adult, and on rarer occasions still, he will tell you that both he and the male adult sexually abused other children together. He never admits to both things at the same time.

Stanley found the company of women challenging, so he frequently sought the company of much younger boys. He was happy to have this behaviour misunderstood by most as homo-sexuality. The unjust laws surrounding this issue have now been changed, but in those days, homosexuality was considered to be one of the most appalling, perverted criminal offences you could commit, punishable by jail. Still, he seemed happier for people to think of him as homosexual than to discover the real truth.

Concerned about him, his adoptive mother and the lady we all called Nanny Claridge, decided to put him in the military to make a proper man of him. He went overseas with the army, working as a cook's assistant and bottle-washer. Unfortunately, Nanny Claridge's plan backfired and Stanley was able to explore his sexuality further while in the army. He often brought young men back to his Aunt Lil's house whilst on military leave.

Now increasingly worried about his behaviour and reputation, Nanny Claridge forced him out of the army and into a loveless marriage that produced two children. The speedy marriage was soon followed by a speedy divorce. As an adult, he was a drunken, violent and abusive man, and had clearly graduated from the same school of parenting as Jennifer. Somehow, though, when the children's mother abandoned them, Stanley was awarded full custody of his two very young children; one eventually went to live abroad, but his daughter, Roma, was left to live with him.

In 1965, Stanley was a manual labourer and lived in a small, grim, three-bedroom mid-terrace house on Tudor Road, in Southall, London. It was a quiet road just off a very busy high street, nestled amid the rows of tiny, identical streets and the rows of tiny, identical houses. Stanley's street had a much-favoured local sweetshop at the top, Tudor Road Primary School at the bottom and a children's play park two alleys behind us.

Stanley was a compulsive liar and was prone to gross exaggeration: he lied about his house, his money and himself. It was his lies that made Jennifer notice him.

Stanley and Jennifer had relations in common – Ken, Jennifer's brother, was married to Pat Claridge, who was Stanley's cousin (whom he now called his sister) and the real daughter of Nanny and Grandpa Claridge. After meeting each other at a Claridge family get-together, and believing every lie that came out of his mouth, Jennifer set her sights on Stanley. When they met, my mother was 20 years old and her children were under four, while divorced Stanley was 37.

Jennifer was still married to my father, Fred, and had heard about Stanley's strangeness, but all she could see were the pound signs he was talking up, a ready-made home and full-time cleaner and babysitter in the form of Stanley's young daughter, Roma. And all this in exciting, happening London. Once my mother had decided she wanted Stanley, there was nothing in this world that could stop her. She almost instinctively noticed Stanley's lack of confidence around women and used her sexual confidence to overwhelm him. She also noticed that the less she appeared to care, the more he appeared to try to make her.

Stanley was excited beyond words to meet her little girls for the first time. He simply couldn't wait and wouldn't stop going on about them. When was he going to meet them for the first time? Can it be soon? He just wanted to care for them, cook for them, wash them, put them to bed – you know, daddy stuff.

From the beginning of Stanley and Jennifer's relationship, Stanley's now 10-year-old daughter, Roma, deeply resented us all, and was not backwards in showing it. That said, what we didn't know about Roma back then was that she had been abandoned and rejected by her own mother and their family, who lived just three streets away.

Roma loved her father as he was all she had and all she had ever known, but he treated her appallingly. She had suffered and had been frequently sent away if she became too difficult. Out of the blue, she was suddenly called back from being away, only to find, upon her return, a new strange-speaking stepmother and new step- sisters, stealing all of her father's attention and turning her into the family's fulltime babysitter and house slave.

All of Jennifer's dreams of grandeur and riches were quickly disappointed once she visited Stanley's home and saw for herself where he lived and worked. Stanley had grossly exaggerated the comfort in which he lived and the money he earned, but far from putting her off, she instead saw his lies as something to hold over him: if he had lied, it was because he wanted to impress her. In any event, anything had to be better than the life she had back in Moreton, so when he asked her to move in with him not long after they met, she packed her bags and moved us all to London before he could finish the sentence.

As far as she was concerned, anyone who wanted to take care of her children was welcome to them. And he certainly seemed eager enough to do that, freeing her to do whatever she wanted. Life, for Jennifer, was definitely on the up.

First Memories

Most people's first memories tend to be visual images; mine are more of senses, smells and feelings, like hunger, fear or distress. The few early visual memories that I do have are like photographs and are accompanied by those feelings. They seem random and patchy.

One memory must be from when I was very young, when my mum and birth father were still together. I remember that small, dark, dank room, with a grubby cot jammed behind the door. The door bashed into the cot whenever it was opened and always startled me. I can recall feeling alone, cold, wet and frightened. I was crying because something kept crawling all over me – in my ears, my mouth, my nose – and biting my already painful skin. I remember that no amount of crying ever made the faces come.

In another memory – it must have been when my father, whom I only recognised back then as the dark-haired man's face, set fire to the house – I see a cleaner, more spacious room. I am standing in a cot, hungry, shivering slightly. There are faces around me shouting, fighting. I feel frightened and there's red stuff running down the dark-haired man's face. He picks me up and puts me in a wardrobe, which terrifies me because it's full of tiny spiders. I hate spiders. I recall a horrible smell that made me cry.

Then suddenly the wardrobe doors burst open. I see a big, nice face with a yellow hat. This man is pulling me out of the wardrobe. He carries me out of the smelly house and into a huge white van. He sits in the back of the van with me. It's exciting and makes a loud noise. We arrive at a hospital and I refuse to let go of the yellow hat man's arm. He's so kind I want him to stay. I scream and grip his sleeve and won't let go. The poor man has to leave his jacket with me to pacify me. I also remember the dark-haired lady's eyes, my mother's eyes. They look right at me, but never seem to see me. She could stand right next to me but not hear me. I'm sure I cried sometimes just to check.

One time I remember feeling pleased, because the dark-haired lady looked like she was going to pick me up when I was crying; then, suddenly, I was being yanked out of the cot by my arm, across the room. Everything went black and I woke up on the floor, still crying. Next thing I knew the dark-haired lady's face was just inches away from mine. She was very angry and was screaming. She was holding me up to her face by my hair as she yelled at me. I had no idea what she was saying.

Then suddenly everything was different. The dark-haired man had gone and there was a man with a shiny head and blue eyes instead. After this, as I reach the age of around three or four, my memory starts to fall into slightly sharper focus.

The first time we all went to visit Shiny Head at his home stands out clearly in my mind. I remember we were all in his living room when he picked me up and sat me on his lap. As I was sitting on his lap, his hands slipped up my dress and I remember a sharp, searing pain in my bottom. I yelped and squirmed, trying to get off his lap, but the dark-haired lady looked angry and told me to be nice to my new daddy. I knew I didn't want the dark-haired lady to be angry, so I sat still.

Shiny Head seemed nice and friendly, although I didn't like how his scratchy face hurt mine, or how hard he held me on his lap and how sitting there made my bum sore. I didn't really know him, but I knew enough to do as I was told, so that's what I did.

Shortly after that, we all moved to Shiny Head's home and everything seemed to change. Most of the faces I recognised disappeared, apart from the dark-haired lady who called herself Mum, and of course Shiny Head, and were replaced by new faces and new places. Shiny Head had a different dark-haired girl with him. She called Shiny Head 'Dad', but she looked cross all the time. Shiny Head also knew a different dark-haired face who was there sometimes; he seemed quite scary to me. It was around this time, in this new place, that I started to see the bright blue and white flashing lights that I would come to know so well.

Just a few weeks after we'd moved in with Shiny Head, when I was three or four, I remember being in a darkened room and lying naked on a table that seemed a long way from the ground. A harsh, bright light kept flashing in my eyes, making them sting and water. I was aware of faces in the room, but I didn't know who they belonged to. A strange clicking sound always followed the flashing light, and I remember feeling cold and worried.

Then I saw Shiny Head and the new dark-haired face walking round the table looking down at me. Suddenly, flashing white and blue lights exploded in my head, followed by the most excruciating, searing pain coming from my lower body. I felt winded and couldn't breathe. I started to scream as the pain shot through me. My eyes were shut tight, and I sobbed when I could breathe enough to do so. I opened my eyes to see what the faces were doing and saw through my tears that Shiny Head was directly above me, moving up and down.

I realised that Shiny Head down meant less pain, so I tried to move away from the Shiny Head up movement. It was then that I realised that I was unable to move my arms. I didn't know why or how; I just knew I couldn't move them at all.

My legs, too, were being squashed by Shiny Head, and I felt unable to fight or move, so I stopped trying. When the movement eventually stopped and I caught my breath, I screamed. Shiny Head punched me hard across the side of my head. He did it again and again. I saw the bright lights in my head every time Shiny Head hit me on it and I started to understand that the flashing lights in my head meant that pain was never far behind. I was too shocked to make another sound.

I was trying to catch my breath when the movement very quickly started again, only now it was the dark-haired face. The pain was the same – it burned its way through my lower body – but this time I felt like I needed to poo.

I couldn't feel my legs anymore and was sure that I was pooing. I could smell it and I could feel it. I tried to look down to see, but the dark-haired face, kept trying to put his mouth over mine, which was making it even harder to breathe. I tried to stay still and quiet, and waited for it to stop.

The next thing I knew I was in the kitchen in the tin bath. Shiny Head and the dark-haired face were standing near to me. They looked very tall. My bottom felt raw, I was cold and my body was juddering with shock. Sitting naked in the bath, with the top of my body above the water, I felt so vulnerable and all I could think was that I didn't want to be naked in front of them ever again.

The bathwater was tepid and making me colder, but it felt like a cover, so I sank down into it, shivering and whimpering. Shiny Head rubbed what felt like liquid fire all over me, inside and outside of my very sore body. I started to cry but Shiny Head just said: "you need to make sure you're clean all over."

I couldn't have known it then, but this was the first of many of Shiny Head's infamous and much-feared tin baths. When it was finally finished and I was dressed again, I went up to my room and curled into a tight ball on my bed and quietly sobbed to myself.

For ages after I walked around like a zombie, dazed and distressed. I was suddenly snapped out of it when I found my little sister, Denise, naked and sobbing uncontrollably in the loft. Her blonde hair was sticking to her face, which was wet with tears. She was unable to speak, but she didn't need to, because I knew instinctively that what had happened to me had happened to her. I don't know what I thought other than that I understood, so I hugged her and dressed her and sat with her till she was calmer.

I felt angry: I didn't want anyone to hurt her, and I just wanted to make her feel better, so I started pulling faces and pretending to fall asleep – leaning on my bended elbow, slipping off and falling face down on to the mattress. She suddenly stopped crying and started to quietly giggle; the more she giggled, the harder I tried to make her. It made us both feel better. It always did.

It happened a lot after that, all over the house. I hated the loft. I remember once resisting going to the loft and the resulting beating from Shiny Head. He took me to the good front room, stripped me naked and took his belt to my backside and legs. It went on forever, and when he eventually did stop, there were tears streaming down my face and I was in a lot of pain. Shiny Head explained that it would have just been my backside if I hadn't moved about so much. So, I made up my mind to really try to keep still next time.

Unsurprisingly, the house didn't feel like a home; it was a poky Victorian three-bed terrace with a makeshift extension tacked on to the back of it and a tiny loft space, which was unrenovated and scarcely suitable for household storage.

As you walked through the front door and down the dingy, threadbare hall, you had the door to the good front room to your left, then the very steep staircase leading upstairs. If you turned left at the top of the stairs, there was a double bedroom at the front of the house and on the right, there were two tiny rooms looking out onto the back garden. Downstairs, at the end of the hall, there was a door that led to the tiny back living room, which had an open fireplace. This then led into the kitchen extension, which also overlooked the back garden. The toilet was outside and terrified me because it was dark and full of spiders, but eventually a corrugated-iron roof was added to join it to the kitchen/bathroom extension.

The garden was small, uneven, unkempt and more mud than grass. It had scrap and rubbish everywhere with a small ramshackle tool shed at the bottom, in stark contrast to all the other houses' gardens, which were well kept and which overlooked each other.

All in all, it was a scruffy old house that had, to put it kindly, seen better days. It had just one well-dressed room, and the rest had been left to years of wear and tear.

In this tiny, cramped house, there was no space that felt safe, nowhere I could hide away or be by myself. We lived on top of each other, and it felt like everywhere I turned I would see bizarre, horrible things going on that disturbed, frightened and confused me.

One time, a few months after we'd moved into Shiny Head's house, I walked into a room and saw Shiny Head standing there and the dark-haired face, kneeling on the floor in front of him. Shiny Head was holding his head and pushing his pee thing into his mouth. Shiny Head didn't see me, but the dark-haired face did. He gave me such a scary look that I ran away and hid. I decided to keep away from him for as long as I could.

However, a couple of days later, the dark-haired face caught me alone and took me to play at the bottom of the garden. He took me into the shed and closed the door. Suddenly he pushed me against the shed wall and roughly grabbed my hands above my head, lifting me so that my feet couldn't feel the floor. Then he used his pee thing to make the pain in my bottom and stomach start all over again. The blue and white flashing lights returned. He seemed angry at me for seeing him with Shiny Head and started calling me names like 'dirty girl and little tart'.

First Memories

After that, he took me to the shed a lot, and every time he did he made me feel like I wanted to poo. One time I pooed on him by accident and he punched me in my bottom till I screamed out for Mum. She didn't come. She was often out, or maybe she just couldn't hear me, but he stopped when I wouldn't stop screaming and let me run into the house. I didn't understand what was happening to me, I didn't even have a name for it besides 'horrible and pain' I just knew I wanted it to stop.

My mother had always been an absent parent, but when we moved into Shiny Head's house, her appearances became less and less frequent. I soon realised that it was pointless to call out for my mother when the faces hurt me. It achieved nothing. No matter how hard I cried or screamed, she never once came.

Daddy Thief

It took months before I began to understand who all the new faces were. I had only just worked out that the dark-haired girl who now lived with us was called Roma, Shiny Head's daughter and our new sister. That might sound strange, but we simply didn't function like an ordinary family. I don't remember anyone introducing me to Roma, so unless I figured it out for myself, they were all just different-shaped faces to me. What was clear, however, was that Roma resented us; she would always tell me that I was smelly, stupid and that nobody loved me, especially not her.

Back then, I never understood why this little 10-year old girl resented us so much, but as a four-year-old, there was little point trying to understand. She was convinced we were stealing her dad, and nothing I could say or do would make her change her mind.

We didn't eat a lot or regularly, but Roma was forced to cook whatever food we did eat. Her food tasted horrible. I particularly hated her breakfast bowl of salt with added porridge. As Jennifer was hardly ever home, Roma was forced to endlessly babysit us and if she ever complained, Jennifer would beat her mercilessly, scream at her for hours and then get Stanley to hit her again when he got home, which just made it harder for us to be friends.

Roma saw herself as a Cinderella and us as her wicked stepmother and stepsisters. She would spend hours telling me why her new stepmother was horrible – and she was right. Mum was just using her father, abusing her and treating her like a slave and Roma hated it.

One time Roma left me with a dead arm for months, after she'd played the 'how far up Karen's back can Karen's arm go?' game. Then there was the time she accidentally set fire to my once long hair, while combing it a little too near the kitchen stove. This really was an accident and Roma felt awful about it; I wasn't hurt at all, but I think I made a bigger fuss just to make sure she got smacked for it. She did and I was immediately sorry for doing it after I saw the beating she got.

That said, we were frightened of Roma – she made no bones about her resentment of us. She used to be her father's little princess until we came along and now she was more like his domestic slave. I didn't want to be her daddy's favourite. I just wanted to be left alone. I didn't, however, realise that back then Roma and I were both talking about a very different kind of favourite.

By the time I was five, in 1968, there seemed to be more and more faces making the pain and the horrible happen – there was a new dark-haired face, hairy face, stinky face, angry face, red face, pain face, big-head face and spitty face... Some would have the machine that made the strange clicking sound when the light flashed. I was sure I once heard Shiny Head call it "a paranoid cammer". They would never let me see what the paranoid cammer did, but I never liked it, because it made my eyes sting.

Sometimes I would see red stuff running between my legs or coming from my nose when I touched it. It made me scared. I didn't know what it was. Eventually, I came to understand that the red stuff was blood, and all I knew about blood was that it was meant to stay on the inside or you die.

I hated what the faces were doing to me; it hurt so much. I couldn't physically stop them. I tried struggling, I tried screaming, I tried to run away, but nothing I knew of worked. Once I'd tried all that, I would just close my eyes and cry, but even that didn't help: it just made some of the faces angrier. Some would just smack me silent; others would tell me to stop crying, open my eyes and look at the paranoid cammer, yelling at me for spoiling their pictures; others would want me to look at them.

But I didn't want to see their faces or what they were doing, so I learnt to keep my eyes wide open and not cry but blur them out. I learnt to stay as still as I could and just pray for it to be over soon.

After a while, though, even staying still and quiet with my eyes open didn't help. I realised it just made some of the faces think that I liked or wanted what they were doing, and then it seemed like it went on forever. Saying no, complaining, holding my breath, fake sleeping or unconsciousness also seemed to make them think I liked or wanted it more.

It was so confusing – they would constantly be telling me that I liked what they were doing and that I wanted it, when I was absolutely sure that I didn't. I remember sitting in my room thinking, why do they keep asking me if I like it, when I tell them all the time that I don't? I say no, but they just say yes I do. They swear it's my fault and that I'm making them do this to me. Am I making them do it?

I'd curl up into a ball on the floor under the bed and rack my brains; I'd spend hours trying to figure out how I made them do it so I could just make them stop.

One morning, I was hiding in one of the tiny back bedrooms when Shiny Head came in with the dark-haired face, sat me up in the bed and took off my clothes. Shiny Head then grabbed hold of my head and put his pee thing in my mouth. He pushed it in and out of my mouth so hard that I started to gag. He stopped after a while and put my hand round his pee thing. Next he put his hand round mine, squeezing it really hard and jiggling it up and down.

The dark-haired face then grabbed my head and some of my hair and started to try to put his pee thing in my mouth. I started to cry and squeezed my lips together tight. This made him pinch my face until I cried out loud. He demanded that I open my mouth properly. Shiny Head said it would be over quicker if I just did as I was told, so I opened my mouth and the dark-haired face pushed his pee thing into it. He pushed so hard and so suddenly that I threw up a bit and couldn't stop crying no matter how much I tried. He was hurting me, but he didn't stop till he squirted hot liquid all over me. It tasted horrible and I started vomiting in earnest. As I was bent over choking and retching, Shiny Head was grumbling at me for spoiling it, but was still jiggling my hand. Then he squirted his hot liquid all over the back of my head and shoulders as I was throwing up.

When it was over, I grabbed my clothes, rushed downstairs to the toilet and carried on retching and throwing up nothing for ages. My mouth felt dirty and I washed it out over and over. My neck and face were throbbing, and my jaw was visibly bruised. I sank down on to the floor. No tears came this time. I was too shocked to cry as I literally sat there for hours.

I had a bruise on my face and my lip was split and later when I winced at the salty food Roma had just given us, she just shrugged and said, "Not to worry – it'll be a pig's foot in the morning."

I had absolutely no idea what Roma meant, but the idea that a pig's foot could grow on my face completely terrified me. All I knew about pigs' feet was that they stood in pig poo all day. Yuck!

I went back upstairs to my bedroom and spent the whole night wishing that morning wouldn't come – I really didn't want a pig's foot on my face! I thought if I stayed awake all night, I could catch and stop whoever planned to sneak into my room and put it on me. Then, somewhere in the middle of the night, I remember thinking, What if it just grows on me all by itself?

Terrified, I started rubbing the bruise until it was a bleeding, seeping, open wound. Then I jammed myself into the corner of the bedroom, with my nighty pressed hard against my face to stop anything from growing out of me, and tried to stay awake. I finally fell asleep in the small hours of the morning.

When I woke up, my injury had scabbed over and fused the nighty on to my face. I cried out in pain and shock as I tried to sit up. At that moment, Roma walked by the door and saw me. She came in and ripped the nighty off my face.

"There you go," she said. "Just give it some air."

I know she didn't know why I was hurting and I knew she wasn't trying to be unkind, but right then I wished I was bigger than her.

After Roma left, I stayed huddled on the floor in the corner of my room. I hugged my knees close to my chest and rocked back and forth. Rocking always made me feel better and I did it a lot.

Over the following months, things went from bad to worse. The faces came to me more often, making me do more and more terrible things. Every time they lay on top of me and made me do the horrible, it made me sore all over again. Afterwards, pee and poo would just come out of me whenever it wanted to – when I was walking, getting up or bending – and it would make me feel bad because I was being dirty, just like the faces told me I was.

Sometimes after the horrible, blood would come out as well as pee and poo, which frightened me and made me cry even more, but Shiny Head would get angry and say, "Fuckin' dirty tart, it's your own fault for moving about too much and not helping when I'm in the fuckin' mood. Just shut up and get on wiv it. If you just kept still and listened to what you're being told, then things wouldn't get like that, would they? What've you gotta make a fuss for, making everyone do it the fuckin' hard way? You bring it all on yourself, don't you?"

One time, I remember crying and resisting because I didn't want to put hairy face's pee thing in my mouth. It smelt bad, tasted bad and had rough bits of skin stuck on it. It was making me gag and I was trying not to do it, but Shiny Head took hold of my head and made me do it properly. My mouth and neck were sore for ages after from where he'd squeezed me, but as Shiny Head said, it was me making this happen.

I was making this happen to me so much that I can't remember a time when I wasn't sore in my pee and poo places, or a time when my body didn't hurt somewhere. I was getting really frightened because small, rough tags of skin were now growing on my hands and in my mouth. Once, when Roma caught me inspecting the inside of my mouth in the mirror she told me, "They're baby pigs' feet waiting to grow up", I completely freaked out and spent weeks trying to rub those things off me.

One day, I came in from playing outside and walked by the other small bedroom at the back of the house. As I turned to go to my room, I looked through the open door of the other little room and saw Roma laying undressed on the bed. The dark-haired face, who had no trousers on, was bouncing up and down on her. His face was all red and to my horror I realised he was doing the horrible to her.

Shiny Head suddenly appeared behind me and moved me into the doorway of my room, took his pee thing out and signalled to me to jiggle it. I don't know why but I thought Shiny Head would be angry at the dark-haired face, but he seemed more excited than angry.

Once he had finished with me, I went straight downstairs to the bathroom and scrubbed my hands and mouth until they were raw – for hours. It helped a little, but I still felt dirty.

The tap we all used only gave cold water at first, then it got hotter and hotter until it was unbearable. So, I asked Roma for some cooler water to rinse out my mouth (she didn't know why I wanted to rinse out my mouth) she picked up the kettle and poured what she thought was cool water into my mouth.

I screamed in agony as the skin peeled off my chin, neck and arm. Roma was mortified and screamed in terrified horror.

My howls of pain brought Shiny Head and Jennifer rushing to the kitchen.

"What the fuck's going on?" he roared.

I was on the floor in shocked pain and Roma was screaming that she thought the water was cold! The fact was, the kettle always sat there with cold water in it and we all often drank from it. Roma really didn't do it on purpose but Jennifer beat her as though she had. She grabbed Roma's hair and pulled it out in bleeding clumps. I tried to tell Mum but I couldn't speak. I never got the feeling that Mum or Shiny Head did any of this to protect me; they seemed more angry that we were taking up their time.

I was bundled into the car and taken to hospital. When we got there, I listened as Shiny Head explained to the people in uniform that I had had an accident and had pulled the kettle down on myself. It hurt to move my face and mouth so I couldn't argue or talk anyway, I just wanted the pain to stop.

When we got back home from the hospital, my face was in bandages and still throbbed. This didn't stop Shiny Head or the horrible; nothing ever did.

Back then we were wetting our beds almost every day and I hated the dreaded tin bath that always followed a dirty bed. The tin bath was a scratchy, oval, skin-stealing tub that would be set down close to the kitchen, for easy access to the water, which came in 'mystery' bucketfuls of either scalding-hot or freezing-cold water, thrown at you if you weren't careful, rather than poured into it. When not in use, the tin bath was kept outside in the garden. This meant that when you got in it, sometimes one side of the bath was so cold from being kept outside that if you touched it your finger would get stuck and a bit of skin would rip off when you tried to let go. The side near the fire would get so hot that it would burn you if you touched it and again steal a bit of skin. So, I learnt very quickly to stay in the middle, which was really hard to do because of Shiny Head's soapy hands.

He would stand me in that tin bath and soap up his hands and arms to the elbows, then run them all over my body, pushing his fingers roughly into my pee and poo places. At first he would pretend it was an accident, but he kept doing it and it would happen every time I had a bath. I would try to wriggle free or move away because it hurt when he was doing it and would sting for ages after he had finished, but it was never very long before he would just tell me to stand still, get his pee thing out and tell me to suck or jiggle it.

If I cried or complained, Shiny Head would just say, "You're not clean unless you wash down there, are you?" Then he would ask, "Do you like what I'm doing now?" I would always say no and he would just say that I wasn't doing it properly, that I needed to stop resisting and just relax. I remember thinking, what is 'relax'? In the end, I decided that it meant, 'Shut up and keep still.' I thought to myself, I will never be able to relax or like it, because it hurts and it's horrible.

One night I was in the tub with my sister behind me, and I was facing the other way. Shiny Head was washing out my poo place with his fingers when I heard my sister crying. I wriggled away from his fingers and turned round to see him trying to make her suck his pee thing.

I was horrified. I remember thinking, please get off her – you're hurting her. How can I stop him? What do I do? Please don't make her cry. Please stop it. She doesn't want to.

I stepped towards Shiny Head, moved her away and started jiggling his pee thing and putting it in my mouth all by myself. She fled upstairs. I stayed for a long time, making everything sore.

When Shiny Head was finished, he smiled at me. It was the first time he had ever seemed really pleased with me after the horrible. He said I did good and that if I did it as nice as that again, I could have a new dolly that was as big as me. I didn't really want a dolly, I just wanted to see my sister, so I thanked him and ran upstairs to find her.

We always wanted Mum, but Mum wasn't around. We never questioned why or did more than wonder where she was. Even when she was home, she didn't speak to me anyway. Most of the time she would say she didn't hear me or couldn't understand me. Mum didn't like me to talk to her or touch her. When I tried to talk to her, she couldn't really hear me. I remember trying to climb up on to her lap for a hug, but she'd always push me away. "I'm not the hugging kind," she'd say, as she moved me away.

One time when she said this to me, I remember thinking, but she hugs everyone else and she can hear them when they talk to her. I decided to see if talking really loud to her would work any better. She suddenly got very angry with me and hit me on the side of the head with her shoe until blood started to trickle from my ear down my neck. When she saw I was bleeding, she got scared and told me in an urgent voice, "You must have banged your ear when you fell down just then." I looked up at her, not understanding. She said even more frantically, "it was an accident wasn't it?" I knew that wasn't true, but I didn't want to make her angrier, so I agreed and she calmed down.

I remember after this she took me to a big, white place. As I walked in with her I looked around and saw there were some strange new faces sitting on one side of the room, near a tall bed, all looking straight at me and smiling. This worried me; smiling strangers near beds were never a good thing.

Mum went over to them and was talking with them. The other side of the big room was full of toys and fun things to do. I had never seen anything like it. I wanted to go over there to play with the toys, but I didn't dare.

One of the men came up to me and asked me to take off my coat and sit down. I started to feel more worried, but did as I was told. Then he asked me to play with the toys and told me he wanted to check some things on me. I looked at Mum, who gave me the kind of look you don't argue with, so I just sat there and let him do what he wanted.

He shone lights in my eyes and ears, put something on my ears and asked me if I could hear things. Next, he covered my eyes and asked me if I could see things. Then he played with some of the toys with me, and I showed him how all the shapes went in the slots. He smiled a lot and kept asking me to look at his eyes; he was very nice to me. He told me that I was very clever and that I had done well.

He asked me and Mum lots of questions. I didn't really understand most of them, so Mum did all of the talking. As they talked, I came to understand some new things like Jennifer was my mother's name; Shiny Head was called Stanley and he was apparently my father and we were apparently all one big, happy healthy Claridge family.

I was confused by much of what Mum said to the man because I already had a face in my memory that I called 'father' and some of the things she told them didn't seem like she was talking about our life, but it was all very fuzzy and I didn't understand, so I stayed silent and rocked.

The man told Mum that I didn't communicate well because I might be a bit deaf and blind; that this might be why I looked at his mouth and not his eyes when he talked to me and why I had such a toneless voice and didn't pronounce all my words properly.

Mum nodded, glancing at me with that 'don't you say a word' look on her face. Then the man asked, "Why does she rock like that?"

Mum said she didn't know. The man turned to me and said, "Karen, why do you rock back and forth like that?"

I just shook my shoulders and stared at the floor; I knew better than to answer. I listened as the man said to Mum, "It's a sign of this dress." He then explained that she could take me to see someone if she wanted to, but she didn't want to right now.

I remember thinking; doing it makes me feel better and what's wrong with my dress?

Then he asked Mum why I wasn't attending school. She said something back to him that made him look very surprised and he said, all worried, "She should be in school, you know." He asked about my bruised ear and Mum explained it was an accident. The man said, "You must be careful and make sure that she doesn't hit her head any more, Mrs Claridge, as it could be what's damaging her hearing and sight." Then Mum got up all of a sudden, said, "Come on you, we're going," and we left in an angry hurry.

From that day on, Mum seemed to be taking a bit more interest in me and I started going to the school at the end of our road, all three of us did. I was wearing a lot more clothes now and eating every day, which I liked and I wasn't being hit on the head as much any more, which I also liked.

School became a haven for me. Nobody shouted at me and nobody asked me to take off my clothes. Even so, I remember being sent home on an almost daily basis in high-waisted green PE knickers because I had wet the ones I was wearing. I had to borrow spare knickers from school, and at one point the teacher asked Mum if she could return some of them, as they were running low.

It was around this time that I was becoming more aware of having grandparents, aunties, uncles and cousins and their names. Aunt Pat was a nice-smelling, light-haired lady who always smiled at me. She was Stanley's cousin and was married to Uncle Ken, who was Mum's brother who was in the army. They had a daughter called Dona, who was my cousin and was two years older than me. I adored their visits. If I knew they were coming, I couldn't hide my excitement. I would rush to the front door as soon as their car pulled up, squealing with delight and hurling myself at them.

I loved their smiling faces and how they looked at me. I loved how they hugged me and made such a fuss of me. If ever

I cried, Aunt Pat would always pick me up, hug me better and then make me laugh with her funny faces. They never smacked me or shouted at me and always seemed so pleased to see me.

On one occasion, I was so happy to see Uncle Ken that I started to cry. He lifted me up. "Why are you crying, my love?" he asked, his forehead creasing with concern. I didn't want to say it was because I was so happy to see them, so I told him about the skin bits growing on me. I told him that pigs' feet were growing on my hand, and I didn't like them. He kissed me on the head and told me that there was no such thing and not to worry. I didn't worry any more because I knew everything he said was always true.

The next time I saw Uncle Ken, he brought with him a special medicine that made warts go away and it made my hand all better. I always felt safe and happy around 'Uncle Pat and Aunt Ken' (whenever I tried to say their names together, I always got it the wrong way around which always made them smile).

Even Mum and Stanley were nicer to us when they were around, but I felt scared for Dona because I wanted to keep her safe from the horrible. We just naturally clicked together, and whenever she came round, I stuck to her like glue. She was tall, kind, funny and very proper. We couldn't go off and play because Uncle Ken and Aunt Pat would never let her out of their sight. I loved her and felt that I should be with her all the time to protect her.

When Uncle Ken and Aunt Pat told me they loved me, I felt like my whole body would just explode; I liked the look in their eyes when they said it. I liked the feeling of having them around me so much that when it came for them to leave, I would sob uncontrollably, in utter despair. Mum and Stanley would only allow me to cry until Uncle Ken and Aunt Pat's car turned the corner at the top of our road. I used to wish the road was longer, or the car would break down, and I would keep staring after them until the very last moment, until the car went blurry and out of sight.

Once they'd gone, it was back to normal. Unfortunately, by then, 'normal' was getting harder and harder to bear.

"Mum, I Have a Secret"

What was 'normal' for me was very hard to understand or say out loud. Every day was different, and nothing stayed the same for very long. My life had no routine, except when I went to school. We didn't eat or sleep at regular times, and I could never count on anything happening the same from one day to the next.

The only thing that I could count on happening was the horrible. It seemed like they were doing it to me every day now. Whenever I knew they were hurting my sister I would move her aside and do it instead. I was more used to the sore and not crying on the outside. Besides, I couldn't stand to hear her cry.

On the occasions that I didn't find her until after the horrible, we would just sit together and I would try to calm her, help her clean up and find some clothes to put on.

One day, when I was about five or six, I was sent home three times in one day for wetting my knickers and Mum was called to the school to talk about it. When we got home and had shut the front door, Mum turned on me straight away. Her eyes looked huge and round. She had a screaming fit. She told me I was embarrassing her.

"You're a dirty girl," she yelled at me.

Her face was red and puffy. I could see little bits of spit at the corners of her mouth.

"Why are you doing this to me? Why the hell don't you ask the teacher for the toilet?"

I wanted to tell her that it just happened and I only knew it was happening when it was happening and that I couldn't stop it, but I knew that every time I got worried it would happen. And I was worried now. I really didn't want to pee myself now because it would make her worse. I didn't know what to do, so I started to cry. This just made her even angrier. I tried crying on the inside, but this just made the pee come out and she went mad.

"For fuck's sake, you're a fucking embarrassment," she shrieked.

Suddenly, out of nowhere, something hit me on the forehead so hard that I was knocked to the floor. A bright light flashed in my head. I couldn't make a sound and I didn't want to move. All I could see was a black, empty darkness. I could feel the hallway carpet prickling my cheek.

I knew something was still hitting me because I could hear noises, but I couldn't feel or see anything anymore. I went limp and completely silent. I opened my eyes as wide as I could, desperately trying to see, searching for something to focus on. The pain was coming now, but I just didn't care. I scratched at my face to see if something was on my eyes, but there was nothing covering them. Panic started to creep over me and I remember thinking, I need to see, to run away. I need to see, to run away. Then everything went silent.

After a few moments, Mum started speaking again. I noticed that her voice had completely changed. She had stopped being screaming angry and now sounded frightened. "Karen?

Karen?" I heard her calling. She sounded far away and muffled. She was shaking me and telling me to stop it. I wasn't sure what she meant, but I was glad the hitting had stopped. Mum was screaming, "Stop it!" at me over and over. I could hear Roma shouting something like, "Stop, I'm telling Dad," as I heard her running out of the front door. Then I fell asleep.

When I woke up, I was aware that I was somewhere else. I still couldn't see anything, but I knew we weren't at home because the sounds were different. It was more echoey, and I didn't recognise any of the voices. I started to cry.

Someone picked me up ever so gently and hugged me. A lady's voice said softly, "Ssh, everything's going to be all right, my darling. Don't be frightened."

The lady smelt nice, sort of sweet and perfumey, and I thought for a moment that it was Aunt Pat. As she spoke, I could hear that it wasn't, but I didn't mind because she seemed kind.

The lady asked me what my name was. I said, "My name is Karen. I live Intruder Road."

"When's your birthday, darling? Is it soon?"

I didn't know what she meant, so I said no. The lady kept holding me to her gently. I really liked being hugged. My body felt like everything hurt. My head was sore, and moving made it hurt more, but I stayed still and let her hold me for a long time because I liked the feeling.

Eventually, the nice lady said, "Now that you're awake, I've got a visitor for you. Your mum is on her way in to see you. She's been very upset."

This made me terrified. I couldn't see anything, so I couldn't run away. Then I heard Mum screech, "Karen!" I instantly peed myself and started crying, but then Mum picked me up and hugged me. I was so surprised by this that I stopped crying and listened hard to her voice to make sure it really was her. Her voice sounded soft – not like her normal voice at all – but it still sounded like her. It smelt like her too, but she was crying, stroking my head and hugging me. It hurt, but I didn't want her to stop. I really didn't want her to cry – it made me feel very sad inside, so I squeezed her with my arms and patted her. I felt so happy, so relieved that she was hugging me and I was hugging her! I had never felt anything like it, and even though it was hurting, I didn't ever want it to stop.

I said, "It's OK, Mummy. Don't cry."

I didn't like to hear that she was upset, but I also wanted to check if I was allowed to talk to her. She didn't get mad or push me away; she just hugged me harder.

Then the nice lady said it was time to change me. This frightened me into panic – I thought maybe they changed bad children for good ones. I heard her heels clicking on the floor, walking away from me.

"I'll just get something to change you into," she called from far away.

Suddenly Mum and I weren't hugging any more. Mum's voice had changed. It was hard again. She pushed me away, but kept hold of me by the shoulders and spoke very close to my face. She said, "Karen, if you want me to stop crying, you have to remember what happened. You fell down the stairs and hurt yourself. You remember that, don't you?"

"Mum, I Have a Secret"

I didn't remember this at all – but I wanted her to hold me again, so I said I remembered falling down the stairs and she went back to hugging me. I was Mummy's good girl now. I got lots of hugs, especially when the nice lady was there.

It took many weeks for my vision to return and they kept me in the place where the nice lady was. At first, I remember seeing shadows, then patches of light. When I could finally see people and objects again, it was the same as looking through some of the windows at school – all fuzzy and smeared. I could see better if things were in the right place, but too close or too far and I couldn't see them properly. This made understanding people hard as well, because unless I could see someone's lips moving, I couldn't really hear them.

When I could see better, I saw that I was in a big, bright room, inside a baby's cot, with high sides. There were cots all around me. Sometimes other people would be there, and other times the room was empty. I remember the nice lady had very dark skin and black hair and a big wide smile. She was easy to see and hear and made me laugh a lot. She told me I was in 'hosterpull' and she was my very own nurse, Anna. She helped me not to wet myself anymore. I could now feel when pee was coming and I would tell Nurse Anna and she would help me get to the toilet. She was so pleased with me when I did this, and I liked that face so much that I used to look forward to feeling like I wanted to pee. When I went all night without going, she gave me a big box of jelly babies and told me I was her big girl, all clean and dry now. I felt warm and happy inside.

I wanted her to come home with me, but she had to stay and look after other children. I cried for her when I had to leave. I was in hospital for a long time, and when I went back home, everyone was so nice to me. Even Stanley said that until I was feeling better I only had to jiggle him.

Mum stopped hitting me as much after that. I was sad that she didn't hug me like she did when we were in hospital, but she did let me speak to her more and she was pleased with me now because I was all clean and dry, and not such a dirty girl. Now that I was back at home, I returned to school. I couldn't really understand a lot of what the teachers said because I couldn't hear them properly, but I wasn't wetting myself now, which made me feel better. I was learning colours, words, numbers and drawing. I liked drawing.

School was a very busy, happy, colourful, noisy place with lots of other children, grown-ups and lots to do. It also served dinner every day – something else we were not used to. There was no such thing as regular breakfast, dinner or teatime at our house, just "Roma's made something! Eat it."

Sometimes, we would only get to eat if we really made a fuss, which was not something any of us liked to do, so when there was no school, we could go two sleeps without eating properly. Some nights I would find it very difficult to get to sleep because I was so hungry. While the other children complained about school dinners, my sister and I would gobble down anything we were given.

I was seeing a lot of new things and meeting a lot of new people, but I didn't feel like I was the same as them. I didn't know why. I looked the same and I tried to copy them sometimes, but I didn't understand them all the time.

School was so different to home. Home was like a long list of things you had to try and avoid. Having said that, things were a bit better for me at home now that I was clean and dry.

One day, I was in our room when I heard Uncle Ken and Aunt Pat's voices downstairs. It was a surprise visit! I ran straight to the front door and told them everything in a flurry of words: I told them all about falling down the stairs, about my eyes, about Nurse Anna and being clean and dry, and doing drawing at school. Aunt Pat was thrilled with me, so I told her again about how I was clean and dry because I wanted to make sure they both knew.

"I knew you could do it," Uncle Ken said, putting his arm round me. "I'm very proud of you."

I didn't know what 'proud' meant, but his face was so happy and his eyes were so pleased that I thought it must be good and I hugged him until he could hardly breathe.

I looked behind him, searching for Dona, but she wasn't there. "Where's Dona, Uncle Ken?" I asked. I was worried because I didn't like her to ever be left alone in the house in case the horrible happened to her.

Uncle Ken said, "She's at home with Nanny Claridge."

I thought, why does Nanny Claridge, have my Dona? I didn't give it much thought, though – I was just glad that Dona was safe and was still so pleased to see Aunt Pat and Uncle Ken that I forgot all about it. They went into the back and I followed, holding on tight to my Aunt Pat's hand.

Mum went into the kitchen and brought out food – something I'd never seen her do before – and we all sat in the good front room and had dinner on a plate. I ate mine fast because I was hungry, but also because I didn't want to drop it on the good living-room floor.

Mum and Stanley were being really nice to us. I felt like we were a family out of a storybook. I was just loving watching

Uncle Ken and Aunt Pat. I was mesmerised by how they looked at me. It was nothing like the way any of the other faces looked at me. They made me feel safe, and they seemed to be the boss of Mum and Stanley, because Mum and Stanley were always nicer whenever they were around.

"We were wondering if our Karen could come and stay with us for the weekend. Dona would love to play with her," Aunt Pat said, looking from Mum to me.

A whole weekend! I nearly exploded with excitement, until I heard Stanley explain that I was too naughty at the moment to be allowed to go away for that long.

"You don't know what she's like," Stanley told them sombrely. "She's not to be trusted. I doubt you'd cope with her, and it wouldn't be right to expect you to."

Aunt Pat smiled at me, but she seemed to look strangely at Stanley.

"She's a good girl. I'm sure she'd be fine with us."

Mum agreed almost straight away. She seemed quite happy for me to have a weekend away, but Stanley still looked worried about how naughty I'd be. He said, "You don't know her she goes all weird and quiet."

Uncle Ken said, "That's alright she's just a bit shy." Stanley said he couldn't promise anything but would think about it.

That night, when I was in my bed and Stanley came in for his jiggle, I was still fantasising about how wonderful it would be to spend a whole weekend with Aunt Pat, Uncle Ken and Dona. Stanley lifted the sheets and I felt the mattress sink down.

I didn't want to jiggle and kept resisting. Eventually, Stanley whispered gruffly, "What's up with you?"

I crossed my fingers for good luck and asked him, "Can I go and stay with Aunt Pat?"

Stanley said, "What do you want to go there for?"

"Because I love them."

I could see in the half-light of the bedroom that Stanley looked a bit worried. Then he explained, "They don't love you. I love you. And I love you the way you want me to."

I didn't understand what he meant, so I asked him. "Remember that time when you sucked me in the tin bath all by yourself?"

I nodded, hoping he could see me in the dim light.

He said, "Well, I never asked you to do that, did I? You wanted to do it, so you chose the way all by yourself."

Then his voice got very low and serious as he added, "What you do to me is between you and me. What you do with the others is none of my business, is it? I won't tell if you won't. I'm only doing what you like, and if you tell other people, they won't understand you like I do. They will call you a dirty girl and lock you away. Do you want that? Do you want them to call you a dirty girl? Do you want them to take you away for being dirty?"

The thought terrified me. I had visions of prison cells and being far away from my sister. I shook my head firmly and said, "No."

Then his voice got a bit nicer as he said, "What we do is our secret. I'll help make sure that no one ever finds out what you're really like and make sure no one takes you away for it. I'm your dad. I'll protect you. And I'll think about Pat and Ken."

I knew he wasn't really my father. I had a father who looked very different to Stanley. I remembered him. Stanley was just my dad, which was different, though I didn't know how. Even so, I felt very relieved that he was going to help me not get caught for being dirty and not get sent away. I thought, He must love me like he says. I tried really hard to jiggle his pee thing until the hot liquid came without crying or resisting.

Stanley was pleased with me. When he was finished, he said, "I'm really looking forward to tomorrow. Tomorrow's going to be a very special day. I've got a surprise for you. Now, don't forget our secret, will you?"

I said I wouldn't. I wanted to ask what was happening tomorrow, but I knew that surprises were good things you weren't supposed to know about yet. I wondered if Aunt Pat and Uncle Ken were going to visit again, or maybe Stanley was going to let me stay with them for the weekend. I felt very excited.

When I woke up the next day, I raced downstairs to find out what my surprise was. Stanley told me that I was ill and wouldn't be able to go to school today. I was confused, because I didn't feel poorly; I always felt fine until after the horrible.

I felt sad that I wouldn't be getting my dinner that day. Once they'd all gone, I realised with horror that Mum was out, too. Now I was completely alone in the house with Stanley and the dark-haired face. I was worried straight away by this – I just knew this wasn't a good thing. As soon as I realised, I panicked, hurtled back upstairs and hid under Stanley's bed. I saw their feet come into the room and heard Stanley shout my name. He used that voice we don't argue with and I knew then that I had no choice. I would only make things worse if I ignored him. I came out. He told me to take off my clothes and lie face down on the bed, which I did. I closed my eyes and waited for the bright lights in my head to start. It wasn't long and everything got sore all over again. I didn't get the surprise I wanted that day.

Shortly after that, I started wetting the bed again, and it was not long after that that I peed myself at school, only this time I knew enough to try and hide what I had done. The horrible was happening all the time, too. I was scared of what everyone would think or do if they knew I was dirty, but having this secret seemed to be making the horrible much worse for us. I didn't like it, I didn't want a horrible secret, and I didn't want a horrible secret to happen to us anymore. I made up my mind I had to do something.

The very next day, I found I was home alone with Mum. This never happened. Mum was always out 'shopping', which was her word for shoplifting, at bingo or with other men, and though Stanley worked from time to time cash in hand as a painter and decorator or a driver, he never seemed to be out working much. This was my chance to tell Mum, and I wasn't going to miss it. I don't know what I thought I was going to do, but I was still determined to do something because I didn't like having this horrible secret.

I went upstairs and peeked through the crack of Mum's open door and saw that she was awake. I whispered, "Are you awake?" to check if it was all right to speak to her today. She didn't move or look at me, but she said that she was awake.

I was relieved and went into her room, stood by her bed, and even though I was really scared, I blurted out, "I have a secret."

This made her turn towards me. She said slowly, "What do you mean?"

I took a deep breath and repeated, "Mum, I have a secret." She looked at me funnily, with her head sort of on one side, and her eyes went a bit narrow. Then she said, "What secret?"

I said I wasn't allowed to say. She said I had to tell her. "I suck Dad's pee thing and jiggle it."

Her face changed. She looked straight at me and said in a quiet, low voice I had never heard before, "Say that again."

I started to cry because I was saying the words out loud, but she just couldn't seem to hear me. She looked angrier than I had ever seen her before. She pushed back the bedcovers and sat on the edge of the bed. I was getting very frightened, so I closed my eyes and waited for the bright lights and pain to start.

With my eyes closed, I stood and waited, but nothing happened – no lights, no pain, just silence. Then I felt her shake me and she said, loudly now, "Say it again."

I opened my eyes and said, "He makes us jiggle and suck his pee thing."

"What does 'jiggle' mean?"

I didn't have the words, so I moved my hand to show her and she just went mad. She flew off the bed, grabbed me and we were downstairs in a moment. She screamed for Roma, who ran in from outside. Mum told her to stay there with me, in the back living room, then ran out of the house.

Roma started saying, "What have you done? What have you said? Why is your mother angry at me?"

I began to cry.

"Shut up," said Roma. "Just tell me what you told her."

For some reason, and without ever understanding why, I stopped crying and started laughing. Roma hit the roof. All I could think was, how can I shut up and tell you something at the same time?

Roma looked scared, though, so I stopped laughing and tried to listen to what she was saying, but she was shouting so fast that I couldn't make out the words.

Eventually, Mum came roaring back into the house.

Mum made us all stand in a row in front of the living-room fire. We were facing her, and she paced up and down in front of us.

"What's been going on?" Mum said, looking at each of us in turn.

We were trying not to cry, but we were getting more scared. We looked at each other and we knew what she meant, but we didn't know all the words and we were just too scared to say anything anyway.

Denise sat down on the floor, sobbing, and I knelt down to help her. Suddenly, Stanley stormed into the room. Denise went quiet and I stood up to get ready for the pain and bright lights. He was wild eyed, and his face was all white and angry-looking. "Why the hell have I been called home from work in the middle of the fuckin' day?" he snarled.

Nobody answered.

Denise stood up again. We didn't know where to look.

Everyone seemed so cross.

Then Mum said to Stanley, "Our Karen says you've been making them 'jiggle and suck your pee thing'." Then she made a motion with her hand.

Stanley roared, "What the fuck is going on here? What's fuckin' being said? I'm hardly ever here, so how can I do anything? She's a lying, dirty bitch. How can I do anything like that if I'm hardly ever here?"

I thought, I'm not talking about when you're not here, I'm talking about when you are.

He kept going on and they screamed at one another for ages, as we stood there, looking at the ground and sneaking glances at each other.

Mum screamed, "Why would she say such a thing?"

Stanley said, "I don't fuckin' know – she's your lying mongrel, not mine!"

I felt Denise standing next to me shaking and we had both already wet ourselves.

Stanley glared at them then suddenly shouted, "Fuckin' ask them, then!"

Mum turned to us and said, "Well, is it true? Is he making you do those things?"

I looked at Roma and Denise and waited for someone to tell Mum all about the horrible. I thought that everything would change and Mum would make him stop.

But they wouldn't meet my eye. They were frightened and visibly shaking from head to toe.

Mum repeated, much more loudly now, "Tell me now. Is he making you do what Karen said?"

They looked at each other and cried, "No."

"So nothing is happening?" Mum asked, her voice becoming shrill.

Faces turned towards the floor, they stammered that they didn't know what I was talking about.

I felt like a vice was gripping my chest. I was so shocked that I couldn't make a sound. Nobody had hit me, but it felt like a big, hard kick in my chest. How could they say that nothing was happening?

Stanley was pacing around now, triumphantly screaming, "See! I told you so! It's her, the dirty, lying bitch! Someone's been teaching her bad habits, but it's not fuckin' me. I try and stop her if she starts on me. I've got you – what would I want to do anything like that for?"

I couldn't believe this was happening. I felt like I was going to be sick. I knew Roma didn't know what was happening to us as she was never there and I had never seen Shiny Head do the horrible to her, so I kind of understood why she had said no. But, even so, knowing everything we knew, I was devastated that Denise had not backed me up. Then, suddenly, the bright lights came, as Mum kicked me across the living room. She screamed at Stanley to take the others upstairs. They all ran out of the room.

Mum rounded in on me, her arms and feet flailing. "You're fucking me up! You're nothing but a dirty, lying bitch! How dare you try to steal Stan away from me, you dirty bitch? You needed to be taught a lesson!"

She stripped my clothes off me and dragged me sobbing across the living-room floor and into the kitchen. Tears streamed down my face as she yanked me by the arm across the carpet, burning my legs.

"I'm not lying, Mum. I'm not lying," I screamed.

Mum span round and shouted.

"I'm going to wash that filthy mouth of yours out."

She grabbed me by the neck, prised my lips apart and poured the stuff that Roma used to wash the toilet down my throat. It stung and burnt my lips. My tongue felt swollen and too large for my mouth. I screamed and pleaded with her to stop. She said

I was a dirty girl and I needed to be cleaned. Then she washed my mouth out and my pee and poo places.

When she'd finished, I lay lifeless on the kitchen floor. Everything felt burnt and red raw. Mum was still screaming at me.

"If you ever speak a word to me again, it will be your fucking last!"

Then she grabbed my hair and thrust her face into mine.

"You must never, ever talk about any of this to anyone ever again! Do you hear me?"

Still lying on the floor, I whimpered, "OK, please stop now, I won't tell."

"You're still talking – I told you not to talk," she screamed. Whack! She hit me hard across the cheek.

"Stop. Please, Mum, stop," I cried out in pain, clutching my swollen face.

Whack!

I yelped, unable to stop myself from crying out. Mum hit me until I fell asleep.

I'm not sure how long I was asleep – it could have been hours or days – but when I woke up, everything had changed again: Roma and Denise had gone to stay with relatives, Mum was nowhere to be seen and I was all alone with Stanley. That night, when I went to bed, I heard the door creak open. A shaft of light fell across the floor.

Stanley whispered, "Are you awake?"

I didn't answer: it didn't matter if I was or not.

"Father, I Have a Secret"

After I tried to tell Mum about the horrible secret, I had been too scared to move off my bed for days. I was black and blue and sore all over, and just lay there silently, trying not to attract anyone's attention. I'd never felt despair quite like it. It just hadn't entered my head that she wouldn't believe me.

I loved my sister, and couldn't understand why she had not told Mum what had been happening, but even then, I understood 'scared' and I knew how hard it was to tell. So I simply accepted it.

A profound loneliness and fatigue descended on me. I was too bruised to go to school, and it felt like I had been forgotten completely. My world narrowed until I felt like the only place I'd ever known was my bedroom.

Everything was different now. My sister wasn't allowed to talk to me anymore and would get battered if she did. Our Denise was out a lot with Mum these days. She seemed to be Mum's favourite and we didn't see her much for a while.

Stanley could now do and say whatever he wanted to, and he did. After telling on him, I had to do even more horrible than ever before.

The only good things were no more Roma food and I didn't see much of some of Stanley's friends anymore, like the dark-haired face or Hairy Face. Even so, these were still dark times, and the rare good days were always spoilt by the horrible nights. It felt like one long, bad time.

Since I'd tried to tell Mum, she wouldn't even look at me let alone talk to me. She only ever talked to me through the others. She seemed to be out more than ever. She was always out with her girl- and boyfriends – Stanley didn't seem to mind, but it meant that we hardly saw her at all. When we did see Mum, it was normally to go out shopping (shoplifting) to buy (steal) stuff with her. She never included Roma in this. She needed us to hide all the things she wanted to 'buy' and if we all went, we could hide a lot between us. Woolworths, on the high street, was Mum's favourite shop. We liked it too, because of all the sweets and toys.

I had learnt to start screaming and crying at the top of my lungs whenever Mum commanded it, which she did with a certain look and a nod. She normally needed me to do it when she had finished hiding what she wanted to buy from the shop and was ready to leave. I had to do this at virtually every shop we went to.

I remember having to sit in the baby pram, which I hated, because I wasn't a baby – I was five or six. I was older than all the other children in prams and it felt weird, but Mum could hide more shopping if I sat in the baby pram, so I sat in the baby pram a lot.

Mum would be in a bad mood until she was finished hiding her shopping and we were outside the shop. Then she would be so happy and we would all have to run as fast as we could to get home and unload the shopping. If you were in the pram being pushed along, this could be fun, but it wasn't so much fun if you were running behind, trying to keep up with her. We nearly got run over loads of times on the main road, and it always seemed more like a mad dash than a fun run, but it put Mum in a very good mood and that was all that mattered.

These days, now that I was six, if I did well with Stanley, I would get a few pennies to spend at the sweetshop at the top of our road, which I was now allowed to go to all by myself. It was when I was returning from one of these trips to the sweet shop that I saw a man with dark hair standing near our house. At first, I felt worried, because usually when strange men came near it was horrible time. When I saw the man's face, though, my heart skipped a beat. It was my real father. I had only seen him a couple of times since we'd moved in with Stanley, but I still recognised him. I flew down the road like a screaming rocket and jumped up at him.

He picked me up, swung me round and looked pleased to see me. I was confused but happy. Was he here to help us? I felt like I didn't dare let go of him.

When he put me down, he said, "Where's your mum?"

"Out with our Denise," I replied.

"Do you know who I am?"

I said, "Yes, of course. You're my father."

He smiled and said, "Yes, I am."

Then his face seemed to cloud over.

"Do you know when your mum will get back?"

I just said, "Soon," and started crying because I wanted to go back to hugging.

He shushed me and said, "Do you know where your mum is now?"

"Yes," I replied, nodding. I knew she was at a friend's house close by.

He seemed pleased with me.

"Hop in the car and take me to her," he said.

I did as he said. It was so good to see him, but when he started driving, he seemed sad and asked me lots of questions about Mum, which I answered until he started crying.

I wanted to ask, "Where have you been? Why did you go? Can you come back?", but he wanted to see Mum. He said he loved her and wanted her back. I just kept quiet until we got to the friend's house.

He told me to stay in the car and left me to go and find Mum. After a while he came rushing back with blood on his face and told me to get out of the car. I sprang out and he speeded off. Mum had followed him out of the house and she smacked me all the way home for telling him where she was. When we got home, she laughed with Stanley about it. She told him that she had beaten up my father before he knew what had hit him. She told him that my father still "had it bad for her". I wasn't sure what that meant, but they were both laughing.

Stanley said to me, "He was no father to ya – he tried to fuckin' kill ya – set your house alight. If you ever see him again, you're to run and hide. And if I ever see that waste of space again, I'll kill him."

Back then I had no real memories of our past together and those memories I did have made little sense to me. I never believed much of what Stanley said about anything but I did believe he would kill my father, so I never told him about the times I would sometimes see him briefly on my way to the penny sweetshop. Sometimes he was just driving by; other times he was parked and we would talk for a few moments, cry, then talk some more. He would always ask me about Mum and tell me how much he missed us all. Mostly, though, he talked about Mum and how much he loved her and wanted to see her. He told me he loved us. I loved him too, and I missed him when I didn't see him and wished he would take us all away.

I wouldn't always see him straight away and I would just hear someone say, "Is that my shy one? Is that you, Shy?" When I heard this, I would search for him, as this was the name he always called me by. One time, I asked him why he called me Shy and not Karen. He replied, "Because in all the pictures I have of you, you're tilting your head to one side and looking very shy." Shy became his secret pet name for me. I liked that he had a special name for me. As I grew older, others called me Shy too, but that was more because I wouldn't say much.

Every time I saw my father he would talk about Mum and say that she had put a spell on him. He would always cry and ask me where Mum was, and I would have to lie and say that Mum and Stanley wouldn't tell me where they were any more. I knew this wasn't true, but I didn't want Stanley to kill my dad, and I didn't want to tell him that Stanley wanted to kill him as I couldn't bear to see him cry. To be on the safe side, I told my father to park further around the corner when he wanted to speak to me. He said OK, and we carried on seeing each other occasionally, but not very often.

After more horrible, I started to wonder what would happen if I told my father what Stanley was doing to us. When I'd told

Mum, I'd made everything worse, but maybe this time things would be different – perhaps my father would stop Stanley from doing the horrible to us. I wanted this more than anything, so I promised myself that the very next time I saw my father I would try and tell him about the horrible secret. He said he loved us, so I was sure he would make everything OK if he knew.

Some time later, I was walking along the top of our road when I saw my father. I was happy and excited to see him and ran straight over to him. I gave him a big hug. I had missed him and had been waiting to tell him about my horrible secret so that he could stop Stanley. I was scared of telling him, but things were getting so much worse.

"Hello, Shy," my father said. "Where's your mum?"

I wished he wouldn't ask me this every time. I lied and said she was out and I didn't know where she was. I really wanted him to ask about me, so I could tell him about my secret, but I knew he wouldn't, so I waited for him to stop talking about Mum. Then he said that he'd better be going.

I panicked, thinking I was going to miss my chance. The words came tumbling out: "I've got a secret."

He looked puzzled. "What is it?"

I swallowed hard. I'd been practising how to say this so that he'd understand and I wanted to get it right. I couldn't explain about the horrible, so I was just going to tell him about jiggling.

"Stanley makes me do things. He makes me jiggle his pee thing. He says it's a secret, but I don't want a secret."

My father didn't say anything. I held my breath. His face had gone very still and pale. Then it crumpled up into little creases and he started to cry.

I hated the idea that I'd made him cry. I grabbed his arm and said, "I'm sorry, I'm sorry. I didn't mean to say it. I know it's a secret," but he got even more upset. There were tears running down his face and he was punching the steering wheel. Then he started to shout really loud. He wasn't looking at me, which was confusing. I turned round, suddenly aware that someone was standing next to me. My heart nearly hit the floor when I saw who it was.

Stanley shouted, "Get home now!" His face was red, and his blue eyes were bulging and huge.

I knew he'd heard me telling my father our secret. He looked furious – even more angry than the time I'd tried to tell Mum. I didn't know what to do, so I ran towards the house. I could hear them shouting at each other as I ran away, crying. I didn't dare look back.

My eyes were so full of tears that everything was blurry and I ran straight into Mum as she was coming out of the front door. She ignored me and stood in the road outside for a moment, looking up the street at them. Then she came back inside and pointed for me to go upstairs. I bolted up to my room.

I waited in my bedroom for what seemed like forever. I heard Stanley come back into the house through the slammed front door, and I crept to the top of the stairs so I could hear what had happened. I listened hard as Stanley told Mum that he had "got him" at the train station and "beat the fuckin' shit out of him". I was terrified. I thought he had killed my father.

I sat down on the stairs, shaking and trying not to cry as I strained to hear their conversation. Then I heard Stanley say that they had a fight, my father had lost and gone away on the train. I was sad, but relieved that he was still alive. I tiptoed back to my room, trying to avoid the creaky floorboard just outside my door.

I sat there waiting for my beating, but it never came. When Stanley came into the room a couple of hours later, it was just to jiggle. I was confused, but I wasn't getting smacked, so I kept quiet and did as I was told.

After Stanley had left, I couldn't sleep. The house was very quiet and still, which I usually loved, but that night I felt more lonely than ever. I hoped my father hadn't gone away on the train for good. Still, now that he knew, he wouldn't leave us here, he would be back for us, I knew he would. I would just have to wait. I started crying softly to myself, feeling my pillow getting wetter under my cheek.

For a while, things carried on as usual. I tried to concentrate on waiting as patiently and calmly as I could for my father to come and get us. The days trickled by, running into weeks and then months. Life at Tudor Road was a horrible blur in which every lesson had to be taught by a smack. You only learnt something was wrong when the smack came and you'd be sent to your room without explanation for the rest of the day. Once you knew it was wrong, you didn't do it again.

I had learnt that when we shopped with Mum, it was called 'shopping', but if we shopped on our own, that was called 'stealing'.

Smack! I learnt that when I got beaten, that was called a 'punishment', but if I hit back, that was called 'naughty'. Smack! Smack! I learnt that when Mum and Stanley told lies, that was called the 'truth', but if I told a lie, that was 'bad'. Smack, smack, smack! Unless they said I could lie, in which case it wasn't a lie, it was a secret, which if you tell you will get smacked. Learning by smack was hard and confusing but it was the least of our worries.

We were coping as well as we could but it was taking its toll on us and we were starting to close down in on ourselves. Our day-to-day life centred around trying hard to avoid all the horrible things that were happening to us. I was very protective of my little sister and always took her turn whenever I could. Unfortunately, this always seemed to make the faces think I wanted what they were doing, but there was no telling them.

One memory of this time stands out above all the others. Indeed, it will stay with me for the rest of my life. Stanley had kept me home from school yet again. He was in the sitting room with me, pestering me to do the horrible.

"I've got tummy ache," I lied, clutching my stomach.

"Stop fuckin' me about when I'm in the mood. It's your tummy ache, not mine. Anyway, I won't be long."

I shouted, "No," and managed to squirm free of his hands as they pawed at me.

Stanley's patience snapped and I saw a sudden flash of real anger. He grabbed me roughly and pinned my arms down to the sofa, his face looming above me. I could smell his breath. It was bitter and rancid. When he spoke, I could see the yellow stains on his teeth. He said, "I'm your father and you will do what I tell you to."

Before I could stop myself, I had blurted out, "You're not my father. My father is taking us away from here. I've told him, you know."

Stanley laughed and said he didn't give a shit about all that and hurled me off the sofa and across the room. I didn't cry even though it hurt. I stayed where I had fallen, knowing better than to try and move. I watched as Stanley came towards me. He knelt down and snarled into my face, "Your father! Your fuckin' father! Your father ain't takin' anyone anywhere! Your father's dead!"

I froze, fear coursing through my body. I knew what 'dead' meant. I knew you were buried in the ground and everyone who loved you or missed you couldn't see or talk to you anymore. I was petrified.

I screamed, "No he's not! You're lying! You're lying!"

Stanley laughed again. "I'm telling ya, you stupid cow, he's dead."

Then I did something I'd never done before. I launched myself at Stanley and started punching his face. I was screaming, "No! No! No!"

Stanley seemed startled at first, but then smacked me back and told me to calm down, but I just couldn't. He finally slapped me hard enough to stop me hitting him.

Stanley said, "Look, Karen, he never fuckin' loved you anyway, he was nothing but trouble, he's dead now, but you've still got me and your mum, so just calm yourself down."

Fear had given me courage. I looked Stanley in the eye and said in a cold low voice that didn't sound like mine, "You killed him at the train station!"

He said, "No I fuckin' never, he died in a car accident, he killed his fuckin' self."

I didn't know what to think, I just wanted Stanley to stop saying my father was dead.

I said, "I want Aunt Pat." I knew that she'd tell me the truth.

"Her and Ken have gone abroad with the army, so you can forget about all that nonsense."

"Abroad?" I repeated dumbly. I felt overwhelmed. I'd lost everyone who could help me and there was no one else to turn to now. I just sat there and whimpered over and over, "My father's not dead." Tears were streaming down my cheeks, but I wasn't making a crying sound.

Stanley shrugged and said, "I've told ya before – he's no fuckin' good and you're better off wivout him and you're not to talk to your mum about him ever, unless you want the belt. Got it?"

I just nodded. I had nothing more to say about anything or anyone. I had no more words and no more sounds to make; I just wanted the world to stop.

Mum suddenly came into the room. I looked straight at her, but she wouldn't look at me, she never did. Then they started arguing. She didn't seem upset that my father was dead, just angry at me for knowing about it. I stayed sitting on the floor in silence.

Mum asked Stanley, "Have you told her he died in a car accident in London?"

He said he had.

Mum glanced in my direction. "Why is she just sitting there rocking?"

"She hit me when I told her about it, so I had to calm her down wiv a little smack."

Mum replied, "Well, remember to mind her head." She paused, then she said, "It's not normal, this rocking. She's doing my head in – tell her to stop it or go to her room."

Stanley said, "Yeah, she should be crying but ya know what she's like, just ignore her."

I could barely hear them anymore. I was locked in my own thoughts. Despair rushed in on me as I realised I was completely and utterly alone. My father had gone, Aunt Pat and Uncle Ken had gone and my sister was drifting further and further away from me. I had never felt a loneliness quite so profound as this.

After a while I went upstairs to my room and sat on my bed, rocking silently and replaying everything that had just gone on. I kept turning over in my head the words that he had said – that I should be crying. I realised then that he wanted me to cry. It was almost as if he liked seeing me upset. This realisation stirred something new in me. For the first time, I felt defiance rise inside me, an anger that I'd never experienced, and in that moment I made myself a promise: I would never cry for Stanley ever again.

Goodbye, London

It was around this time, in 1969, when I was about six, that my life took yet another unpredictable turn. I was sitting in the back garden with my sister when Mum and Stanley announced that they were getting married and that Stanley was going to adopt us. I didn't know what this meant, so I didn't really care. What I can remember about married is that I had to spend the whole day before having my straight hair roughly pulled and twisted by this lady who said she was trying to make it curly. She put stinky stuff on my head that made my eyes sting and told me off the whole time. Then she stabbed a comb into my newly curly hair and said, "There you go – you look very pretty." Then she did the same to my sister.

We got to wear a pretty dress that we couldn't get dirty, rip or sit down in, and we had to hold some flowers all day. I remember I met a lot of relatives and faces, some I knew, some I didn't, but most of the day itself is a blur.

The evening stands out more clearly. That night, his wedding night, Stanley came into the bedroom I was sleeping in and told me, "I'm your real daddy now."

A slow smile spread across his face as he undid his trousers. It hurt like it always did, but he had insisted that I keep the dress on, which I had been trying so hard to keep clean and pretty all day. After he was done it wasn't clean and pretty any more.

It was after this that I first remember being introduced to a very grey-haired old lady and man that I was told to call Nanny and Grandpa Wallbridge. Mum told me that Grandpa Wallbridge was a Reverend and Nanny Wallbridge was a headmistress. She was a strict, devoutly religious woman, a very bossy lady that everyone was scared of. There wasn't anything she didn't have a rule for, and it was the smacky punishments for breaking the rules that made her very difficult for me to understand. Her husband was a kind, smack-free man with the patience of 10 good men.

Not long after the wedding, we visited Nanny and Grandpa Wallbridge in a house that didn't have an upstairs and was on wheels. It had sliding doors and was right next to a huge white house full of people and children; it had massive gardens and bluebell woods all around it. It was a beautiful 'horrible free' place that I liked visiting.

When we were very young, we were each other's comfort and protection, but as time went by, things changed. Denise had always been Mum's favourite, but these days she got her full attention. Mum would dress her up like a doll and parade her blonde-haired, blue-eyed angel around the place as if she had won her in a competition. Denise just liked being close to Mum and away from Stanley, so she put up with it.

As for me, I continued to be invisible to Mum. She still never spoke to me, and mostly I thought this was a good thing. I just wished I was invisible to Stanley as well. He was the same with all of us: horrible.

Unfortunately, my mother's favouritism towards my sister and obvious dislike for me had a very negative effect on us. If my sister played with me, Mum and Stanley wouldn't play with her. She needed to get Mum and Stanley to like her, so over time she stopped playing with me.

Most of the relatives we met during our time at Tudor Road lived up North in Merseyside. Before I even met them, it seemed most of them had decided they didn't like me either. Thankfully, my beloved Uncle Ken and Aunt Pat had recently returned from being abroad with the army, though I didn't see them much as they were now living in Birkenhead. They lived just across the street from Nanny Claridge, who was Aunt Pat's mum and had adopted Stanley when he was young. Nanny Claridge lived on the aptly named Queen's Street, and Aunt Pat lived just up the road across from her house.

Around this time, I can remember being able to see better and only realising that it had been bad before, because of how much easier it now was to see things that were too near or too far away. I had been experiencing blurry tunnel vision; what I didn't learn until much later was that this had been brought on by multiple traumas to my head. My eyesight continued to be poor for a while, but it was definitely much improved.

My poor eyesight and hearing had, however, made me very isolated at school. Other children would come up to me and try to play with me, but I couldn't hear what they were saying and sometimes I didn't even know they were standing next to me. In the end, they thought I was ignoring them and would leave me alone. This was alright by me; I no longer yearned for friendship like I used to. I always felt as though I was watching a movie of my life rather than living my life. With no friends, no relatives nearby and growing ever further from my sister, I felt incredibly alone. I was different, but I didn't know why.

I saw and understood much more than I ever said out loud. I understood that I was naughty, dirty and bad and that if I could just somehow change and make the horrible go away I could maybe get Mum to like me a bit. In spite of the distance between us, I knew I loved my sister. I knew the truth was whatever you could see happening in front of you. I knew secrets were things that Mum and Stanley would beat you up for, if you ever told anyone else. I knew that the family doctor had told Mum and Stanley not to punish me on the head anymore because it was bad for my ears and eyes, and that they were trying not to. I knew that the horrible was a secret. I knew that telling anyone about the horrible made people hate you and die. I knew I loved my mum and really wanted her to love me, but she couldn't and that was the end of it. I knew Stanley thought I was dirty, but you could learn a hundred ways to show him you didn't want to be dirty and none of them would work. I knew Stanley was trying to protect me by not telling anyone how dirty I was. I knew lots of things, but nothing ever made any sense.

Home was a dark, painful, lonely place. I was missing my father and wanted to see him to say sorry for killing him, but I wasn't allowed to talk about him. That was OK, though, because I was getting really good at not talking about all kinds of things.

Like I'd promised myself when my father had died, I didn't cry in front of Stanley anymore. I felt shut down on the inside.

He said I was getting argumentative, uncooperative and cheeky. Once, I accidentally (on purpose) called him Shiny Head to his face. He went mental and turned me all black and blue as he screamed at me to call him father. I remember thinking, you're not my father, but I'll call you anything if you just stop hitting me. After this, I didn't even call him Shiny Head to myself just in case I forgot and said it out loud: I called him Stanley in my head, but Dad to his face.

It was during this terrible, depressing time that out of nowhere came a ray of hope. For no apparent reason, my parents agreed to let me spend some time alone with Uncle Ken, Aunt Pat and our Dona at their home in Birkenhead. What's more, I wasn't just going for a weekend but for a whole two weeks! I couldn't believe it. I'd been wishing for years for this to happen and now it was.

Mum and Stanley gave me hours of warnings about what I could and couldn't tell them about what went on at home. I agreed to everything and anything. I just wanted to go! Stanley took me to one side and said I couldn't talk about our secret. I remember thinking, When I'm with them, there is no secret, so what are you talking about?

All the warnings were unnecessary; they didn't need to say any of it: I knew that people either hated you or died if you told them about the horrible, and I wasn't going to let that happen to Uncle Ken, Aunt Pat or our Dona.

I counted the days, and after an eternity the day finally came. I waited by the front door for hours for their car to pull up. I was wearing a coat and shoes, and I even had knickers on, which I was never given to wear unless I was going to school.

When I saw the car appear at the top of the road, I raced out straight away. Uncle Ken and Aunt Pat wanted to say hello to Mum, so I waited in the car for them.

When we got to Birkenhead, Aunt Pat was worried about how much I could see and took me for an eye test, but I don't think I did very well. Staying at their house was like living in a different world – nothing was the same. Their home was bright and beautiful; everything was happy, fun, laughing and full of hugs and kisses. Uncle Ken would play with me and Dona and chase us through the house, threatening to tickle us to death if he caught us, which he always did, because we would laugh too much to run away fast. He made the funniest faces and you just couldn't help it.

I remember that they had a proper time for getting up, going to bed, washing, meals (three a day!), toys and television. Dona had her own room and always slept in it – at our house, sometimes I would share with my sister and sometimes I'd be on my own or in the loft. It was like another world.

I loved them so much I used to pretend I was really their daughter and would call them Mum and Dad in my head. Aunt Pat used to let me call her Mum sometimes. She would just smile and say, "Don't let your mother catch you saying that." And I would always promise that I wouldn't.

As for my cousin Dona, I loved everything about her and wanted to be just like her. She had friends! Friends are people who play with you just because they like you. Dona was funny, clever and very grown-up. She would read and draw with me and show me how to add up.

They lived on the steepest hill in the whole world, next to the longest, steepest steps in the whole world, which we all called the Monkey Steps. Slim, tall Dona could stride up them like a rocket, right to the very top. I would try and keep up with her, but could never make it more than halfway without collapsing in a heap, laughing breathlessly at how impossibly hard it was. She would stand at the top and laugh till she cried at my pathetic attempts to reach the top, which just made me laugh more.

One time, we were at the bottom of the hill, about to climb up, when she called out that I had "old-lady legs" and then bolted off up the hill. I didn't make it past the first step, because I was in a heap on the floor laughing at the very idea of me with old lady's legs stuck on me. She won again, but she made trying to win a lot of fun.

Staying at their house was incredible, but it was also very confusing. I used to wonder, how come when they tickle me, it doesn't hurt? Why is there no horrible? Why doesn't Uncle Ken make me jiggle him? Doesn't Aunt Pat mind me being naughty, dirty, bad? How come they can always hear me and understand me? It didn't matter that I couldn't answer all these questions, though – they didn't do the horrible, and they said they loved me, and I was very pleased about that.

When the time came to return home, I was very sad. I couldn't tell them why I was so sad, so I kept quiet in the car on the way back to London as I tried to think of ways to die before I got home.

When I got back, life seemed even more grim than before. Horrible was never far away and I seemed to be trying to protect my sister a lot these days. I started to wish my father had taken me with him.

I recall that around this time, when I was perhaps seven or eight, I started having to make regular special 'office visits' to play with Plasticine and toys in front of the smiling grown-ups.

Upon reflection, I realise now that these people were outside professionals taking an interest in my life. I recall being taught to speak by a white-haired lady, and I remember the nice man who checked my ears and eyes a lot. I remember the family doctor; he was a very old man in a posh suit. He gave me medicine for mumps, chickenpox and for the smelly, itchy stuff that was coming out of my pee place. We mostly talked about wetting the bed and if I could see and hear all right. Nobody ever seemed to really want any more than this. Nobody asked me questions on my own, away from Mum and Stanley, but even if they had I don't think I would have told them anything.

Except for these few disconnected memories, I just can't remember enough about the professionals to say any more. Although I didn't know it, my life was about to change once again and very soon I'd never see any of them again.

Because I was 'pretend ill' so much for Stanley, I missed a lot of school. Eventually, the school said they wanted to see Mum about it. Suddenly, I was being told to keep my mouth shut – "If anyone asks you anything about home, you're not to say a word. Got it?" Got it.

I didn't need or get to say anything, because not long after the big meeting with the school, Mum came storming home and said, "Right we're moving."

At the time, I didn't think much of it, but I now realise that the school and the professionals had probably been asking awkward questions about us, about the incontinence, why we were off school so much and why we had so many bruises.

Mum simply announced that we were moving and that Roma wasn't moving with us and that was it. Mum said that we would be moving to Birkenhead and would be living just a short way away from Aunt Pat. I felt so completely happy that I actually screamed.

If you have questions about my life so far, then you are pretty much where I was at this point, having spent most of my life wishing or praying to stop bad things happening. I had lots and lots of questions and no real answers. Everything I knew or understood to be true always left me asking, "Why?" or, "How come?"

Hello, Merseyside

Merseyside has some of the most breathtaking landscapes in the UK. Admittedly, it has its share of eyesores, but it is also filled with many beauty spots. The whole region is steeped in stunning architecture, and has so many incredible features – from its rolling countryside to its bustling towns, from its stunning, tranquil waterways to its hectic, fun-filled beaches, its wealth of wildlife and its unique flora and fauna make it a very special area of interest. It has a little bit of everything, and more than enough to make you miss it when you leave.

Birkenhead is a much-loved historic town and sits on the banks of the Mersey, directly opposite the city and docks of Liverpool. You can reach Liverpool by land (the long way round), or through the Mersey Tunnel or, indeed, by 'ferry… cross the Mersey'. You have to stand on the banks of the Mersey on a clear night to fully appreciate the stunning picture-postcard view of the city of Liverpool.

Liverpudlians called everyone across the water from them 'woolly backs'. Birkenhead accents aren't as guttural as the Scouse accent, and we weren't as progressive (or as aggressive) as those racy city folk, but we really didn't have any more hair growing on our backs than they did. (I know because I checked.)

Hello, Merseyside

When we first moved to Birkenhead, when I was about eight, we lived in a flat on Park Road South. My only memories of living there are of the wonderful inside toilet (which, unlike our toilet in London, didn't have spiders in it), playing in the beautiful park that our home backed on to, and the stunning white blossom on the cherry trees that lined the street you walked down to get to the bus stop.

I do remember walking alone to and from school, but not a single thing about school itself. I remember learning how to catch the bus on my own and only caring about how far it was to Aunt Pat's house – two buses and five stops – and I can remember how pleased I was that my hearing had started to improve, as I didn't have to look at people's mouths so much to hear what they were saying anymore.

Horrible was the same and part of my everyday life. It was mainly only Stanley at this time. I don't remember any new faces – apart from a horrible man called Reg, who worked at the market – but this didn't seem to make it feel like it was happening less.

The only way to make Mum like you was to be the best at 'shopping'. Luckily, when it came to stealing, I was really good. Still, things were getting a little bit confusing, as we seemed to be shopping everywhere we went. One time, Mum shopped at Aunt Pat and Aunt Violet's house, which made them very angry at Mum and they wouldn't talk to her for ages. I heard Mum tell Stanley that if they kept it up, she would have one of her dizzy fits and sort them all out.

I knew exactly what she meant because if she thought the shopkeepers were angry at her for shopping with them, she could 'pretend faint'. Once I had got through the shop door with the shopping, then she would get better quickly and come to find me. Aunt Pat and Aunt Violet didn't start talking to her again, so Mum had a pretend faint and everyone was soon speaking to her.

She still didn't speak to me, and nobody seemed to notice that she always 'told them to tell me'. After a couple of months we moved out of our flat on Park Road South and into a house above and behind the hairdresser's on Queen's Street. It was five doors down from Nanny Claridge and one tiny street away from Aunt Pat.

When we went to view the house on Queen's Street, I was horrified – it was a bleak two-bed with an outside (spider-filled) toilet. To get in, you had to go through the tiny back-yard gate and then up some steps and in through the back door, which opened into a tiny room. This single downstairs room had a small open fireplace and a cupboard for a kitchen, which was on the right and had only cold running water. A killer staircase – even steeper than the one on Tudor Road – was enclosed in the far-left corner. This killer staircase was practically a sheer drop from the top floor to the ground floor and had a series of knee-smacking, three-inch-deep steps that even our little feet would frequently miss. On the way up, we would miss and slip, then knee-smack every step-edge on the way back down to the bottom. On the way down, if you didn't wedge your heel into each step, you would slip and surf the rest of the stairs on your heels and backside, slapping unceremoniously into the door at the bottom. I managed to do this on the very first viewing, much to our Denise's continued amusement.

The house was cold, small, dark and surrounded by derelict houses. I hated it, but I would have lived in a bin bag if it meant being this close to Aunt Pat, so I just smiled and said it was very nice, thank you, and when can we move in?

We moved in soon after the first visit. I shared the front bedroom overlooking Queen's Street, directly above the hairdresser's, which sent up the most terrible smells during the day. The hairdresser's dog was a very yappy, tiny little thing that looked more like a bee on a string than a dog, but it was a sweet, frightened, shaky-looking thing and I liked taking it out for a walk.

We lived opposite the grubby local pub, and as you looked out of our bedroom window, you could see the steep Monkey Steps to the left and Aunt Pat's street to the right. It seemed there was a noisy pub on every corner of every street this close to the shipping docks.

As I lay awake at night trying to get to sleep, I was to learn a lot of new swear words and a lot about why the lady (two doors down) always wanted her husband, whose name was Feckin' Eejut, to stop drinking all the wages away and try paying the rent with it. I learnt from her husband that apparently she could kiss his arse. Apparently, she could always kiss his arse no matter what she said.

The pubs chucking out, the cars going by, the big ships coming and going past Camel Lairds (just behind our house) on the Mersey were all new but very welcome sounds. I liked being quiet on the outside, but not on the inside, so any noise was a welcome distraction.

I can see in my mind's eye a school with a playground on the roof, but again I can't remember anything about the school itself. I had a lot of unwelcome memories that would just flash into my mind and make me feel like I felt when I was there and it was happening. I could now make it so that when the pictures came into my head, I would use my imagination to chase them away, but this took a lot of concentration, which made me look like I wasn't paying attention to the adults. I got into a lot of trouble for doing it, and when the adults yelled at me to concentrate, I remember thinking, I am concentrating, just not on what you think.

As well as being naughty, dirty, bad, I was both old beyond my years and stupid beyond all reason. The family GP said that I was an elective mute. I remember thinking to myself, I don't know what that is, but whatever it is, I'm not that! And don't think I'm gonna talk to you because you can't make me and I won't!

Silence had become a defence mechanism. Stanley could beat me black and blue and he could do any horrible thing to me and I could just lay or stay there, still and quiet, till he was done. Sometimes he used to hit me extra just to see if he could make me cry and sometimes I nearly did. It drove him up the wall when he couldn't get me to, but crying was the one thing I could control, that he could not. So, no matter what he did, I would save the tears for later when I was on my own.

Until we moved to Birkenhead, I thought Christmases and birthdays were things that happened to other people. I had seen Mum, Stanley, Roma and Denise have birthday and Christmas celebrations, but I was never really part of those occasions. To be honest, I never really thought about them that much and don't recall feeling particularly left out. I just didn't think they were anything to do with me and felt happy that I was being left alone.

When we moved, though, I recall that Dona, my sister and I all had birthdays close together. They both had special treats on the day, but I didn't. I remember thinking, Why don't I have birthdays or Christmases? I recall this moment well because it was the first time I ever remember thinking hard about what was and wasn't fair.

According to Stanley, I got everything I deserved and would have got a lot more if I wasn't so naughty, dirty, bad. Besides, if I didn't muck around when he was "in the fuckin' mood, things might turn out better". When I asked Aunt Pat, she said that Father Christmas decided who was good or bad and she would make sure that he knew I had moved and that I wanted a music box. That year, Father Christmas found me and sent me a music box, just like Aunt Pat's. I was so excited when I unwrapped it. Mum let me open it all by myself and have a look at it. Then she took it away to her bedroom and I didn't see it again. That year, I had my first Christmas dinner, too, which Stanley cooked because Mum never did cooking. It was very special.

That Christmas was one of the very few good moments I can remember. I was still struggling to manage day-to-day living. I was eight by now but was still trying to keep clean and dry. This was even harder than ever because I always had to go to the toilet in the night or I'd wet my bed. I was desperate not to do this, so I'd have to get up in the night. Unfortunately, because we had an outside toilet, we also had an inside family pee bucket for the night-time. Stanley put the bucket in his room and you had to be careful not to disturb him when you used it or the horrible would start.

Emptying the pee bucket always seemed to be my job, as was cutting up old newspapers into hundreds of squares for the outside toilet. I remember one time when I was trying to carry the pee bucket downstairs to empty it. I was at the top, with the bucket full to the brim with week-old, cold family pee. I could see the door at the bottom of the killer stairs was closed, which made things even more difficult.

Our Denise was on the stair landing, thanking her lucky stars she didn't have to empty it. I held the bucket steady and slightly above my head so that I could watch where my feet were going. As I ventured gingerly down the first step, my left foot stayed stuck where it was but my right foot proceeded down the stairs. I did the splits and slid down the rest of the stairs, desperately trying to steady the bucket above my head. The steps burnt the skin off my thighs as I went down. When I hit the bottom, my foot booted the door so violently that it swung straight open. For a moment I thought that I had made it without spilling the pee, but just then the door swung back and smacked the pee bucket out of my hands and all over my face and my now screaming open mouth.

Our Denise, although genuinely horrified, helpfully fell about in hysterical fits of laughter at the top of the stairs as I proceeded to scream the house down. Mum heard the screams from Nanny Claridge's house and so did Nanny Claridge who was telling her off for leaving us alone all the time. Mum stormed in, hosed me off and then smacked me for getting her into trouble with Nanny Claridge.

The Day I Found Death and Chased Our Denise with It

I was singled out as the cause of anything and everything that went wrong, and Mum and Stanley's growing dislike for me made it increasingly difficult for me to spend time with Denise. It got to the point where she simply wasn't allowed to play with me at all, which is something I found very hard to accept. When Mum and Stanley weren't around, though, Denise and I would snatch some time to play together, and would spend hours just messing about. I would love these stolen opportunities to be normal. Sadly, these moments were few and far between, and the two of us would be punished severely if we were ever caught.

I loved my sister and missed the days when we were closer. Slowly but surely, Mum and Stanley were chipping away at the thing I held most dear: my relationship with Denise. I was very fond of her. She was my little sister and I always felt protective towards her. Whenever I took her place with Stanley she would cry for me until I returned. In those days, I could make her laugh so hard that she would forget about the horrible. We would spend ages trying to make the other laugh out loud. I always won.

If you frightened our Denise, she would burst out laughing, which was just plain funny. She would laugh at everything

– being scared, being happy, being sad, anything. She didn't mean to laugh; it just happened. I knew why she laughed, but the adults didn't really understand her and would get mad at her. I loved her, but I also enjoyed teasing her.

One day, I was playing on my own among the derelict houses behind our house when I came across the body of a dead cat. It had no eyes, and was flat and stiff as a board. I wasn't afraid or squeamish, so I took a closer look.

Just then, I saw our Denise standing at our gate, calling me to come and play with her. I saw an opportunity to tease my little sister! Without a moment's thought, I told her that I had found 'Death' and that I was going to touch her with it.

She looked at me, all cocky, and said, "No you haven't. You can't catch me, anyway – I'm miles away from you."

In our language, this meant, "Catch me if you can."

I had absolutely no intention of actually touching her with Death – I just wanted to tease her with it. Within seconds, I had picked up the stiff, dead cat by its stiff, dead leg and was bounding across the derelict buildings towards her.

I was giggling so hard I could scarcely see straight and was over halfway to her when I looked up and saw her face go from all cocky and 'you can't catch me' to abject terror. I had stumbled, but managed to catch my step and steady myself. As I did so, however, the stiff body of Death somehow snapped off in my hand and the body half propelled itself straight at her. She screamed, I screamed, and we both just lost the plot as Death flew past her head and landed directly behind her.

She went mental! I was mortified. I had a dead cat's leg in my hand and had just emotionally scarred my baby sister for life.

Only now did I realise how disgusting picking up dead things was. I dropped the dead cat's leg and we both ran away crying in shock. Our fear quickly turned to laughter, though, and by the time we got to the end of our street, we were both laughing so hard we couldn't take another step.

When we got home, I washed my hands over and over again because I didn't want Mum or Stanley to know what I had done, but also I couldn't bear the thought of dead cat juice on my hand.

I chased our Denise around the house with "dead cat juice hand" for months after, and we even got some secret pleasure out of the fact that Stanley had "dead cat juice hand" on his pee thing, but I did learn to never play with dead animals again.

I was the main focus of Stanley's horrible attention at this point in time. He would ask me to come over to him and I'd have to do as he said. If I refused, he would look at me with his cold, blue eyes and say, "Where's our Denise then, Karen?" Even writing those words sends a shiver through me. He knew exactly how to get me to do what he wanted. Looking after my little sister was more important to me than anything, and he knew this about me and took full advantage of it. I was aware he was manipulating me at these times, but I felt powerless, so I would just take a big breath and go to him every time.

We knew, without ever saying the words out loud to each other, that we hated the horrible. We didn't like it and we wished it wasn't happening, but we had no idea how to make it stop. I used to wish I was Dona because Stanley never did the horrible to her and she had a lovely mum and dad who were always kind.

Stanley never laughed much. If he wasn't punishing you or doing the horrible, he was sitting there grumping on about losing on the horse racing, the pools or wrestling and about how much he hated working.

As I grew older, Stanley's twisted mind managed to find ever more inventive ways to get me to do the horrible. I had to do it to get anything I wanted or needed in life: to eat, go to school, get dressed, breathe in and out. Everything any normal child took for granted was used against me as a means to manipulate me into doing the horrible. He used it like a currency – do the horrible and you can play with your sister; do the horrible and you can sleep. What was more, the punishment for not doing it when he was "in the mood" had always been a beating, but unfortunately Stanley said this wasn't working on me anymore, so I had to do more horrible instead. The horrible was now both carrot and stick, a punishment as well as a currency. It pervaded every aspect of my life, everything I did or didn't do.

My vision was now twenty-twenty, my hearing and speech had vastly improved, but the more I could see and hear, the less I wanted to. The more I could understand, the more I longed for the days when I wasn't really aware of what was happening to me or around me. The more I could speak properly, the less I wanted to say. I felt like I was disappearing inside myself.

Although my sight and hearing were much better, I had begun to realise that I had problems with my memory. I had to concentrate really hard now to recall things that I used to be able to remember easily. As I wasn't speaking or sharing my thoughts with anyone, and was starting to forget simple things, I started writing things down in code. I say code, but I didn't write well so it was more words and little cartoons. I called them my secret scribble notes. I kept these bits of paper with me everywhere I went and would even hide them in holes I would secretly dig outside. They were like my coded diaries that had tons of my thoughts on them, and I spent a great deal of my time and energy keeping them a secret.

I hated and loved our time at Queen's Street. I hated it because of my life and loved it because of Aunt Pat and Uncle Ken. They never told me I was "naughty, dirty, bad". They never did the horrible or the punishments, no matter what. They loved me, but they never knew what was happening at home, because I never told them – I just couldn't. I couldn't tell them, but I couldn't lie to them either. If ever I thought I was in danger of letting out a secret, I would just fall silent.

I adored cartoons at this age, and they gave me brief moments of the escape I so craved. They were brilliant, colourful, bright, funny, fast and, most of all, violent. In cartoons, the characters could smack things flat and blow them up and never get hurt. I loved Bugs Bunny, but my favourite was Road Runner. I related to both Wile E. Coyote and Road Runner. I knew what it was like to constantly fail to stop something you really wanted to stop, and I loved the way Road Runner always managed to dodge Wile E. Coyote and get away. I used to wish I was him. When I watched cartoons, I would imagine that I was one of the characters that always won – in my head, Stanley was the character that got flattened. When things got bad at home, I would imagine I was in a cartoon, in which I'd save my sister and make the horrible go away. Being able to escape into cartoons in my head also helped with the terrifying flash memories that had started to invade my thoughts.

I knew that I was different from everyone else; I could just feel it. I couldn't get people to understand me and I couldn't understand them, especially if I was concentrating on blocking out the memories, so I did a lot of not speaking and imagining being in a cartoon in those days.

I was trying to spend as much time as I could with Aunt Pat, Uncle Ken and Dona, but the more I did, the angrier Mum and Stanley would get. When Mum and Stanley were out or weren't looking, I'd sneak over the road to see them. I learnt to keep quiet about how much I saw them, loved them, missed them, or how I secretly ached and prayed to be their daughter – still, at least they were now just a street away.

I had settled into a sort of routine. Now that we had Aunt Pat, Uncle Ken and Dona over the road things were a little better. Life was still hard, but I found comfort in some things being the same for a while. Little did I know things were about to dramatically change yet again.

One night, when I was about eight, I was sitting in my bedroom when I heard Mum and Stanley talking in low voices in the sitting room. I crept closer, making as little noise as possible, and listened intently to what they were saying. Mum was telling Stanley that she didn't like being this close to Aunt Pat, Uncle Ken and Nanny Claridge, as they were always poking their noses in and asking too many questions. She said she had heard about a new council estate up near her mum and dad's home and wanted to move there. My heart skipped a beat when I heard this. The last thing I wanted was to move again. Mum dropped her voice a little and I strained to hear as she explained to Stanley that she could tell the benefits and housing people that I had special needs and then they'd give us a home on the brand-new Noctorum estate, on the other side of Birkenhead.

"Do you think they'll buy that she's special needs?" I heard Stanley ask.

"They'll buy anything I tell them," laughed Mum.

I was horrified to hear this. Even at that age, I knew I wasn't special needs. I had fallen behind at school because for so long I hadn't been able to hear what the teachers were saying or read the blackboard and was isolated from my classmates, but I had never been considered special needs.

I listened with growing horror as Mum continued: "The only problem is, we don't have enough kids to get the biggest house."

As always, though, she had a solution: they would have to get our Roma back! Roma had been away and was happy at her boarding school. It was the only time she felt free of all the pressure being put on her at home and the only time she was ever able to enjoy being a child herself. She used to dread having to come home. They didn't seem to care about this, as I could hear Stanley eagerly agreeing with Mum that it would make it cheaper all round for him. I was devastated. I could not imagine living so far away from Aunt Pat and Uncle Ken; they were all that made life bearable and now I was going to lose them. I just couldn't bear it.

Naturally, I had to pretend that I knew nothing of Mum and Stanley's plans, and when they didn't say anything about it to me or Denise for the next few weeks, I started to believe that maybe it wasn't going to happen after all. My hopes were dashed, though, when Mum announced that she had got us a lovely big new house on a brand new estate and we were all moving.

I pleaded with them to let me stay with Aunt Pat. I begged them and promised that I would be good. They seemed immovable, but I was so desperate to stay that I persevered: "I won't tell them anything," I said. "I want them to be my mum and dad now. Please let me stay with them, please!"

I knew before the words were even out of my mouth that I had just made a very serious mistake by saying what I had. Even so, by this point I just didn't care anymore. As Mum screamed, "I'm your fucking mother and you'll do as I…" everything went into slow motion and I saw the punch coming and for the first time ever, I ducked the punch, ran out of the front door and headed for the Monkey Steps.

Stanley chased me out. I could hear his laboured breathing and heavy tread. Thanks to our Dona, though, I could run to the top of the Monkey Steps like a whippet, and I'd got halfway up before he was even across the road. I bolted to the top and looked down. He was still at the bottom, screaming something at me, and had gone bright red. He didn't follow me up, as I knew he wouldn't be arsed, so I stayed there for ages, smiling to myself. I wasn't sure what to do next because I had nowhere else to go, but I was pleased I'd got away and was considering running more often when, all of a sudden, I felt a hard kick in my lower back, sending a searing pain through my body. A vice-like hand gripped my neck. I didn't need to look round to see who it was, I could smell Stanley with my eyes closed. He had driven round the long way in his car and come up behind me; it took five days 'off school' to get over that beating.

The coming weeks were very difficult for me. The worry about moving away from Aunt Pat, Uncle Ken and Dona was making everything else even harder to cope with. I felt lost, alone and very frightened. I knew people and even loved people, but none of them knew about the horrible and I just couldn't speak to those who did.

I often wondered if Mum knew about the horrible. I had tried to tell her and she hadn't believed me. Deep down, part of me thought she must know – how could she not? But the more I thought about it, the more I began to realise that she was never actually in the room when it happened, and Stanley would never refer to it when she was around. When she wasn't there, he'd say things like, "Let's do it," or, "I'm in the mood." We would say, "He wants me to do something." These expressions were never used in front of Mum, though. All of a sudden, I realised that she probably didn't know about the horrible. This realisation completely changed the way I viewed and treated Stanley after this. If it was a secret from Mum and she wouldn't believe me when I told her, maybe she would believe it if she saw it for herself.

I turned this new thought over and over in my head and finally came up with 'the loud plan'. The loud plan was, essentially, to make loads of noise when the horrible was happening, to see if I could attract Mum's attention and make her catch him. I thought this was a brilliant idea and couldn't believe that I hadn't thought of it before. The very next time that Stanley was doing the horrible and I thought she was close by, I put my plan into action.

Big mistake! After just a few attempts at trying to alert Mum, I realised that making noises when the horrible was happening just excited Stanley beyond words and made him think I was really enjoying it. Now that he thought I was enjoying it, it went on for much longer. He called me even more bad names and wouldn't leave me alone for bloody days. As usual, there was no sign of Mum. I don't know if she heard me or not. I quickly abandoned the loud plan, but the damage, I'm afraid, had already been done.

After the loud plan had failed so catastrophically, Stanley started mithering me and nagging me to do the horrible more and more often. He used to always hit me, and he still did it as a punishment, but when it came to the horrible, he would whine on and on about being "in the mood" and making out that I was the cause. "It's all your fault – you're getting me in the mood. Are you going to sort it out?" I would do my best to ignore him, but it never made any difference.

Because I felt so isolated at this point in my life – unable to tell anyone my secret or talk to those who knew – I started to seek out noise and distraction. Despite being so quiet and intro-verted myself, I now felt very uncomfortable with inner silence and would constantly seek out sound and visual stimulation whenever and wherever I could. It was a soothing distraction from what was going on in my head. I had already become fixated with TV, and cartoons especially. I loved the constant changing images, although I didn't much like the radio, as I couldn't understand or relate to many of the sounds coming out of it. It was a bit like listening to a foreign person who sometimes said words that sounded like English.

I was about to change my mind about the radio, though.

One day, Stanley had pulled me off school as pretend ill again to do the horrible. When he had finished, he went out and left me alone in the house for the rest of the day. For some reason, I felt particularly dejected that day. I didn't understand the world, the world didn't seem to understand me, and I didn't know how to change it or make it better.

I made up my mind to ask Aunt Pat if I could live with her when my parents moved, so I snuck up to her house and asked, very tentatively, whether it would be OK. She said she would love it, that she had even tried, but that Mum and Stanley would miss me too much. I remember thinking, no they fecking wouldn't – they didn't even like me!

Then she told me that they were planning to move as well, and if I moved with them, I would be miles and miles away from my Mum, Stanley and everyone. She thought this was a bad thing, but I thought it was brilliant! I really thought she might let me go with her, but she said she couldn't because Mum just wouldn't let her. Then she got upset, and it broke my heart to see her cry so I stopped talking about it.

Just as I was leaving, Aunt Pat put her hand on my arm. "Are you OK, love? You seem very quiet, and... well... I just want to know if everything's all right."

I looked up at her, swallowed the hard lump that had risen in my throat, and nodded gently. I desperately wanted to tell her how I was feeling, to tell her everything, but it seemed like an impossible obstacle. I had learnt to keep my feelings hidden away deep inside of me. No matter how I felt on the inside, I was strong enough now not to cry on the outside. I couldn't tell anyone how I felt about anything, let alone Aunt Pat. I didn't know the words and I didn't want to make her or Uncle Ken hate me, like Mum, or die, like my father.

"Well, if you're sure, love," she said doubtfully.

I nodded again, more decisively this time, and she gave me a kiss as I stepped out on to the street.

As I walked away from their house that day, I knew in my heart that I wouldn't be seeing much of my Aunt Pat and Uncle Ken anymore. I felt an ache growing inside me, like a great big lump in my chest, but I knew there was no point in crying.

I went home and sat on the stairs leading out to our back door. I was doing a little bit of secret inside crying when I heard a voice from the radio say, "Up next, the golden-oldie hour, after these messages."

I was intrigued, so I started to listen and before I knew it, a 'boom, dat, boom, boom, dat' had started and some bloke called Jimmy Ruffin started to sing: *"What becomes of the broken-hearted…"*

I froze to the spot. I knew and understood every single word this man was singing; even the long words I didn't know, I knew. All I could think of was, who is this man? How does this man know my secret feelings? How did he get inside my head? And why is he telling everyone? As I listened to the song, I was hit by wave after wave of overwhelming emotion, which I was trying to keep in control of, so that I could listen.

When the song had finished, the biggest tears and the loudest sobbing came out of me from nowhere. I couldn't stop, no matter what I tried. I felt exposed and betrayed. I just couldn't believe that someone else knew how I secretly felt, but somehow it didn't feel like a comfort; here I am trying to hide my thoughts and feelings and here he is telling everyone about them. It just felt like yet another thing I couldn't control, and I was totally furious.

I suddenly rushed at the radio, picked it up and threw it at the wall, but it simply bounced off and fell to the ground, undamaged. I stood there and stared at it as though it had just stabbed me, and sobbed until I thought my heart would break. I remained there for hours, sobbing and replaying the words of the song in my head.

After that day, I would sometimes listen to this song on purpose. I had pushed my feelings so far down that it was getting hard to find them, so I would listen to *What Becomes of the Broken-Hearted?* to help me reach my sadness, to see if it was still as bad as the last time I looked. It always was.

When I felt I needed to release some of my pent-up emotion, I would scan the radio, searching for the song. Luckily for me, that particular radio station only ever seemed to play golden oldies, so I got to hear it many times, and each time it would have the same effect on me.

It wasn't long before I realised that the writer hadn't read my mind: Jimmy Ruffin had brought out *What Becomes of the Broken-Hearted?* years before and was just an incredible singer whose song had touched the sadness inside me by accident.

After discovering that song, I got hooked on music and the radio. I found it comforting. I still loved the television, too, and Stanley had said that when we moved the family would have one of our own, so at least I had some escape to look forward to.

The Noctorum

It was the early 1970s. The radio was playing T-Rex and Rod Stewart, Benny Hill had recently introduced us to Ernie, the fastest milkman in the west, and some ugly, sweaty old Elvis fan in a bad wig who called himself Gary Glitter was in the charts.

The Two Ronnies, *The Partridge Family* and *The Liver Birds* were on TV, the cinemas were running *Shaft* and *Love Story*, and the kids were playing with Space Hoppers and Chopper bikes. Ted Heath was still our prime minister, the newspapers were reporting on Vietnam and Northern Ireland, and Mr Heath had captained his team to win the Admiral's Cup on Morning Cloud. I was nearly nine years old, going on 45.

Changes were afoot in Merseyside. The local council was busy clearing away old pre-war housing to make way for their rejuvenation project. The Noctorum estate was being built on the foothills of the historic and beautiful Bidston Hill. The Noctorum was surrounded by similar housing estates, which between them shared the local schools, pools, parks, shops, pubs and off-licences. The whole area was being revamped. The council had lofty aspirations for their new community and were trying to cater for 'working' family-oriented residents. Mum pitched herself perfectly to the local council – selling us as ideal tenants for this new development. In 1972, when the Claridge family moved in, the Noctorum was a muddy building site, with many part-built houses and just four finished ones. We were the very first family to move in.

Number 29 Stratford Way was a modern, ultra-bland, four-bedroom, end-of-terrace house, with a proper indoor bathroom, central heating, hot and cold running water, a tiny open front garden and larger fenced back garden. It was indeed a heavenly palace compared with our previous homes.

At the front of the house was a large communal triangle of grass, which would eventually have similar houses along each side. Our house was on the bottom left of the triangle, right next to the part-built shop that was to be called Billy Rainbows.

In order to ensure she got a house on this modern estate, Mum had to completely reinvent herself as the model parent of a model family. That meant that she and Stanley had to get jobs, because she needed to prove to the housing people that they were a working family, and of course Roma was moved back in with us to make up the numbers. Once they had signed the tenancy agreement, Mum left her job… to pursue her bingo-playing and shopping career.

Her whole life revolved around shoplifting and the many bingo halls in Birkenhead. Her day-to-day existence was determined by the bingo halls' opening times (day and night), and if you wanted her for anything during those times, you would have to go find her and get her 'called out'. Most times, we would have to wait for the end of the game for her to come out, often very late into the night.

Mum did occasionally take paid work, but she never stayed anywhere for long. Everywhere she went, someone else always stole the money she was in charge of and she would always lose the job.

When Mum first met him, Stanley was a manual labourer, but for a long time he had been a painter and decorator. His work was always cash in hand and very casual, so that he could get his state unemployment benefits every week. In order for us to get the house on Stratford Way, however, he had had to come off the dole and get a proper paid job. He was now working as a full-time short-distance lorry driver. Having said that, it wasn't long before the benefits people started paying him 'accidentally' all over again. He would claim that he'd told them that he was in work, but that the payments just kept coming through. Honestly, what could he do? He had better things to do than keep telling them, so all he could do was keep his head down and spend it.

Over the following months, more people moved on to the estate. Building work continued at a pace. The funny thing about the estate was that it had professional builders as well as the 'professional unbuilders'. These were people who would come at night and take down, or 'unbuild', what the builders had spent all day building. Now, to be clear, the unbuilders never took anything – they just unbuilt it for fun. The bizzies (the police) were there most nights trying to catch them, and it was entertaining to watch out of my bedroom window.

We nearly got kicked off the estate shortly after we moved in, when the builders found out that Stanley had been 'shopping' on their building site for a cement-mixer, and windows that had already been fitted. We were allowed to stay, though, after he'd convinced them that he took the stuff to protect it and now he was giving it back and promised to inform the police if anyone else tried to take things. After that, he didn't keep stuff for long: anything he took, he quickly sold to his work friends, so that "poor people could have jobs".

Mum always spent money (even money she'd earned) like she had stolen it. She had a sort of 'quick, get rid of the evidence' attitude to the family's finances. As far as 'shopping' was concerned, her thinking was very clear: the shop had 20 and she had none, therefore the owners could spare one; don't get caught, and if you do get caught, lie, cry or flee, because you will get punished for getting caught and not for stealing. Despite all the legal and dodgy ways that my parents made money appear, we were always broke, always in debt and always having to hide from Bogeyman Bill. Bogeyman Bill was anyone who knocked on the door for overdue payments or for services like the electric, gas, water, rent, the Provident, the catalogue or to empty the meter on the back of the TV. It was also any friend or family member they owed money to.

Whenever the door was knocked on unexpectedly, the whole family would have to dart into their hiding places, keeping still and quiet until whoever it was got bored and went away. Sometimes bill collectors would peer through the letterbox or living-room windows to see if anyone was home. In the end, Mum nailed some carpet over the letterbox and kept the front curtains permanently closed to stop them peeking in. If she was in a good mood, she would send us to the door to tell them our parents were out.

On our estate, the milkman probably got the hardest time. That poor sod was robbed each way from Wednesday. Residents stole milk and food from his cart as he delivered; they robbed him of his money bag; they never paid him for what they ordered, always telling him it wasn't there when they opened the door and they even nicked his lunch from his cab if he accidentally left it open. If they weren't robbing him, they were robbing his customers, who really did find the milk and food missing when they opened their doors. I bet he hated coming on to our estate.

I think our estate also managed to get most of the poor postmen sacked for theft, fraud and deception, as many, including Mum and Stanley, would often get their benefit Giros, cash them, then swear blind they never did, which would always make another one come, which they always received without any problem. In the end, the poor postman would not part with the post unless he personally identified you and took your fingerprints himself.

We did indeed get our own TV. We loved cartoons. We would be scattered around the house and the shout would go out: "Cartooooons!" Before the opening credits had finished, we'd all race from wherever we were and plonk ourselves in a row, bellies down, elbows on the floor and heads resting on hands. You just had to be careful whose voice was shouting it or you wouldn't find cartoons at all. On more than one occasion, I heard, "Cartoooons," but rushed through all excited, only to realise it was Stanley and the horrible.

Billy Rainbows, the shop next to us, sold a little bit of everything except for booze, which was fine by us, as nobody in our family ever drank – in fact, except for Mum, who was always on prescription medication, my parents' only obvious social vice was to smoke like chimneys. Most of our generation grew up in someone else's 'lung cancer cloud'. Back then it was both cool and very grown-up to smoke. Everyone smoked as soon as they could; those who couldn't, faked it; and those who wouldn't... were just babies.

I remember we'd always be sent to the shop to buy cigarettes. The magic sentence for any child to walk out of any shop with booze or fags in those days was "Mum or Dad sent me".

As 1972 came round, and I turned nine, life in the Noctorum took a turn for the worse. Roma was going from a girl to a young woman and didn't want to be treated like a skivvy by the stepmother cow, nor did she want to babysit her bloody kids all the time. To be fair, who could blame her... well, actually, for a while I did.

Roma loved Rod Stewart and played his album over and over on the family portable High Fidelity record player (shopped from T. J. Hughes) until I couldn't bear to hear his voice ever again. She dressed the same, bought all his records, covered her walls with his posters and even cried when she saw him on telly.

As for me, I was a Motown girl at heart. Every time I saw or heard Rod Stewart, I would see our Roma trying to look like him, playing his songs over and over again. That was until one day when I accidentally (on purpose) cooked her Rod Stewart album in the oven. When it came out, it looked nothing like an ashtray, as I'd heard it would. I was becoming angry inside and was starting to do things like this even though I knew what the consequences would be. I spent the rest of the night taking a beating from Stanley, until I looked nothing like Karen, but it was worth it, not to have to hear *Maggie May* one more sodding time.

We did get more visitors at Stratford Way but not too often and only under the strictest conditions.

One day, Aunt Violet was visiting and she was a Category 1 visitor.

Visitors were split into three categories, though essentially you would never tell or talk about the horrible to anyone, ever. The other rules for each category were as follows:

Category 1 (Aunt Pat, Uncle Ken, Nanny and Grandpa Wallbridge and other friends and family who were law-abiding): smile, pretend to be happy and well fed, do not say anything, deny whatever is said and act all distressed if ever Mum or Stanley were taken out of our sight.

Category 2 (Social Services, professionals and authority figures): smile, pretend to be happy and well fed, don't speak unless spoken to and lie through your teeth if you are.

Category 3 (relatives and friends who break the law): smile, pretend to be happy and well fed, it's OK they are as bad as us and we can talk about whatever they are talking about.

Aunt Violet was Mum's snobby eldest sister, who had lived in the flat above us when I was a baby. She was the boss of Mum. She was very strict and, most importantly of all, married to a policeman. Aunt Violet was a real relative, not a fake one – no matter who we met back then, we were told we were related to all of them. We had to call them fake names, like Mrs Wallbridge who was 'Nanny Wallbridge' or Stanley's friends who did the horrible, like fake Uncle Reg from the market and so on. It confused us no end and I hated how much fake relatives were allowed to do to us, but there was little we could do, as we were never sure who we were really related to. In any event, it seemed anyone could do whatever they wanted to us, more so if they were called family.

All of my immediate family spoke a strange hybrid slang of swear words, grunts and gestures, hardly ever using real words, and we all had broad Merseyside accents. Stanley was the odd one out as he had a Cockney accent. Mum had shopped at all my real family's houses in the past, and none of them liked Stanley because he was always on the scrounge, but us kids got on with them all OK.

By this point, I was hardly going to school at all, as Stanley would take me to work with him in the lorry. The first time it happened, in my naivety, I believed I really was going to work with him, but I quickly realised that this was just another excuse for him to get me alone to do the horrible. These days the horrible seemed to be happening practically every day. I withdrew further and further into my own head, my own world, as I was introduced to more and more fake uncles.

Stanley got a sadistic pleasure out of me doing the horrible with someone else, because it seemed to prove to him that I was the dirty one, which was always his argument to make me do it when I didn't want to – which was always. Stanley told me that I was a dirty girl and that he was stopping me from being caught for being naughty, dirty, bad. He said he was protecting me because he didn't want Social Services to put me in care. As a nine-year-old, I just accepted this.

I hated this new stuff called Vaseline (which Stanley secretly called 'wet' – as in "Put some wet on it"). I hated being woken from my sleep with him already hurting my pee and poo places, even with the wet. I hated bathtime, bedtime, getting- up time, daytime

– all the time, really. I hated the night visits the most. I would lie in bed praying that he would leave me alone, just for one night.

As my life became harder and harder to bear, I did my best not to cooperate. I had taught myself to wake up at the slightest smell or sound, like the sickening mixture of hot liquid, wet and fags, or the jingling of Stanley's belt buckle accompanied by the strange heavy breathing. Then I would roll myself in my quilt or pretend to be in a deep sleep or thrashing nightmare. Then I might get in a sneaky smack, after which I'd pretend my arm was asleep or that I needed the toilet, and on it went. Sometimes it worked, sometimes it made things worse. I was simply overwhelmed by the daily horror that my life had become.

Mentally and emotionally, I was shutting down.

Running

I have spent so much of my life trying to forget what happened next that it has affected my ability to remember it well at all.

Some of my memories of those days are incomplete or too painful to recall, while others are terrifyingly crisp and vivid. All my recollections are nonetheless jumbled up like jigsaw-puzzle pieces that won't stay where you put them, never allowing you to see the complete picture at any one time.

Over the next couple of years, I continued to stay silent. I had discovered that it was safer and easier. When I did speak, I spoke in both ordinary speak and fluent swear. In my head, my thoughts were defiant and full of swear words. I always thought things I would never say out loud – like, for example, if I was asked, "Put this in your mouth," I would think, "Put it in your own mouth, you bug-eyed fuck monster," but I would always just say, OK, switch off and get on with it.

As disconnected from all that as I could sometimes be, I had also developed an intense sensitivity to other people's feelings. I simply couldn't bear to see anyone cry or watch someone hurt someone else, not even on the TV. I always felt I should do whatever it took to make it stop. It was an overwhelming instinct, and because of how it made me feel, I got into a few fights on the estate. I just didn't cope well with sad people or cruel people.

Despite everything that was going on in my life, and all the horrible, confusing things that my family said and did, I loved them and wanted to make them happy with me, so if they needed something and I could get it or do it for them, I would. Any child wants their family's attention and approval and I was no different. I was starved of affection and love, and consequently whenever my family wanted something, I would do whatever it took to get it. They wouldn't even have to ask, I would simply see that they were upset and I would try to fix it – that's just how I was.

Most of the time, my family seemed to hate me, but when I was stealing something for them or doing a job for them, they seemed to like me, and I liked being liked, even if it was for just a short while. It breaks my heart even now to think how desperately hard I tried to make people love me. The horrible seemed to be everywhere I went these days. I had grown to hate the sound of the front door. Stanley was not only doing it himself and inviting his friends to the house or to his lorry, but now he was also dropping me at his friends' houses and leaving me there. Whenever he did this, they seemed to want to do the horrible to me as well. I was sure he was doing it on purpose.

He would tell Mum he was taking me to work with him on the lorry because he needed the help. When we got on the road, however, he would then say that he couldn't take me with him today because his work insurance didn't allow for it and he would need to drop me off at his friend's house for the day. Some of the people he left me with were very violent and would force me to pose for still and moving pictures, which I hated.

Late on in 1972, something inside me snapped. Anger had been building inside for so long now. Up until this point, I had kept a lot of my frustration and angry thoughts to myself. I recall one particular day very clearly, because it was the first day I'd ever really properly stood up to Stanley. We were sitting in his lorry and he was about to take me to visit the man who lived near the caravan park. I knew this man was very violent and I hated visiting him. I told Stanley that the man was hurting me.

I'll never forget his response. He said, "Don't be such a fuckin' twat – there's not a mark on you! I only interfere when they really fuckin' hurt you, like stab you or somfink. You gotta remember, you don't behave, so what do you expect?"

His words kept flashing through my mind. I couldn't believe he said I didn't behave – all I wanted was to be good and please people! He meant that he wanted me to stay still while people hurt me. I was furious; anger bubbled up inside me. Before I knew what I was doing or thinking, I just screamed at him, "If not screaming and crying when you're fucking hurting me is not 'behaving', then I don't know what is! Why have you got to make it hurt?"

Stanley was shocked at first, then went a funny colour, then lost the plot and nearly crashed the lorry. He was so angry at my outburst he couldn't even swear properly. He pulled over the lorry abruptly. His bald head had gone bright red and looked like it was going to explode.

My brain just went into overdrive. This is the first time that I remember thinking and arguing with myself, which must have happened in a few seconds, but felt like it took longer at the time. I was overcome by an overwhelming urge to hit him. A defiant, angry voice inside my head was saying, "Smack him. Smack him quick and run away," but the rational part of me said, "No, he'll kill me." Then the defiant voice said, "Not if he can't catch me he won't. Remember how fast you ran up the Monkey Steps. Unlock the cab door and have it open and be ready to bolt. Go on, smack him and run away."

Before I knew what was happening, I'd punched Stanley with one hand, slapped him with the other and was off out of the lorry cab like a rabbit. Stanley's face was imprinted in my mind as I ran – it had gone from furious red to astonished purple to shocked white. I was running as fast as my legs could carry me and I was not going to stop for anyone.

I looked back and saw him nearly fall out of the lorry's cab and start after me, but he didn't make it past the back of the lorry before he had to stop to catch his breath, so I just kept going. I ran faster than I've ever run in my life. My lungs were bursting, and my throat burnt. I felt so good, so alive.

I was fast and agile, and felt like I could run forever; my brain was going even faster than me, as I suddenly became acutely aware of my surroundings. I was on a narrow country road and had deliberately run in the opposite direction to the way the lorry was facing. I reasoned that running away from the back of the lorry was best as Stanley wouldn't be able to turn the lorry round, and if he tried to reverse, I would hear him and dive into the field. I was frightened, but elated.

My intention wasn't to run away forever; it was just to avoid having to do the horrible with the man from the caravan park, and give Stanley a bit of a fright. I knew that I would get a beating once I got home again, but I didn't care.

Running

I kept checking behind me and couldn't see him so I started to feel a bit calmer and slowed down. Like Denise would when she was scared, I started to giggle uncontrollably. I don't know why – I didn't think anything was funny – I just couldn't stop laughing.

I'd slowed down to a fast walk now and was planning my next move. I was thinking that I would get home and stay near Mum for as long as possible because Stanley wouldn't ever talk about the horrible in front of her, so wouldn't be able to tell me off, when – SMACK!

I was hit square in the face. The beating continued for ages. It was Stanley. Like with the Monkey Steps before, he had driven the long way round, come back down the other end of the country road and hidden in the lay-by ahead of me. Stanley beat me black and blue for running away – he said he was teaching me a lesson "for my own safety", which Mum later accepted, when she asked about the marks on my face.

I did learn a painful lesson that day, but something else had happened, something else had changed: once he had stopped hitting me, Stanley didn't even mention my smacking him or asking him why he had to make it hurt. It was then that I understood that Stanley was off his head (mentally ill). He couldn't refer to what had really happened only a few minutes before. It was like he couldn't cope with anything real. That got me thinking.

It was a long drive home. Stanley was talking to me, but I couldn't hear him. My mind was racing with the sudden realisation that Stanley was sick in the head. As Stanley jabbered on at me, I sat staring through the windscreen, thinking. As I thought things over, I asked myself a series of questions: he makes us do the horrible, but he never says it out loud. Why? He's afraid of

Mum finding out about the horrible. Why? He never admits that other people do the horrible to me, even though he knows they do. Why? He always says it's my fault, when he knows he makes me do it. Why? He never admits that he is doing the horrible, even when he's doing it, even when it's me he's doing it to. Why?

Suddenly, it felt like all the questions I had been asking for years now had an answer: he's crazy.

Stanley and I never spoke of this again, and although he tried dropping me off at friends' houses a few more times after this, he eventually gave up, when I started running away, hitching a ride home and waiting at Judy, our neighbour's house, at the top of Stratford Way, for him to get home. He never told me off for running away, but he did always make me pay.

Stanley and his friends did most of the horrible, but I also happened upon some of it on my own. I recall a very old man called Steve, whose flat was just across from Nanny Scott's. He always left his door slightly ajar and the local kids would sneak into his hall and nick the loose change out of his coat, which would be hanging in his hallway.

He'd often ask kids to go to the shop to buy his newspapers. I was pleased to do this because he gave me some sweets in return. I was only about nine at the time and free sweets were a very big deal.

One time when I went to see Nanny Scott, Steve was standing in his doorway. As I passed, he asked me in. I stepped inside, all excited because I thought that he was going to ask me to go to the shop. Before I knew what was happening, though, Steve had grabbed me by the back of the neck and pushed me into his bedroom. His hand felt like a vice, taking my breath away and I yelped in pain. The next thing I knew I was naked, face down on his bed, and squeezing my eyes shut tight to block out the horror of what was happening to me. He hurt me for ages. I didn't fight, even though he was hurting me; I just lay as still as I could, praying to anyone who might be listening for it to end. No one was listening. I lay there for an eternity until he finally pushed himself off me and wheezed, "Go make us a cup of tea, will ya?"

I staggered to the kitchen, too stunned to speak, and my hands trembled as I poured out his tea. When I returned, he grunted, "D'ya want paper money or sweets?"

I remember thinking I had never had paper money of my own before, so I agreed to take that.

He smiled, like we were friends again, "Now don't go telling anyone about our arrangements, will ya?"

I shook my head. "Promise me now?"

'I won't tell anyone, I'm used to it,' I said.

This seemed to please him even more. He patted me on the bum with his bony hand and told me to go. I left and ran across to the toilet at Nanny Scott's flat.

By this point in my life, I was so used to the horrible happening every time I met new men that I simply accepted that it was going to happen. I didn't encourage it or initiate it, but I did always expect it. I felt that I couldn't do anything to change or alter it, I might as well just accept it. It had become something I thought all men would do to me, and although I knew that it didn't happen to everyone (Dona never had to do the horrible), I believed that it would always happen to me. I still hated it, but at least with Steve, I was given sweets or paper money. I thought I was lucky, as with Stanley I didn't get anything.

I would take my sweets and rush off to Leasowe Beach to recover and eat my sweets. I liked it down there; it was calm and tranquil and it gave me time to gather myself. From then on, whenever I went to see Nanny Scott, Steve would be standing in the doorway to his flat beckoning me in. It had become so normal that I had long stopped questioning it.

After a few months, however, I went to visit Nanny Scott (having done the horrible with Steve beforehand) and left her flat to nip round to my Aunt Joan's, who lived nearby. When I returned to Nan's, though, I noticed that Steve's door was ajar. I had already been down to the shop for him when I'd done the horrible, so I was surprised that it was open. I went in and, to my horror, saw that he was on the bed doing the horrible to someone else. I couldn't believe it; I thought I was the only one he did that to. As I edged closer, I realised that he was on top of my baby sister. I felt sick. Denise was undressed, crying and had blood on her legs. I went mental!

I knew they knew each other, but I did not even consider that he would dare to hurt my baby sister and besides, I had already done the horrible! The realisation that it was happening to my little sister sent me into a blind rage. Without a second thought, I rushed to the kitchen, picked up a big pan and flew back to the bedroom. Then, with every single ounce of strength I could muster, I smacked him right across the head with it. He was so shocked he didn't even try to stop me as I pounded his head, a word per smack. GET smack OFF smack MY smack SISTER smack! I finally hit him hard enough to get him off my sister and long enough to get us out of there.

We rushed out of there and on the long walk home we talked and decided we were telling Mum. When we got home, I took a deep breath and said, "Steve, who lives across the way from Nanny Scott, has been dirty with us... down there," pointing at my pee place. I expected her not to believe us and do nothing in any event, but she flew up in a rage from the sofa and started ranting with wild, blind fury.

Suddenly we were at the hospital, doctors were looking at our pee places, we were taking a foul-tasting medicine for something we had caught, and special policemen were asking us questions about what had happened. I couldn't really understand what all the fuss was about – I had told Mum before about bad things happening to us, but she had never done anything like this before.

Mum was so furious about what had happened that one night, we even saw her being brought home by the police and warned to stay away from Steve's flat or she'd get herself arrested and charged.

Shortly after this, someone from the police – a Category 2 visitor – came to see us and told us that what Steve had done was called child abuse, and that child abuse was a crime and a bad thing, and that you could go to jail for doing it. I was so confused. Why was this time so wrong, when it happened all the time? A few weeks later, Mum told us all that Steve had indeed been sent to jail for what he had done to us. I was dumbfounded.

Shortly after, a Category 1 visitor came and asked a question that seemed to stop Mum and Stanley dead in their tracks:

"Why aren't the children at school?"

All of a sudden, we were back at school. I was now going to Hillside Primary, which was just a few short streets away from our house. The authorities brought me a school uniform, shoes and a coat. My new headmistress was called Mrs Cook, and my teacher's name was Mrs Titley.

It took her no time at all to realise that, even at the age of around nine years old, I couldn't read or write very well, nor could I understand most of what she said. It wasn't long before I was at the back of the class, on my own, and teaching myself out of her special-needs learning box.

I hated this school. Whereas before school had been a haven, I was now so far behind my classmates and found it so difficult to understand or communicate that the teachers simply wrote me off. Mrs Titley spent most of her time trying to hit me with the blackboard rubber and sending me to Mrs Cook's office, where I would be told off for raising my hand to ask "Why?" too many times. They felt I was doing it on purpose to disrupt the class. I was indeed doing it on purpose, because I didn't understand. Apparently, nobody is that thick. They said I was attention-seeking. I knew I wasn't attention-seeking, but I believed I was that stupid.

Mrs Titley would ask me things like, "If two trains are travelling at 50 miles per hour, one makes two stops and lets off 10 people at the station and the other does not, what time do they all go to dinner?" I wouldn't have the faintest idea what the question meant let alone what the answer should be. The questions were so far removed from the reality of my life.

If she'd asked me, "If two men were standing in a room, which one could you run the fastest from − the big, fat smoker or the weedy little gym freak?" then I would probably be more able to answer. I gave up trying to answer their impossible questions. I'd just say, "Sorry, miss," and walk away.

One day, I got home from another tortuous day at school to find Stanley in the hallway. He looked worried as he told me there was a social worker (CAT 1) in the living room who wanted to talk to me about stuff. I had never met a social worker before. All I knew about social workers was that they could take bad children away and we were most definitely not allowed to talk to them.

Social Services had never shown an interest in my life up until this point and I was frightened. This was the first time I remember hoping that Stanley would stay silent and not tell them how naughty, dirty, bad I was and he sensed this fear in me and told me, "it's OK if we just keep our mouths shut, you understand." I nodded.

Stanley sent me to my room to change out of my school clothes. As I did so, I started thinking about Steve and everything the police had told me. I remembered that the police had told me that a man's pee thing is a 'penis', my pee thing is called a 'vagina', and everyone has a poo place called a 'bottom'. Everyone calls them their 'privates', because they are supposed to be private. I'm not to let anyone touch mine, not until I'm 16 and not until I say so. Then I thought about how Stanley (and all the others) didn't want anyone to know about the horrible – just like Steve, who was wrong to do what he did. If he was wrong, then maybe Stanley and his friends were wrong too… Stanley had drummed it into me that he was allowed to do the horrible because he was our adopted dad, but at that moment it struck me for the first time that if he was allowed to do it, then why wouldn't he simply tell people he was doing it. I turned this new thought over and over in my head. Is Stanley allowed to do it or not?

Broken

I sat down on my bed and tried to work out what I should do. I could simply tell the social worker and see how Stanley reacts. If he was allowed to do the horrible to me, then surely nothing would happen, but if he's not allowed to, then maybe they would stop him. Even though telling them seemed like the logical thing to do, I was absolutely terrified of putting it into words. Every time I'd told anyone in the past, terrible things had happened. Were things going to go wrong again? When I had told Mum, she hadn't believed me, had stopped loving me and hadn't really spoken to me since. When I told my father, he had run away and died. Was this the right thing to do? Then I realised that things couldn't be any worse, as I already had to do the horrible for everything and I just needed it to stop. It took me all of my courage to go downstairs.

A tiny bit of me was thinking (just for a brief moment) about a life without Stanley and all his horrible and how wonderful that could be, but it didn't seem like something that could ever be real.

Now that I had made up my mind, I felt strangely calm. After everything the police had told me, everything I had seen on TV and all that had happened to Steve, I knew that if Stanley wasn't meant to be doing the horrible to us, then a social worker would sort it out. All I had to do was say the words out loud in front of them both. I curled my fingers into fists, took a deep breath and opened the living-room door.

The social worker was a tall, thin lady with dark hair. I was glad it was a lady and not a man. She was standing next to Stanley, but she was smiling at me.

"Hello, Karen," she said. "I'm Mrs Potter."

I wasn't used to being called Karen, as most of my family now called me Kaz or Shy, but I said hello back. Mrs Potter looked quite nervous, but she asked me lots of questions, like whether I liked my new clothes, how I was finding school and whether I had any trouble understanding the teacher. I was getting more and more frustrated because I wanted to tell her so badly but was having to answer all her questions as politely as I could. Suddenly, I blurted out, "Stanley makes me suck his penis!"

Mrs Potter nearly fell over. Stanley went white with rage and sat down on the floor.

The lady looked at me very hard. "Karen, what did you just say?"

I repeated it, a little more slowly this time so that she would definitely hear me. Then she turned to Stanley, who was still sitting on the carpet, looking at the swirly pattern. "Is that true?" she asked.

Stanley didn't answer straight away. He was shaking his head. Then he sighed heavily, stood up and looked the social worker lady straight in the eye.

"It's kind of true but not the way she says it."

The social worker lady didn't say anything, but she was looking at Stanley.

"She keeps pushing herself on to me, trying to force me into letting her suck me off," he said. "I've tried to stop her, but didn't always manage it; she nearly got me a couple of times." He told her he would welcome some help with my crazy sex behaviour.

I looked at him in sheer shock and thought, she's never going to believe that bunch of old –

"Karen, is it true? Have you been trying to force yourself on your father's privates with your mouth?"

The lady's voice had changed. It was harder now and not as kind.

I just stood there, speechless. Then I stammered, "No, I haven't! He makes me do it – he knows he does!"

"That's not what your father tells us."

"He's not my father!" I burst out.

Stanley replied, "That's what she always says, she's just saying this to punish me, she just hates me because I'm not her real father."

Then he said, "Her real father tried to kill her, then he killed himself, gassed his-self to death in a car a few years back."

I was stunned. What did he just say? My father tried to kill me? Then he killed himself! Nothing made sense to me anymore.

Stanley was shaking his head and looked serious.

"The only one who abused her was him, that nutter father of hers," he continued, "and she's just blamin' me for it because she doesn't like me. Mrs Wallbridge – she's a friend of the family – knows all about it. She's been tryin' to help us get Karen's sexual urges under control, but we're not sure what to do about it. It's like she's out of control."

I couldn't believe it. How could he make it sound like it was me who was doing this?

Mrs Potter was nodding sympathetically, and then she started talking about how it might help if I always wore lots of clothes and that I should take cold baths if I felt funny in my privates. I didn't take in what she was saying; I was reeling. Then she said something about Nanny Wallbridge and just left. I didn't understand most of what she said or what had just happened.

 as still trying to come to terms with the fact that she had

believed Stanley over me. But even that didn't really register as all I could think of was what Stanley had said about my father killing himself, "gassed his-self in a car."

I was numb for days. I barely felt the beating I took that night.

I never learn, as Stanley told me between bouts of smacking and horrible. "You must be dead thick," he said. And it was true: even the teacher had asked me that very day just how someone with such a "smart mouth" could be so very stupid. Nothing anyone said or did could break through my confusion. What Stanley had said about my father – "Her father tried to kill her, then he killed himself, gassed his-self to death in a car" – kept repeating itself over and over in my mind.

Unbeknown to me at the time, Mrs Potter had made a note on my Social Services file regarding her visit. Somehow, Stanley had persuaded her that at nine years old, I had a distorted attitude to sex and had been making sexual advances to him. Little did I know it, but a chain reaction had been set in motion that was to have disastrous, life-long consequences.

Not long after Mrs Potter's visit, Mum was made to take me to see the new family doctor about a rash on my backside that was very itchy. He made it go away and said something about it being a disease from sexual something. He said he was going to make a note on my file. I didn't really understand, but he said that he had spoken to Mrs Potter, the social worker, and she had told him what had been going on. I didn't like the way he said that – it was like he was cross with me. Even so, I liked our doctor because he was safe.

A few weeks after Mrs Potter's visit, Nanny Wallbridge came to visit again and spoke to Stanley and Mum. After a long talk they called me into the living room. Nanny Wallbridge didn't seem very happy with me.

"Your poor parents are being driven mad trying to control you, young lady," she said, pursing her lips. "Your father has been ringing me, telling me what you've been trying to do to him."

I wanted to say that he wasn't my father and that I hadn't been doing anything – Stanley had been doing it to me! – but before I could say anything Nanny Wallbridge was explaining that she had spoken to Social Services and had suggested that I be sent away to school. Apparently, this would help me master my "sexual behaviour". I had no idea what this meant, but the next thing I knew, I was in a convent.

St Mary's Convent was an all-girls boarding school. I was encouraged to turn to this all-knowing and all-seeing God, who was apparently everywhere, and repent my wicked, wayward ways. Some scary, angry-looking people dressed in black and white told me that God knew everything that everyone had ever done or thought and that I had to tell Him I was sorry for trying to suck Stanley's penis. I remember telling them that if God knew everything, then He would know it wasn't me and wouldn't want me to say sorry. He would know I was telling the truth. I asked the nuns why God didn't come and help me if He was so good. Apparently, He can't help in individual cases, but He would still like to hear me say sorry.

In my frustration, I became a disruptive and obstinate pupil.

From the moment I got to St Mary's, religion was everywhere. They tried to teach me stories from the Bible, but I couldn't understand what they were trying to teach me. I would respond with questions like, "If we all come from Adam and Eve, does that mean we're all related? Isn't that illegal?" and, "How do you get pregnant without sex?" I admit my questions made the class laugh and that I was disruptive, but I wasn't trying to be funny or undermine their faith. I honestly couldn't understand their book. I felt like the world had gone mad around me and that they were all allergic to the truth.

The nuns didn't like my attitude and just as quickly as I had arrived I was leaving. Suddenly I was in a car with two strangers being driven to Yorkshire to see Nanny and Grandpa Wallbridge.

Pately Bridge

I woke up in the back of a car. It was pitch black and for a moment I thought the people sitting in front were some of Stanley's friends. I felt a familiar lurch in my stomach and could hear my heart pounding in my ears. It was a freezing – cold night, and there were strange sounds and smells. I had no idea where I was and started to panic.

The car pulled into a field and someone got out of the passenger seat. I asked, "Where are we?"

A lady's voice snapped, "You're in Pately Bridge. Be quiet and follow me!"

I got out of the car, but asked, "Why? Where are we going?"

"You will only get one warning. Be quiet and follow me."

"Follow you? I can't even fucking see… "

Smack!

"You never use that language in this place. Understood?"

I nodded, even though it was dark and I knew the lady wouldn't be able to see me.

"Is that you, Nanny Wallbridge?" I asked.

Smack!

"I said, be quiet and follow me."

We crunched down a path. I was aware of strange sounds about me as we passed around the back of what looked like a bit of a train with the lights on. I felt the ground beneath me change and we stepped through a doorway. It was so dark I couldn't even see my hands.

The lady said firmly, "Right, madam, here is your torch. Don't switch it on. Here's your blanket. Don't get it wet. This is where you will be sleeping and you will be locked in."

"Locked in? Why? What are you doing? Why am I here?"

Smack!

The lady switched on her torch and I could see it was Nanny Wallbridge and we were standing in a tiny shed, stacked to the roof with tools and boxes. There was just enough room to walk alongside the tiny bed. There were cobwebs everywhere. I've been terrified of spiders ever since I was a little girl. I felt a panicky sensation in my chest.

"Here you go. You can use this when you need to go to the toilet."

She passed me a bucket and some loo roll.

"You will be woken up early every morning to do the chores. I will tell you what the chores are."

I listened to her list of commands without interrupting.

"You must never remove all your clothes at any time. I mean that. Never."

This was absolutely fine by me.

"You are never permitted to go anywhere or do anything without permission. You must never speak unless spoken to."

I was a bit confused by this: how could I ask for permission if I wasn't allowed to speak?

"Furthermore, you must use the fewest words possible, when you are allowed to speak."

"What the – ?"

"You are to wash yourself three times a day – morning, noon and night – in the stream outside. You are not permitted to remove your clothes when washing."

"Wash with my clothes on in a freezing-cold stream!" I said, "But it's bloody freezing in here. Why can't I wash in your… "

Smack!

"'You have already had your warning about your language and about speaking. Understood?"

I nodded. I didn't dare say anything back.

"Now, sit on the bed until we say you can move."

"When you're gone, can I switch on the tor – " Smack!

"You will learn."

She slammed the door behind her, leaving me alone in the darkness. I imagined spiders crawling over me, which made my skin itch uncomfortably. Alone and unable to see around me, my brain started to go into overdrive. Although a few months had passed since Mrs Potter's visit, Stanley's words still repeated in my head whenever I was confused: "Her father tried to kill her, then he killed himself, gassed his-self to death in a car." It was like I no longer had any control over my thoughts. Images suddenly started to flood into my head of things I hadn't thought about for years, like the wardrobe, the stinky house, the man with the yellow hat and his jacket, but I didn't know what any of these memories meant.

My thoughts were now racing. My mother never loved me after I told her about the horrible. My father gassed himself in a car after I told him. My family don't want me to tell them about the horrible, and everyone thinks it's my fault anyway. Oh, dear God, why did I tell? Why can't I keep my big mouth shut? What's wrong with me? I've killed my father! Stanley always says that loving me makes you do bad things, so I really must be the cause of what has happened! Is that true? Is it really me? It must be me – look who is sleeping with the spiders tonight. My thoughts were interrupted when suddenly the door opened and there was Grandpa Wallbridge, holding a lamp and a tray with hot tea, soup and some cheese sandwiches.

He said, "Hello, Karen. I thought you might like something to eat and some light in here."

His voice was gentle, soothing. I nodded, but didn't smile. I was thinking, here we go, this is where we do the horrible. I knew I wouldn't fight him. It wouldn't do any good.

"Look, Karen, I know it is a little cramped at the moment, but we weren't expecting you, so this was the best we could do in a rush. Don't worry – we'll sort it out as we go. Here, eat this, then settle yourself down for the night. It is very late and you must be tired."

I didn't move and he continued, "Wrap yourself in the blanket to keep warm. You can leave the lamp on for a while, but you must turn it off before you go to sleep."

"There are a lot of spiders in the room," I said, very quietly. "Where?"

I showed him and he took them away. I was grateful but confused. Why hadn't he done the horrible? And why was he being so nice?

"Try to settle down now, Karen, and I'll be back for the tray." Then he left.

OK, he probably prefers morning horrible.

As he closed the door, I just couldn't help it: the tears started to flow. I knew how to cry without making a sound, so I just let go and had a bit of a cry. It didn't last long because I was starving and it was hard to cry and eat at the same time. As I calmed down and ate, I started to look at where I was.

I was in a squarish, oblong shed. The bed was against the back wall. The wall opposite the bed was really the outside of an old-fashioned, green train. The tool shed had been built against and around a thick, heavy train door. The door had a big brass handle that looked like a little dog's bone and which you had to twist to open the door. The door had a large window that you slid open (from the inside only), and there was a leather strap attached to the bottom of the sliding glass bit. It had two more narrow windows on either side. There was a large window in the wall to my right, and on the left was a door (definitely locked) with a window at the top. The door could be opened in full or in half. Neither windows had curtains. I was used to curtains – in the Noctorum, my mum had kept the curtains shut all day – so this seemed very strange to me. All the boxes, suitcases and tools had been neatly stacked under the bed or against the wall, and as I peered through the big window to my right, I could not see a thing in the ink-black night.

I was just starting to notice how much quieter it was than normal when the train door swung open and I nearly leapt out of my skin.

"I'll take that," Grandpa said, gesturing towards the tray. I handed it to him and he said, "Now it's time to turn off the light and go to sleep, see you in the morning. Goodnight, God bless."

Pately Bridge

I switched off the light, lay down and closed my eyes. Then he closed and locked the door. I heard shuffling, followed by the sound of another door being closed and locked.

I kept my eyes tight shut for ages, but I couldn't sleep. My mind was racing again, and there were unfamiliar and disturbing sounds outside. Somewhere, in the distance, there were babies crying. I could also hear water gushing, trees blowing. I even heard a real owl. (I had until then only heard them on TV.) The sound of the crying kept returning and seemed to be getting louder, then it stopped abruptly.

I didn't want to open my eyes, as I didn't like the inky black, but the sounds were worrying me, so I opened them and was surprised at how much I could see. You could see outside through the big window. It looked like a black-and-white cartoon of the countryside and seemed a little scary. The moon was only half full, but it was still really bright. My face was hurting where I had been smacked, so I lay down and closed my eyes. When I opened them again, it was daylight.

The Child's Cry

When I woke up after that first night in the tool shed at Pately Bridge, the sound of crying had started again. In the light, it seemed even more disturbing and was now very close. I was scared stiff; it seemed to be coming from just outside. Without thinking, I sprang up to see what was making those poor children sob and cry.

I looked out of the window. Just inches away from my window and staring straight at me were 10 or more sheep and their lambs. The sounds I had heard were the baby sheep calling for their mums. Having grown up in the city, I had never been this close to livestock before and was genuinely terrified by their proximity. I screamed my head off. The poor sheep ran away, equally startled, and I fell over backwards.

Grandpa came to the train door and asked what the matter was. I said there were sheep in his garden, just outside the window.

"Can I come in?" he asked.

I hesitated, thinking that perhaps the horrible was about to start, but I was still frightened of the sheep, so I said yes.

He stepped into the shed, smiling. "Good morning, Karen. Calm down. There's nothing to worry about." Then he said that the countryside belonged to all the animals and they very kindly let us stay with them, so we must be polite and kind and must never scream them away. I said I was sorry.

Then he said, "Now, collect your wash bag and toilet bucket, empty that in the pit, then go to the stream and wash yourself. When you're finished, come back here and wait for your breakfast."

I nodded, confused. When was the horrible going to start? I couldn't bear waiting for it. I just wanted to get it over and done with.

When Grandpa had gone, I grabbed my wash bag and bucket, and emptied it in the pit behind the train. Then I went to the stream alone. As we had arrived at the tool shed in the darkness, I was overwhelmed to see the area in the daylight. It was breathtakingly beautiful.

I could see now that the old green train was a traditional steam train, part of which had been converted into living space. I didn't know it at the time, but this was Nanny and Grandpa Wallbridge's holiday home for when they weren't living at the school. The train was situated at the bottom of a lush, green, part-wooded valley, and was positioned by a stream, the start of the stunningly beautiful River Ouse. There were a few holiday log cabins dotted around. The sun was bright and warm, and seemed to turn all the colours up to 11. The stream had a rickety wooden bridge over it.

As you looked upstream, just beyond the bridge, you could see little waterfalls cascading over rocks and flowing downstream, where the water became tranquil and flat. Here, there were smooth rocks of all shapes and sizes, moving around in the deep, crystal-clear water pools. I loved the sights and sounds immediately.

The riverbanks were overhung with trees, and were steep and rocky in parts and flat and grassy in others. On the opposite side of the bank to me was a little cave hidden in the clay bank beneath a tree root. There were birds and bugs flitting about the place. The riverbank was teeming with wildlife getting on with its day. I was absolutely mesmerised. I had simply never seen anywhere so captivating and peaceful. I plunged my hands into the water and splashed it on my face. It was freezing cold and woke me up in an instant. I was surprised, but I didn't care. I thought it was just wonderful. When I got back to the shed, I looked out of my window. It was as if someone had captured the most perfect countryside scene ever and framed it just for me to look at. As I stared out over the hills and the stream, I was glad now that there were no curtains, as it seemed wrong to ever cover up such a beautiful view.

Grandpa soon arrived with the breakfast tray, told me not to take too long, as there were chores to do, and then left. I was again puzzled that no horrible had taken place. I started to think that maybe it wasn't going to happen, but then caught myself. I thought, well, that just can't be true, so we'll just wait and see. I ate my breakfast.

The door swung open and Nanny was standing there. She said, "Good morning, Karen. Did you sleep well?"

I nodded.

She said, "Follow me."

She took me to the living-room part of the train, sat me down and fixed me with a stern look. She repeated all the rules she had told me last night and asked me if I understood. I nodded. Then she said in a very clear voice, "Your mother and father (he's not my father) want you to get better and they have asked me to see if I can help. I have agreed to try. I believe in discipline and a firm hand, and that is what you will get. Do you understand?"

I nodded, but I didn't. Whenever anyone mentioned Mum or Stanley, all I could think was, what are they doing to my little sister; is she alright? It always sent a jolt of panic through me. My brain started whirring and I tr...

"Karen!"

"Yes, Nanny!"

"Are you listening?"

"Yes, Nanny."

"We are elderly people who do not have the time or the energy to run around after a naughty child. You must listen and learn quickly if you want to get better and get back to your parents."

This struck me as strange. I didn't really understand what she meant by "better", but I knew that I definitely didn't want to get back to Stanley.

"You want to get back home, don't you?"

I hesitated, thought about our Denise on her own with that lot, so I said, "Yes, Nanny," I said. "Is my sister alright?"

She said, "Extraordinary question!"

I explained that nobody would tell me anything at St Mary's and that I just wanted to know.

"Of course she's alright. Now that we know what's been going on, we are taking care of everything."

Genuinely puzzled, I said, "What do you mean? What's been going on?"

Nanny looked a little uncomfortable as she said, "Well, regarding your inappropriate behaviour with your father."

I couldn't help blurting out, "I don't have behaviour on my father – he has behaviour on me! And anyway he's not my father, I killed my father. He's just horrible Stanley who does the horrible and neve…"

"Karen, I am not going to tell you again."

I couldn't stop, though. The words rushed out: "But he's not my fucking father. He does the horrible and real fathers don't do that."

Smack!

"Karen, I gave you a warning, but you refused to listen." She pronounced my name 'Carron'. I would soon learn that when she said my name like this, it meant she was very angry and I had 10 seconds to back down or get smacked down, but I hadn't learnt this yet.

Smack! Smack! Smack!

"Stop," I squealed, running away from Nanny's hand. "Please, I'll do whatever you tell me, but you've got to believe me – I didn't do it. He blames me for it, but it's not me. Honestly, it's not me. I don't know how to make him or any of them stop. I just want them to stop. I know I make them bad, but I don't know how."

All of a sudden, Nanny had stopped smacking me. Her face had gone white. Grandpa stepped in from outside. Nanny stared at me. She still had a strange look on her face and said she begged my pardon. I didn't know what she meant, but I realised I had said too much, so I just gazed at the floor and shrugged my shoulders, as she begged my pardon some more. I kept quiet and she told me in a soft voice to go to my room and wait to be called. I nodded and left.

As I walked around to my room in the tool shed and passed under the train windows, I could hear Nanny and Grandpa talking. Nanny sounded really shocked and Grandpa was saying, "You should never have smacked her like that, Vera. She's only a young girl, and clearly very disturbed. She's very young to be talking this way. I don't fully understand what's going on, but it's clear the child needs our help."

Grandpa's voice was very serious as he said, "They are not words from a child's mouth, Vera. The child was terrified. I think there's something very wrong here."

Nanny said, "I've got a horrible feeling that Stanley and Jennifer haven't been entirely honest with us. We're going to have to tread very carefully. The child swears blind that she isn't doing anything wrong, that it's Stanley who's doing things to her. I just don't know what to believe." Her voice was trembling.

Grandpa said, "I agree, she sounds honest, but frightened, have you noticed how much she rocks? Let me talk…"

I couldn't hear any more. I was trying to work out how to get Nanny Wallbridge to stop smacking me. I had already worked out that less swear words equaled less smacks, so I was going to try that. And even though I'd said something about the horrible that seemed to have got through to someone for once, no part of me believed that anything would change as a consequence.

Back in my room, I sat on my bed and rocked back and forth for comfort. I was thinking, I never wanted to be Karen the daddy killer. I don't want to be someone who turns the grown-ups bad or angry with me all the time. What is wrong with me? As I sat on the bed rocking, I realised that I understood nothing. I couldn't understand why people reacted the way they did to me and what I was doing to make it happen. I didn't know what to think. I didn't know anymore what was real, what was right, wrong, good or bad. I chastised myself for telling them that I killed my dad. Could I be sent to jail?

Just then Grandpa knocked on the door, interrupting my thoughts. He still looked serious, but I didn't see any anger on his face. He said, "I know there are some things we need to talk about, Karen, but there is plenty of time for that. For now, let's get on with the chores."

I nodded mutely, afraid to speak in case I blurted anything out again.

Grandpa took me outside. "This is Biddy, our dog. She is a lovely old lady who likes to be walked slowly twice a day and must be fed three times a day." Then he asked me to follow him inside the old train. "This is Paulus, Nanny's guinea pig. He likes his tray to be cleaned and to be given fresh food and water every other day."

Again, I nodded, as he continued, "Nanny can't walk very far, so this is Nanny's commode, which you must empty every day. This is the kitchen, which must be cleaned four times a day, including any washing-up, which must be washed, dried and put away.

"We wake at 6.30 prompt. We eat breakfast at seven o'clock, brunch (which is tea and biscuits) at 10.30, lunch at 12.30, high tea (tea and cake) at three, followed by tea at half six and finally supper (hot chocolate and toast) in time for bedtime at eight o'clock sharp. You help prepare the food but always eat in your room. Any scrap food goes on to the bird table, which must be done daily."

Grandpa paused, looking at me, then said, "Follow me."

We went back outside again and he said, "This is where you collect the post. This is the milk urn, which you must take to the farm up the hill for milk and eggs, as required. This is the laundry, which must be washed in the stream every other day. These are the boundaries you can walk to – you're not allowed to go any further than that without permission. These are your clothes, and here are some books for you to read when you have any spare time. Do you understand?"

Suddenly, and for the first time in my whole life, I completely understood. As he had spoken, my mind had been writing down his words in an indelible mind book. Until this point, I felt like I had simply bounced from one horrible to another. With this new idea of having some rules, though, I felt like I knew where I was – just don't do or say certain things. I now had a clear understanding of exactly what I had to do and where my place was in everything. This felt like a huge relief. I smiled and said, "Yes, Grandpa, I do understand."

He smiled. "Now," he continued, "I know that there are some other things you might like to talk about, but there is no rush."

"Like what?" I asked.

"Well, like anything that is worrying you."

"I'm worried about my sister and about when I will have to do something with you."

Grandpa looked taken aback, but soon composed himself. "Your sister is fine, and as for the other thing, well, there will be none of that sort of thing in this place. Good grief! Certainly not!"

On hearing this, I flung my arms round him and gave him a massive hug. I even let out a little cry. I couldn't help myself: I felt so relieved and so delighted at the same time.

He hugged me back for a second and then pushed me away. He seemed awkward and blustery. He said, "OK, now. That's enough of all that. We'll talk about how you can overcome these – " he paused, looking like he was a little lost for words "– problems of yours another time. For now, let's get started with the chores."

I didn't know what he meant about my problems, but I was so happy that he had said I wouldn't have to do any horrible. After this, I would have walked across hot coals for Grandpa, as I could just sense he was my friend. He knew about things and was very wise. He even heard me cry and he still liked me. He was never angry with me and was very fair, plus no horrible. For the first time in my life, I felt like I finally had a life to live in a safe home.

Learning to See

My time at Pately Bridge may seem like a hardship to some, but to me, it was heaven. I could write an entire book about this period in my life and still not touch on the impact the people and the place had on me. It was like I learnt to see the beauty of the world and understand my place in it for the first time.

I was taught so much during the months I was there, like how to read. I was given a whole stack of books, including a dictionary. Nanny and Grandpa would often say words that I didn't understand and I would make a mental note to look them up later. I read everything and could soon read most books in a few days. I read Blyton, Lewis and Dickens, and even tried Shakespeare, but that bloke talks in riddles and takes about a month to say what he means so I didn't persevere.

I studied art from Da Vinci, Constable, Rembrandt and Monet to Gainsborough, Picasso, Bosch and Brueghel. Now, when I say 'studied', I mean I looked at the pictures and read the captions below. I can tell you now some of those painters certainly know how to paint my idea of hell, but on the whole I loved the way they could take a picture out of their mind and make it appear in such glorious detail, with their hand.

It seemed like pure magic. Bosch's paintings, shocking as they are, really spoke to me. His three-panel painting The Garden of Earthly Delights was a horrific revelation. The right-hand panel represents Hell and shows humans, their bodies stripped naked, being tortured and abused by animal-like monsters. If anyone ever asked me to pick a picture that best represented my life so far, it would be this one.

Nanny also encouraged me to listen to classical music. Together, we listened to Mozart, Beethoven, Brahms, Tchaikovsky, Rimsky-Korsakov, Elgar, Debussy, Strauss and Rachmaninov, and I ended up liking some of it.

I learnt how to cook and clean. Through looking after Biddy, the dog, and Paulus, the guinea pig, I also learnt how to care for animals, as well as people. I loved debating with Grandpa. He was very well spoken and I liked copying the words he said. It made me feel very grown-up.

I grew to love the countryside, the views, the wildlife, particularly birds and, most of all, the River Ouse. My secret spot, where I'd go to be alone with my thoughts, was at the bottom of the garden, where a gentle, sandy slope met the water's edge. The water here was calm and tranquil, and was no deeper than a foot all the way across. I'd often go here to cleanse my mind. I'd sit and watch the water, and for the first time in my life, I felt truly happy.

One evening, after I'd been at Pately Bridge for a month or so, I was returning to my room when I overheard Grandpa and Nanny Wallbridge talking in the train. Their voices were low and urgent, and I struggled to make out every word they said. I heard Nanny Wallbridge whispering, "What are you saying?"

Grandpa paused for a moment, then I heard him say, "From what I've seen of her, and the concerns she has, I believe that she's telling the truth. It sounds like it really isn't Karen who's initiating these things, it's Stanley. You will agree that she hasn't exhibited any sexualised behaviour around us?"

Nanny agreed. "Indeed she is almost over proper. She is by no means stupid or unteachable, she is extremely intelligent and learns faster than anyone I have ever taught. She is no more special needs than you or I, Vera. All this time, we've been led to believe that she is the delinquent one, but I rather think we've been misled."

He sounded more sad and worried than I'd ever heard him.

"Do you mean you think that all these things that are happening to her... that she doesn't want them to happen? You mean she's being forced?"

"That's exactly what I'm saying."

"Good grief, Percy."

Nanny went quiet for a while. I think she was still speaking, but I couldn't really make out the words. "We're going to have to help her manage him, Vera. She can't be left to cope with things on her own," Grandpa said. Just then I heard a noise and, fearful of being caught eavesdropping, I slipped back to my room and jumped into bed and wrapped the covers tight around myself. For the first time, I started to feel that maybe, just maybe someone believed me.

In Pately Bridge, everything was wonderful and nothing was horrible. The only thing that haunted me were the bad thoughts and fears for my sister. One time, I asked Grandpa how to stop the bad thoughts in my head. He asked me what they were about and I told him that they were like little films and pictures of bad things that had happened to me that would just pop into my head and make me feel sad. He asked me if I wanted to talk to him about the bad things and I shook my head.

He told me that until I was ready to talk to him about them, he thought it might help if I went to the stream and washed my face. When I did, I was to imagine washing the bad thoughts away down the stream.

I thought, I'm not putting those horrible, dirty things in my beautiful, clean stream! I asked him, "Won't that make it dirty?"

He looked at me as if I was crazy and said, "You, make the river dirty? Dear child! You are a funny little thing. You speak utter gibberish at times, yet still manage to make some sense." He told me that I was the innocent victim of someone else's sickness. He said, "It seems certain people have tried very hard to convince you that this badness you speak of is your fault, but the truth is, it's not."

Grandpa said that he and Nanny Wallbridge had been told all kinds of things about me before I came to stay and that he was delighted to find out for himself that none of it was true. He said, "I know you hide yourself behind that fuss you sometimes make, but you are a very kind little girl and I think others, less kind, see this in you and take advantage. I think you know very well the difference between right and wrong. You should have a little more faith in what you think and stop looking to others to decide your mind for you. I certainly trust you to make the right choice. I feel sorry that you don't trust yourself a little more. Do you understand?"

I thought, yes, I understand. I understand that you just said that it was not my fault and that I shouldn't let anyone boss me into thinking that something is good when I know it is bad.

I asked him, "How do you stop someone from making you do things that you don't want to do?"

Grandpa paused before asking, "What sort of things?"

I looked away, fearful that he would be able to read in my eyes the secret I was holding, and said, "Just things."

"Are these the things that give you sad thoughts?"

I hesitated. "Yes."

Grandpa nodded to himself and said, "I hope that one day you will trust me enough to speak to me about them, but until then you should know that nobody is allowed to make you do something you know is wrong and that you should at least try going down to the stream."

I went down to my secret spot at the edge of the stream and wished I could wash all of my horrible thoughts away, but I was sure that if I did, I would leave a dirty ring of bath scum round the edge of my wonderful stream, so I plucked one horrible thought out of my head and splashed my face with water. As I did, I imagined a dark cloud evaporating into the water and being washed away, and I must say, I did feel a little better. For a while there, I had the cleanest face in Yorkshire, but I was always careful not to wash too much horrible into my stream, just in case.

I started thinking about what Grandpa had said about it not being my fault and I agreed with him. The problem I had was that I really didn't know why it wasn't my fault, just that it wasn't. Whenever I tried to think hard about this, my thoughts would jumble up, so it was very hard to think any of that stuff through properly.

I started off my time at Pately Bridge waiting to see if I could trust Grandpa enough to tell him my secret and everything that Stanley made me do with him and other people. In the end, though, I ended up loving Grandpa too much to tell him the truth. I hated to see him upset, and whenever I would start talking about bad thoughts, his face would crumple up with concern. I didn't want to see his face look unhappy, and I loved it when he smiled and didn't want to spoil it. Deep down, I didn't want anything to change at Pately Bridge, and I knew that telling him about the horrible would change everything.

As I had done when I lived in the Noctorum, I wrote down all my feelings and worries in code and hid them. Here, in Pately Bridge, I kept my secret scribble notes in an old tea tin, which I buried in the garden. It made me feel better if I knew nobody could find them, but I was always worried someone would, so I moved them around a lot.

Over the months I'd been in Pately Bridge, Nanny seemed to have changed towards me. She no longer sounded cross with me, but would talk to me gently and kindly. She never smacked me anymore, and she explained to me that I would have to try to avoid getting into any "situations" with Stanley. She said that Stanley had a sickness that I needed to try to control and that she would help me to "manage" things a little better.

She also said that although I learnt things at the speed of light, I needed to slow down a bit to take in the details, and it was true: I loved finding out about anything I didn't already know. As soon as I came across something new, I had to know all about it: how it was made, how it worked, how it didn't work, how it felt and smelt. I was never happy until I could discover how things worked. This natural curiosity once got me into hot water, though: most of the time I could put the things I'd dismantled back together, but not Nanny's garden radio. As a punishment, I had to stay outside with Biddy and Paulus all day, but she did say I could keep it as it was now broken. I didn't tell Nanny when I later fixed it and started listening to it in secret.

One night, Nanny told me that if I kept my good behaviour up, I could go home for the weekend. She knew how much I missed my sister. I did miss her, but I absolutely did not want to go home. All I wanted was to stay in Pately Bridge with Nanny and Grandpa. I thought, I'm doing as I am told, so why do I have to go back?

I knew I had to avoid a home visit at all costs. That night, back in the shed, I wrote myself a note as a constant reminder: "Ruin all chances of a home visit."

Unfortunately, Nanny got hold of the note soon after and I had to do some fast talking. "What is the meaning of this, Carron?"

My brain had thought of the answer just before she finished her question: "I'm sorry, Nanny – it is meant to say 'don't ruin all chances of home visit'."

Nanny wasn't at all sure about that. "Why would you write that?"

I didn't answer, and Grandpa said, "Your parents want to see you and the only way for us to keep you with us is for you to go back home for a weekend."

My heart sank. I suspect my face must have given away my feelings because Nanny said, "Would you be happier if the family came here to visit you?"

This was even worse! I thought, oh, dear God, no! Stanley and Mum, in my happy place! I don't think so!

I said, "No, no, it's all right. I'd love to see my sister. When are you thinking of sending me back?"

They weren't sure and said, "We'll see."

That night, every single one of my horrible thoughts came rushing into my head. Memories of how being at home made me feel came flooding back. It just made me want to cry, but I couldn't. I felt like I was being strangled and made to swallow a beach ball at the same time.

I sat on my bed and rocked for hours. I held Nanny's garden radio so tightly against my ear that it left lines across my cheek. I was waiting for my favourite song, *What Becomes of the Broken-Hearted?* I really needed Jimmy that night to comfort me. Then, as I scanned the frequencies back and forth for the zillionth time, I finally heard the familiar 'boom, dat, boom, boom, dat'. I threw my face into the pillow and sobbed like a baby.

Going Home

On the journey back to the Noctorum estate for my weekend visit, I wished for storms, car accidents, plagues, war, heart attacks, everything, but in the end I was forced to face the inevitable reality: I was going home.

Nanny and Grandpa had told me that they knew what had been happening with Stanley and had sorted it all out. I knew they didn't really understand the extent of what had been going on, but I also knew that Stanley was scared of the Wallbridges and they seemed so confident that nothing would happen that, despite my dreading the visit, I was looking forward to seeing how my little sister liked life without horrible in it and was curious to see what Stanley was like, now he wasn't horrible any more.

Even though I thought things would be different, I wanted to make absolutely sure that nothing was going to happen. Nanny had told me that Stanley had a sickness and that this is something I could try to manage by not putting him in situations where he would "get urges". I wanted to do anything I could to avoid the horrible, and if it was something I could control, I would do whatever it took.

Over the days leading up to the weekend visit, I'd devised a plan that would help me to manage Stanley and make sure the horrible never happened. I had decided I mustn't use the toilet because Stanley might come in and see me. Unfortunately, this would mean I couldn't eat or drink because then I'd need to use the loo, but I knew I could manage for just two days. I decided I'd need to keep all of my clothes on at all times, so I wouldn't be able to wash. I was already wearing three pairs of knickers under my jeans and wouldn't change my clothes at all until I got back to Pately Bridge. Like Nanny had taught me, I'd also try to do as I was told and only speak when spoken to, using as few words as possible. I wouldn't make any eye contact, and I planned to stay in Mum's presence at all times. Because Mum didn't like me, I'd have to remain completely silent and still, so I had taken a book to read. If it wasn't possible to stay in the same room as Mum all the time, I would just start cleaning. I felt happy that I had a plan. I would have done anything if it meant not having to do the horrible.

Nanny and Grandpa Wallbridge had arranged for a family friend to take me home. I sat in the back of the car in total silence, turning over in my mind what I had to do to make it through the weekend. As the car turned down Stratford Way, round the bend and left into the car park, I saw that the estate was finished and people had moved into all the houses. It was brand new but already looked 40 years old.

I saw our Denise and Stanley waving through the dining-room window at me. I was excited to see Denise, but because Stanley was with her, I kept a straight face and just nodded. Denise looked sad, but as soon as Stanley moved away from the window, I gave her a great, big, toothy smile. I switched straight back to deadpan as Stanley came out of the front door.

Denise was thrilled to see me and we hugged at the door. I was a little surprised to see her, as it was nearly lunchtime on a school day, but she looked well and happy. I went inside and Mum said, "Hello, Karen, would you like a drink?"

I was completely thrown: she had just spoken directly to me! And she wasn't frowning. I wanted to say yes to make her happy, but I remembered my plan, which meant I couldn't drink anything, and so I said quietly, "No thank you, Mum."

Roma asked me how I was.

I said, "I'm very well, thank you. I hope you have all been well."

They all hooted and laughed at the way I was speaking. I hadn't realised until then, but my accent had changed a lot and I now articulated my words more slowly and clearly. They said I had gone "all posh" and Stanley suggested I "ang me fuckin' coat up". I said I was fine and would like to unpack, then asked for permission to leave the room. I didn't want to stay, as the room seemed dark and smelly. Stanley agreed and I left. As I went upstairs, I could hear them trying to talk like me and giggling.

I couldn't believe how dirty and grubby the house was. There were clothes on the floor, washing-up all over the kitchen – in fact, there was dirty crockery throughout the house. The beds were unmade, and everything seemed worn or broken. Up in my bedroom, I looked out of the window and suddenly felt very overwhelmed, like I wanted to run away; but I knew if I wanted to remain in Pately Bridge, I needed to stay here for the weekend.

I cleaned my room, and while Stanley was outside messing with his car, I cleaned the bathroom. Then I went back downstairs and did the washing-up. I tidied around, then sat down and read my book in the same room as Mum. She looked shocked to see me being so industrious.

A little while later, she turned to me and said, "I'm glad you're here, actually, Karen." I immediately became suspicious. Mum was never glad to see me. "I need you to come with me to the social, as they're going on about stopping my money for you." I wasn't surprised any more. "You have to go there with me because they need to have your special needs assessed."

Mum always wanted me on record as being special needs as it would entitle her to more money for me.

I didn't know what to say. I didn't want to be special needs. I listened mutely as Mum explained that I wasn't "special needs enough" and told me not to answer any questions they asked and to just sit there, rock and "try and look a bit more mental".

I didn't really want to go, but she was speaking to me and I didn't want to do anything to make her stop – it was nice that she wasn't ignoring me, and I thought it would help keep Stanley away from me, so I did as I was told. She was pleased with me when we left the dole office, but by the time we got home, she went back to saying to my sister, "Tell Karen…" After that, Mum didn't really speak to me again over the weekend.

In fact, I didn't see anyone much. Denise was busy with her Brownies and her friends, but we had some fun together practising Mum's new religion. Mum changed religion all the time: they would give her charitable help for a while, until they found out that she wasn't a believer at all and was just in it for all she could get. Mum had joined this new religion because she was chasing some bloke who was a member. They had given her a tambourine, which you'd beat yourself half to death with, while singing God songs.

It was a little hard to understand my family anymore, because they spoke with such strong accents, at such a speed and hardly said any real words, but I got the gist. I just didn't feel like I belonged there.

Denise and I went to the shop, and when we got back, Mum asked Denise, all expectantly, "Well, did you get anything?"

I thought, no we did not. That's stealing and that's wrong! I lied and said I nicked some chocolate that I had really bought and gave it to her.

Stanley hardly said a word to me, let alone looked at me. He seemed uneasy and passed most of his time outside, fixing his car. Even so, I spent the entire weekend terrified that something was going to happen. In bed at night, every creak of a floorboard made my heart pound. I kept pinching myself to stay awake.

It was only on the car journey back to Pately Bridge that I had a chance to think about my weekend at the Noctorum. Although we hadn't talked about it openly, my sister didn't seem to be getting the horrible. Though I did learn that he had been seeing a lot of other people's kids on the estate who had made friends with Denise, but no horrible seemed to be happening and I was pleased about that. Mum had spoken to me, even if it was only at the beginning. Most importantly, there had been no horrible and no smacks, but even so, I didn't feel like I was a part of them anymore. I felt different and very uncomfortable.

I had spent the entire weekend in a state of anxiety, forever looking over my shoulder to make sure that Stanley wasn't nearby. I had tried to keep myself busy, but as a result was now totally exhausted. I hadn't slept at all, because I had been so anxious in case Stanley slipped into my room while I was sleeping. Hunger had kept me awake, and I now felt dizzy and sick.

When I got back to Pately Bridge, I flew straight down to the stream and cleaned off three days of not washing and as much of the Noctorum as I dared put into the stream. Then I went to the toilet for about an hour.

I was starving and nearly bit Grandpa's arm off when he brought the dinner tray in. I couldn't wait to finish it and go and run around all of my safe places, but I hadn't slept for two nights and as soon as my head touched the pillow I was fast asleep.

I was never happier than I was when I was in this magic, safe place. I learnt so many things. I knew and trusted all the animals, and they knew and trusted me. I felt like I belonged. It could only be topped if Aunt Pat, Uncle Ken and our Dona moved in next door and adopted me.

With the help of Grandpa and Nanny Wallbridge, I now understood the world differently. The truth is, normally it's the bad things that the grown-ups don't want anyone else to know about. Taking things that don't belong to you is definitely stealing. Acting is only acting if it's done to entertain; otherwise it is just plain lying, and lies put your soul in prison. Others may choose to do bad things, but it is up to each individual to choose if they want to be part of that badness. Anyone forcing another to do badness should be reported to the police. It is their job to stop and punish bad people and even put them in jail.

I had started to learn how to ignore all the noise and distractions in my head and was more able to think things through. Life was complicated, but at least I had an opinion on things, which

Grandpa said was important. Grandpa taught me so much about life and helped me understand the world a little better.

I learnt that my vagina and bottom are private, and there is no need for anyone, except the doctor (if you are ill down there), to ever need to touch them. What's more, the grown-ups should not be asking any child to touch their privates. Grandpa explained to me that when fathers do the horrible with their daughters, they will go to hell. Because Grandpa was a reverend, he knew all about God and what was right and wrong. I listened with wide eyes as he explained to me how God had created the world in seven days and liked to help people who were in trouble. I wondered why He had never helped me, no matter how much I'd needed Him.

I thought maybe God was a bit of a wino, who made everyone go to his house on a Sunday and only gave them booze to loosen their wallets, but Grandpa said I was being cynical (I made a note to look that up) and that the booze was wine and the wine was Christ's blood!

I said, "Yuck! Why does He want everyone to drink boozy blood?"

Grandpa laughed and said, "No, it represents Christ's blood." Then he asked, "Do you believe in God?"

I shook my head and said, "No, not really."

I told Grandpa I had prayed to Him a million times and He had never helped me. Grandpa studied my face, then asked, "How do you think you came to be here with us? Maybe He was listening after all."

I thought about this for a moment and answered, "No, Grandpa – you and Nanny brought me here."

He said, "Dear child, I am a reverend. Who do you think guides Nanny and me?"

I knew he wanted me to say God, but I didn't believe this was true. I said, "You, Grandpa – you're just good inside. I believe in you, but I think this God's off His head." I hesitated before asking, "How come you haven't got a God's house? How come you never go and see Him on a Sunday?"

"Because I'm officially retired from being a reverend now. Then he said, "Most people believe in the same God, but all have different ways of talking to Him. Our way, the Quaker way, is not the same as most, but I couldn't imagine my life without my faith."

I gazed up at Grandpa and thought, I can't imagine my life without you. I loved spending time with Grandpa. I couldn't agree with him about God, but when he explained things to me, he made the world seem so much simpler.

I rarely looked at people's faces, let alone their eyes, but I always did with Nanny and Grandpa. I loved looking at them. Their faces and eyes always matched what they were saying: when they spoke, their eyes weren't saying something else, and what they said was always what happened.

Grandpa and I had many chats. Most helped me understand things better, though occasionally he left me wondering what on earth he was talking about. He tried very hard to help me talk about the horrible.

One day, after I'd been in Pately Bridge for about six months, we were sitting looking at my stream and watching the birds flitting over the water, when he said, "Do you feel like you're ready to talk about some things now?"

I turned to him and said simply, "I like your face the way it is."

He scrunched up his nose to bring his glasses nearer his eyes and peered at me, all puzzled, then said, "What on Earth? Dear child, do you realise that keeping this sort of thing bottled up inside is very bad for you? It's like a spiritual poison that can eat you up, and the only way to get it out is to talk about it."

I said, "I understand, but I can't bear to watch the change in your face when you hear what I have to say."

Grandpa nodded and said, "I understand your fears. When ever I have to say something that is difficult, I go away some-where private, where nobody can hear me, and practise. Why don't you run up to the top of the hill and sit on the gate you like, and after you have made sure nobody is around, practise saying the words out loud. Once you've done that, it might be easier to talk to me about them. Plus, you would still be getting it out, which would be beneficial."

This struck me as a good idea. I thought, yes, the wind will carry the words away and nobody will ever hear them. So I hurtled to the top of the hill and waited for a big gust of wind before I started talking and at first I just whispered. I managed to get a fair bit off of my chest on that gate, but I don't know that it made it any easier to tell Grandpa about the horrible.

I had grown to love Nanny, now that she understood that I wasn't naughty, dirty, bad. She was still strict, but she was also kind and loving. As much as I adored and trusted them both, I didn't ever tell them the whole story. I don't think they realised that the horrible had always been there ever since I could remember. It felt like almost every day, every night, everyone I met and everywhere I went. Even though I knew 'telling' always made things worse, I did try to tell them, many times, but I just couldn't bear to see their faces change or, worse still, lose them because of telling them. I couldn't imagine my life without them in it. Little did I know that my time with them was rapidly drawing to a close.

"Tell her, Karen!"

After nearly a year of calm, healing and smack-free learning, in the autumn of 1973, I was suddenly told that I would have to spend another weekend at the Noctorum. My first thought this time was, Oh, great! What does Mum want me to get for her now?

I didn't dread it half as much as before, but I just didn't want to leave Pately Bridge for any reason. I had built my own secret garden down by the stream and it had seven potatoes growing in it. I didn't want to leave my stream. I had bathed in it, played in it, learnt to swim in it, and I knew every bit of it for at least a mile either way. I had seen it in every season, each one as beautiful as the last. I had seen the stream gush and torrent, and I had seen it calm and lazy. I had grown completely accustomed to its soothing sounds, its constancy.

I loved the days and the nights, and all the day and night animals. I had watched little animal families build homes and have babies, and I had seen those babies grow up and go off to build homes and have families of their own. Even though Grandpa had told me that I wasn't supposed to interfere with nature, I couldn't help myself when a blue-tit couple decided to build their nest in my favourite secret place: the tree root and clay cave on the far side of the stream. I saw what they were collecting (moss and little twigs), so I collected some and put them on a rock on my side of the stream. The blue tits started to collect what I had put there and I loved the idea that I had helped them build a safe home to have their babies. Then I saw what they were feeding their chicks, so I looked for worms and moths and put them on the rock. The blue tits took them and gave them to their chicks. I loved this place and ached at the thought of having to leave it, even for a moment. I was able to reassure myself, though, because it was just a weekend. I'd be back soon enough, and Grandpa said that when I got back, we could dig up the potatoes and eat them for lunch.

Just as I'd done on my first weekend visit back to the Noctorum, I got my plan together to avoid the horrible and manage Stanley, then scanned the radio for Jimmy Ruffin's song. Except for the intrusive images, I could almost entirely blank my childhood from my mind and live in the moment, but whenever I listened to *What Becomes of the Broken-Hearted?*, it was like opening the door to all of those horrible memories and feelings. Even so, I was strangely compelled to listen to it. It was therapeutic for me, however painful. No luck this time.

Although I felt stronger and wiser these days, whenever I thought about the bad old days, I would plummet straight back into those lost, lonely feelings, where I felt I was free-falling into an endless darkness, spinning wildly out of control, but I also knew that if I blanked it out, I could keep the lights on and at least see what was happening to me.

This time, I took the train back to the Noctorum on my own, as Grandpa and Nanny Wallbridge couldn't come with me and their friend who had driven me before was away. I returned to the Noctorum to a hostile reception. No one answered the front door when I knocked and I could hear raised voices inside. I pushed open the door and saw that a lady from the social was arguing with Mum in the living room. Nobody else appeared to be in.

The lady turned to me when I walked in and said, "Do you live at home all the time?" Mum was always on the take in one form or another – she was continually fiddling her Giro – and social were clearly checking her out.

I looked at Mum, but she had her back to me and was arguing with the lady. Then Mum spun round, quick as a flash, and said, "Tell her, Karen!" She shot me a sharp glance and held my gaze.

I didn't want to lie, so I told the truth but did it in a way that would get Mum what she wanted. I said, "I live at Pately Bridge and only visit when my behaviour allows – I have special needs." Then I sat on the floor, stared at my feet and started rocking.

"Seeeee!" Mum screamed, her eyes blazing. "I told you – she's my daughter and she's not right in the head. So when are you going to give me my Giro?"

The lady from social didn't look very pleased. She said that if I wasn't living with Mum all the time, she wouldn't get paid for me. The lady looked directly at me and said very slowly this time, "Do you live here all the time, Karen?"

I didn't answer; I just sat and rocked.

Mum shrieked, "She lives here all the time, so give me my fucking Giro!"

The lady sighed and replied, "Well, Mrs Claridge, that's not quite true, is it? She says herself she lives in Pately Bridge, and Karen isn't registered at any school."

Mum hissed something like, "She is so special needs that she has a very special special-needs teacher who she calls Pately Bridge. Ask Social Services if you don't believe her!" Her face was red and puffy. She looked like she was going to explode. "If I don't pay my gas and electric bill, they're going to cut me off. I don't have anything for my poor children!"

The woman asked me, "Is this true?"

I ignored her and carried on rocking. Then she said, "We will pay you for Karen, but only from today and only if you send her to school. I can put you in touch with the local education department to arrange that, and we will come to visit now and then to see how things are going."

I sat there dumbstruck. I was completely lost for words. Surely they couldn't make me stay here? Surely it couldn't happen?

As the lady left, Mum screamed all kinds of swear words at her and demanded an apology and her missing payments, but the woman was out of the door like a flash.

Mum rounded on me the moment the front door had shut. "You'll be the death of me!" she screamed, and threw her metal pill box at me. It scratched my face and made it bleed.

Clutching my cheek, I blurted out without thinking, "You lied to the lady, and hitting people is wrong and the police can put you in jail for it."

The look on Mum's face instantly made me realise I should have kept quiet. She went absolutely mad and lunged at me, grabbing me by the hair. By the time it was over, my lips were bleeding, my legs were bruised, and my head was throbbing. Mum hissed, "There's no way I can send you back to Nanny's now, not if you are going to be this naughty."

Hearing this was far worse than any beating. I could have kicked myself for saying what I had. I had given Mum just the opportunity she needed to keep me at home and use me to claim benefits. I begged and pleaded with her to let me go back, but she simply wouldn't listen. She called Nanny and Grandpa and in her sweetest voice explained that I had been so naughty since I had got there that morning that I would have to go to a special-needs unit close by and that the local education department had demanded that she send me to the one they had chosen.

"I'm so sorry to have put you to all this trouble, but I'm afraid I've got no choice in the matter – I can't send her back. It's out of my hands now."

Mum's voice sounded like silk.

Even so, I was sure Nanny and Grandpa wouldn't believe Mum. They knew she told lies. I waited at my bedroom window with my bag packed for Nanny and Grandpa to come and get me back. I heard a car pull up outside and my heart leapt for joy, but I slumped back down when I saw it was just a neighbour. I kept up my vigil at the window for two days and two nights before I realised that they weren't going to come. I felt completely and utterly abandoned. My sense of devastation was total.

To this day, I still don't know if they believed Mum's story or if they simply thought that I had learnt enough to be able to cope with the situation myself. They were an elderly couple and everything they had taught me in Pately Bridge had been to help me manage Stanley; the intention was never that I'd live with them for ever, though this is what I'd hoped for. Even so, at the time I felt very betrayed. It's possible that Mum had persuaded them that I was happy and that things were much better, but this is something I'll never know. One thing was certain: after all that had happened, all that I'd learnt, and all the happiness I'd enjoyed, I was back living in the Noctorum – living in my idea of hell.

It took no time at all to realise that nothing had changed; in fact, it had got much, much worse and my poor little sister had just been too afraid to tell me.

On my first night back in Noctorum, my heart sank as I heard the familiar creak of my bedroom door being opened. Stanley came over to the bed and demanded I suck his penis. I felt sick at the thought and resisted so hard, but he went on and on at me. He said, "Talk proper. None of that snooty ol' bollocks will work wiv me, so get on wiv it! I don't give a shit what you fink. I ain't got all night! If you're gonna start all this again, I'll take me fuckin' belt to you."

Eventually, I gave in and did what he said. Slowly but surely, I began to slide back into the darkness.

Epileptic, My Arse

I was around 10 years old at this point in my life. It's still hard for me to comprehend all that had happened in what felt like bloody decades. To this day, it remains difficult for me to put it in the right order, but I will try to give you an insight into how I felt.

To begin with, back in the Noctorum, my whole body ached for the sound of my stream. I would have done anything to be back there. Even though I had lost all of my tea tins full of secret scribble notes, I knew they would be safe enough where they were. As the months passed, though, Pately Bridge began to seem like nothing more than a fantasy, a place created purely by my mind. It seemed so cruel that I could have had this glimpse of what life could be like, this taste of happiness, only to have it taken away. I didn't even see Nanny and Grandpa Wallbridge for quite some time after I left Pately Bridge. They seemed to think that they had equipped me to cope with Stanley and that the local authorities were now taking over, so they took a back seat in my life. If only I'd told them how bad things really were.

Now that I knew how wonderful and secure life could be, my own life seemed even more perverted and twisted. In the end, the only way I could cope was to completely blank out Pately

Bridge and pretend it had never happened. Everything I had learnt there seemed so at odds with the hell I was now living in, and it was all just too confusing. The dark times grew darker.

In order to get her Giro money, Mum let the local authorities send me to various local special schools. I didn't cope well with all the other special needs children or the teachers. I had clearly fallen so behind that I just didn't know or understand what was being asked of me most of the time.

Ironically, even though I'd been sent back to school, the lady from the social never gave Mum all her Giro money. Mum called the local papers, then took us girls and dumped us on the steps of the Social Services office, claiming she was being forced to abandon her children because she couldn't afford to feed us and saying that was due to the gas company and the social. The local newspaper even took her picture with the gas and electric bill.

The problem was, I knew Mum had loads of money, as she was either stealing it, conning it out of someone or out playing her beloved bingo with it. When she was at home, she was apparently always on the brink of death. She was perpetually claiming to have one sickness or another, and was permanently on prescription medication – tablets to sleep, wake up and everything imaginable in between. She was part hypochondriac, part con artist, and she was always faking illness to get her own way. She always had only three or six months left to live (depending on what she had done or what she was avoiding doing). The first few times she said it, I freaked out – we all did – but after a few years, you just got used to it.

Roma had moved out for good. She had got married and was now living in Aldershot with her new army husband. I think it was around this time that I first realised that throughout everything, Denise and I had each other for support, but Roma had always been completely on her own. This thought had only occurred to me as I noticed how empty her family's side of the church looked on her wedding day. I tried to make sure I was a little kinder to her after this realisation. She had less and less to do with us, as she started a family of her own, but she always opened the door to me whenever I knocked – no matter what she'd heard about me.

I still watched TV a lot and enjoyed the escape it afforded me. The TV helped in other ways, too – like for example, at night, we knew that when we heard it go off, it meant Stanley had stopped watching it and the horrible was coming, so I would leave my bed against the wall, but pull my mattress away, leaving a gap along the side. I would then wrap our Denise in a blanket, lay her in the gap and sleep on top of her. That way, if Stanley tried to get her in the night, I would wake up and take over.

In the daytime, if Stanley wanted to do the horrible, I had also found a new tactic. I knew Stanley would not want Jennifer to hear him looking for us, so, I would hide our Denise, who was now nine, in the airing cupboard and then go and hide in the potato cupboard in the kitchen. This was the only place he never thought to look for me, as I would always make a fuss about going anywhere near it, saying it was dirty and full of spiders. It was, but it didn't have him in it, so it was better. He must have walked right past me dozens of times and never realised I was just at his feet, behind the grubby little curtain.

More often than not, though, I didn't have time to hide before Stanley found me and I'd be forced to do the horrible.

I tried everything from being sick on him, pretending to faint (which just made him worse so I didn't keep that up for long), wetting myself on purpose, pretend coughing fits, arm ache, tummy ache, bum ache, jaw ache – I was practically a medical miracle at one point. The problem was that no new thing I thought up to avoid it ever lasted very long, as Stanley would quickly lose his rag and just do it anyway.

In my own right, I was now a feisty and very vocal girl and had become far too difficult to easily manipulate or bully into doing the horrible. As a result, Stanley was getting increasingly frustrated with me. Violence no longer worked on me – I didn't care if he hit me anymore so he couldn't use the threat of a beating to make me do the horrible. I think this was because I'd become so used to being beaten that I could shut my mind off to the pain. I'd make my body go limp and act like a doll. Because Stanley couldn't hurt me that way anymore, he was now using Social Services as his main threat. If I did anything to piss him off, he would say he would call them and get them to take me away for being naughty, dirty, bad.

"If you don't get on wiv it, I'll call the social and tell 'em what a filthy little slut you are," he'd growl.

The horrible had escalated to a point where Stanley was no longer being careful about what he did and when. At one point, when I'd just turned 11, I found myself in intensive care after contracting an STD. It seems absurd to think that no one would question why an 11-year-old should have an STD, but no one seemed unduly concerned. I remember having a very heavy period while in hospital. It wasn't until many years later that I would discover that my heavy period had actually been a miscarriage. I would suffer two more miscarriages by the time I was 14.

It was a terrible time for me. I missed Grandpa and Nanny Wallbridge and my old life in Pately Bridge desperately. I realised that no one was going to come and save me. I could no longer imagine a future without the horrible.

One night in 1974, shortly after I'd turned 11, I woke up retching. I was horrified to realise that Stanley's penis was already in my mouth and he was holding my head by the ears. Still half asleep, I tried in vain to fend him off, but he had my head gripped painfully firmly. I struggled and tried to push him away. Then I was startled to see a figure standing behind Stanley, in the doorway. Mum had come up the stairs and was behind him. My heart leapt with joy. This was it! She was finally going to find out what was happening, that Stanley really was making me do the horrible. I started to flail my arms about to show I wasn't participating and Stanley said stop fuckin' about. Mum moved slightly and the floorboard just outside my room creaked, startling Stanley. Quick as a flash, he jumped on top of me and pretended to wrestle me. He ground his elbow into the centre of my chest to make me cry out in pain, then he started throwing me about the room, saying it was me fighting him.

Mum came further into the room and said, "What's going on here?"

Stanley gasped, "I don't know... I think she's having an epileptic fit."

Mum rushed over to restrain me, shouting, "You hold her arms, I'll get her legs."

Stanley hastily pulled up his fly and helped to restrain me. At that moment, with a sickening lurch, I finally realised once and for all that Mum already knew what had been going on with Stanley: she must have seen what he had been doing, but she'd chosen to ignore it. It was the most crushing blow. I couldn't believe it. What kind of mother was she? What had I done to make her hate me so much? Any shred of hope I had that Mum was going to save me and protect me disintegrated in that instant. Somehow, it was clearly easier for her to pretend that she was ignorant of what he was doing. She helped Stanley to hold me down, playing along with the charade that I was having a fit.

I felt completely powerless as Stanley said he was going to phone an ambulance.

"I don't know – I reckon she's 'aving a fit. She's thrashin' about all over the place," I heard him tell the operator.

When we got to hospital, he and Mum whisked the doctors to one side and informed them that I had special needs and had now started to have epileptic fits. Given that my special needs, although fabricated, were on record and the persistence of my parents' claims, the doctors didn't hesitate to believe them. I watched as I was given an injection, not realising it was a sedative. A cloud enveloped me. My eyelids became heavy and I struggled to fend off the drowsiness that was descending on me. Eventually, I gave in.

When I woke up, I found myself lying in a bed in a long room with grey walls. Slowly I turned my head to the left. It felt like I was moving through treacle and everything looked hazy. It took me some time to establish that I was on a mixed adult mental ward in a completely different hospital. In my sedated state, I was unable to move or protest. I was completely powerless.

The drugs they gave me were terrifying – they made it so I could hardly raise my arm, let alone try to explain that I didn't need them. They made it hard to concentrate on anything, but also made it so that you were still fully aware of what was happening to you.

After seven horrifying weeks on the ward, Stanley came to collect me. I had seen my parents just once or twice during my time on the ward. Stanley was given a prescription of drugs, along with careful instructions on what amounts to give me. I saw his sly smile as he put the medication into his pocket and knew then that I was about to enter one of the darkest times of my childhood.

Because of all the drugs Stanley was giving me, the time following my return from hospital is particularly difficult for me to remember. I spent months lying in bed falling in and out of consciousness. I once again stopped going to school and would fall asleep in my room and come round to find myself in all kinds of different places with all kinds of different sweaty faces doing God knows what to me. I can recall the men from the caravan park and the bungalows, the men from our estate, like Dave King from the top of our road and Reg from the market. Stanley would make us help out on Reg's stall all the time, and Reg would rape me in the back of his van. Sometimes I'd come to in other people's houses, with no idea of how I'd got there.

I remember once escaping and running home from one house on the estate. As I reached the corner at the bottom of our street, I heard footsteps pounding behind me. I ran like the wind, but as I neared our house, a boy called my name and as I turned to see where he was, half a house brick smashed me straight in the mouth. The pain tore through me as the brick split my mouth open, knocked out one of my front teeth and chipped a few others. Blood was pouring from my mouth. Just then, Stanley opened the door to me and roared, "You probably deserved it for running off like that! Now get to bed." And I remember thinking, how did you know I had run away?

My teeth were in a bad way, but no one took me to the dentist. When I finally did see a dentist, he said it was too late to help me and asked why I hadn't been brought in when it happened. Mum had a screaming fit at him and we never went there again. Whenever anyone questioned what had happened to me or asked something tricky, Mum or Stanley made sure that we never saw them again.

It was during that terrible, bleak time that Stanley started dropping me off at the docks. I remember the men on the ships chaining my foot to a metal bed, filming and photographing themselves making me do things to them or raping me. I knew this word because Grandpa Wallbridge had taught me that when someone makes someone else do sex against their will it was called rape.

"Smile!" the men on the ship would say. "Stop hiding your face! Come on, you're famous. Pictures of you are like gold dust – everyone wants them. You're a big product in the black market, a top seller. Come on, give us a smile."

I think they thought all their talk was making me feel big or special, but I felt ashamed and humiliated, and didn't care about any of it. I just wanted them to stop. I remember trying to use my eyes to send 'help me' messages down the lens of the various cameras, hoping that someone good might see them and come and help. Nobody ever came, and it wasn't long before I realised that nobody good was looking at these pictures, and absolutely nobody was looking at my eyes. I didn't understand the real cost of this kind of abuse, not until I was much, much older.

One sickening incident that haunts me to this day took place during this time. I recall going to sleep in my own bed, drugged to the nines, then dreaming that I was somewhere else and trying to fight these men off who were raping me one after another. Then as I started to wake up, I began to realise it was true. I was in a strange room, hidden away somewhere. I don't know if it was on the ship or the caravan site. They were hurting me so much I could hardly breathe. I started to fight like I had never fought before and the next thing I knew I woke up in a field, miles from anywhere, mostly naked, covered in bruises and blood, my head aching like never before. A bit of my skull was sticking up under my skin. Everything looked blurry, and I was so cold all I wanted to do was fall asleep. I was overwhelmed by tiredness and felt incredibly heavy and lethargic. The voice in my head said, "Get up and start walking, otherwise you're going to die."

I managed to haul myself up and began to walk, though I had to practically drag myself. Eventually, a car stopped and the kindly driver gave me a lift home.

When I finally got back, the others seemed surprised to see me, as when I was left anywhere, I was usually gone for a while.

Once, I was left for four weeks and only knew that I'd been gone that long because I'd missed Bonfire Night. Everyone had simply assumed I'd been put into care again.

Stanley reassured the driver, who was very concerned about me, that I was fine, just a bit mental and special needs.

"Don't worry. We'll look after 'er from here," he said, putting his arm round my shoulder. The moment the driver had left, Stanley roared, "Fuckin' great! Now you've put 'em off. What's wrong wiv you? If you just behaved yourself, things wouldn't turn out like this, would they?"

I was too dazed and shattered to respond. Besides, I'd long ago learnt that I was powerless to stop bad things happening to me.

Some time later, because I was in such a state and my vision was so bad, Mum took me to hospital and told the doctors that I'd fallen off a swing. As usual, they swallowed her story and, after treating me, told her that I had a fractured skull and needed to rest at home in the dark. It took me many months to regain my sight. Even though I was trying to recover, Stanley never left me alone. The drugs had already made me vulnerable, but now I was even more so. Stanley took full advantage of my weakened defences.

I began to understand that the drugs were giving Stanley more power and making everything worse and I just had to find a way to stop taking them. I became so desperate to stop what was happening that I started to pretend to take the tablets, squirreling them in the side of my mouth, then spitting them out when no one was looking. Slowly my head started to clear and I woke from my drug-fuelled nightmare to the very real horror that was now my life.

Even without the drugs, over the following months Stanley's abuse became progressively worse. He had always used sex as a currency, telling us that we had to do it to get food, water and clothes, but now we had to do it even if we wanted to speak to each other. It had reached the point where anything you said he twisted and made sexual. It was his weapon. In fact, I had to have sex with him for not having sex with him.

What was more, Stanley had access to even more children now. Stanley had budgies and he would use them to start up a conversation with children coming to the shop next door or visiting our house. As the months went on, our house became a child magnet.

Just when I was starting to believe that things couldn't get any worse, a ray of hope appeared in my life. One night, I was lying in my bed trying to 'sleep off' one of the pills I had not managed to spit out when I heard a voice from heaven: "Where's our Karen? Karen, hon, are you up there? Wake up. Come down, sweetheart. It's your Aunt Pat."

I thought I was dreaming at first and started to cry because it wasn't real, but then as I woke up, I realised it was her; Aunt Pat was calling me from downstairs. I hadn't seen her for ages because they had once again moved away! I practically fell down the stairs and lobbed myself at her as though my life depended on it.

"Oh, Aunt Pat," I sobbed, "please stop Stanley from giving me any more tablets, I'm not epileptic! Honestly I'm not! I can't wake up properly. Please tell him, Aunt Pat – tell him to stop."

Aunt Pat went ballistic.

"What in God's name do you think you're playing at, Stanley? Jennifer? I'm told she hasn't been out of bed for months, she's not going to school, and you know she's no more bloody epileptic than I am! Why are you giving her these tablets? You can't give a child these sort of tablets! I'm reporting you. What are you doing to her?"

I'd never seen Aunt Pat so angry.

Stanley looked frightened and stammered on about how he was only doing what the doctor said.

"Maybe you're right, though, Pat... Maybe the doctors have got it wrong. In fact, I'll tell them so at the very next case meeting at the hospital."

Mum sat there looking scared and said in a pathetic voice, "I don't know what's been happening, Pat. I've been so ill, and Stanley's been taking care of everything – as best he can, he's a good man."

Pat retorted, "You're well enough to go to the bingo all the bloody time, so don't give me all that rubbish, Jennifer!"

She then grabbed the bottle of tablets, rushed through to the downstairs bathroom and flushed the whole bottle down the toilet. When she came back, she said, "That's it, Stanley! You give her no more tablets, do you hear me?"

"Y-y-yes, Pat," he stammered.

Aunt Pat was one of the few people who Stanley was afraid of. She was a straight-talking woman and he knew that she wouldn't tolerate his lies.

"If I find out anyone's knocking her about or giving her any more drugs, they will have me to deal with. Do you understand?"

"Y-y-yes, Pat."

She said, "Why won't you give her a break?"

Stanley shrugged, looked helpless.

"You don't know what she's like. She's a little fuckin' bastard, always getting into trouble everywhere she goes. She steals, and she tells lies just to try and get me into trouble all the fuckin' time."

Aunt Pat's face was a picture of fury. She screamed at him, "She is nothing like that with anyone else! We've had her stay with us and she's as good as gold. Everyone says she is very shy, but she doesn't lie or steal from them or us! You're always picking on her! She doesn't do all the things you say, so why are you so hard on her?"

"But she's very clever, Pat – she knows how to be good around others. There's somefink wrong with 'er head. She's a little bitch. She gives people the silent treatment and it winds 'em up, and she don't do as she's told."

Exasperated, Pat said, "No, she doesn't."

Mum tried playing the sympathy vote again: "I've been so ill, Pat, I can't always know what she's doing, but I'm sure she's got something wrong with her head. She's special needs. You know she can't even read or write properly. She's so naughty they can't even teach her – just ask the school."

Now Aunt Pat went mad at Mum: "Listen to you! We've been telling you for years that she couldn't hear or see you properly. She's not thick, but you're always keeping her off school. No wonder she can't understand what they're saying to her. And she can read – watch this." Aunt Pat turned to me.

"Karen, sweetheart, read this for me."

She passed me a newspaper and I read part of the front page. Aunt Pat turned to Mum triumphantly and said, "See, she can bloody well read!"

She pointed at a word and said what does that mean? I responded that construct means build. See! She's not bloody stupid either. Then her voice softened as she said to me, "Karen, sweetheart, Uncle Ken will be here soon to say hello. Can you go and sit in the dining room and watch out for him and let me have a chat with your mum and dad?"

I went next door, dashed to the central-heating vent that ran throughout the house, flicked it open, pinned my ear against it and listened. I was crying inside, but outside I was shaking like a leaf, my jaw was shuddering as if I was cold, and I felt like I was going to explode with excitement. I had no idea what was about to happen, but somehow I knew things were about to change in a very big way.

Aunt Pat was talking quietly then suddenly said much louder, "Right, you two, I'll be back in a moment, I'm just popping to the shop." She left for a few moments.

Next I heard was Stanley and Mum speaking totally unguardedly. Even to this day, I have never been able to wipe this conversation from my mind. Because what they said shook me to my very core.

"I told you not to smack that little twat so much – now look what you've done!" Mum spat.

"She gets on my fuckin' nerves!"

"Mine too. She makes my skin crawl, but if she's not here, they won't pay us!"

"She don't know when to keep 'er fuckin' trap shut, that one," Stanley complained. "Why don't you just stick 'er back in the nut house?"

"Because there's nothing wrong with her."

"Well, make somefink wrong with 'er, for fuck's sake! We'll have to tell 'em all we're movin' again or people are gonna start sniffin' around. Fuckin' 'ell! See what she does to us all the fuckin' time? I fuckin' hate 'er. We should have let Fred fuckin' kill 'er! We wouldn't have all this bother, would we?"

"No, I know. You know I can't stand her, but leave her alone for a bit. I'll come up with something," Mum retorted, trying to keep her voice low in case Aunt Pat returned from the shop. I fell back against the wall as though someone had just punched me in the face. My own mother truly hated me and wanted me gone. Despite everything I loved my mother and even though I suspected she didn't love me back, I never realised just how much she despised me.

I couldn't focus or hear what they were saying any more. I felt dizzy, and my head and heart had started pounding. My whole body began to tremble and my mind started screaming, "They hate me! I make her skin crawl. They wish I was dead." I felt strangled and like there was a beach ball in my throat, chest and stomach again. I tried to say a word, but it just came out like a moan. Then a kind of mental fog came into my brain and I howled out loud.

They didn't hear me: they were too busy arguing.

The howl was a horrible sound that I had never made before. I felt an all-over pain surging through my body, and things flashed through my mind that I hadn't thought about in years. I simply could not control it. Not Pately Bridge, not Jimmy Ruffin, not even rocking could help me now. I was freefalling into the darkness and I couldn't stop myself.

I was crying more out of fear than anything else, but then suddenly I heard this tiny voice at the very back of my mind saying, *Listen. Please listen to me. Will you please listen to me?*

I instantly became very quiet and still – no freefalling, no pictures, just the fog and this voice. It was a kind but firm female voice.

In my head, I said, "OK, I'm listening."

Sit back where you were. OK. Breathe slowly, calm down and listen to the grown-ups.

I said, "I can't. It hurts."

"Listen to them! I will hear it and store it, but you have to listen.

I was so shocked I just did as I was told and the fog started to clear. Aunt Pat was back in the living room and Mum and Pat were talking about how Mum and Stanley always said we were moving but never did. Then Uncle Ken turned up. He found me curled up next to the vent and came straight to me, hugged me and asked if I was OK.

I faked a smile and said, "I am now."

Then he said, "Wait there, sweetheart. Let me go talk with the others."

He patted me on the shoulder and left the room. I put my ear back to the vent. I heard them all argue for a while, then Uncle Ken said something that made my heart soar: "Why don't you just let me and Pat adopt her, you're always saying you will, why don't you?"

"Yes!" I screamed from my hiding place by the vent before I could stop myself.

Stanley, alarmed that I was eavesdropping, shouted, "Go away!" but Aunt Pat said, "No, let her in – it's about her anyway."

I flew into the living room. Mum was glaring at me and Stanley was angry as hell.

I sat down and Mum turned to me, pursing her lips, and said, "Pat and Ken want to know if you would like to go and live with them for good. They want to adopt you. What do you think about that?"

I blurted out straight away, "I'd love it. I promise I'll be good. I wouldn't be far away. I would come back to see everyone. I would do good at school. I would do everything they told me to do. I won't talk unless I'm talked to. I…"

Mum cut me off abruptly. "Well, it looks like she wouldn't mind."

She looked like she didn't care one way or the other as she said, "Yes, all right, if that's what everyone wants, I can't see why not."

Stanley was clearly not quite so happy to see the back of me, and grumbled, "It can't be today. I'll sort a few things out and do it later this week."

I felt a huge surge of relief. Aunt Pat and Uncle Ken were so pleased they hugged each other. Then they gestured for me to come over to them for a hug, too. I fell into them with such joy that I started to cry with sheer happiness. This was my ultimate, best ever dream come true. I was finally going to escape this life, these people, the horrible and the darkness.

I was laughing and crying at the same time, when I said thank you to Stanley and Mum. Mum said, "That's all right. Now go wash your face and let us talk for a bit." By the time they left, everyone was happy and friends again, and I was on another planet.

For the rest of the day I did exactly as I was told. I didn't want to do anything to upset Mum and Stanley. I was so happy I wanted to run to the top of Biddy Hill and shout at the top of my lungs. I couldn't quite believe that Mum had let me go so easily. She normally seemed to want to keep me around because she got benefits for me, but I'd heard her give permission, so had Aunt Pat and Uncle Ken. I was on cloud nine.

That night, Stanley got me on my own and whispered, "Now listen to me good. If you wanna move in wiv Pat and Ken, you gotta promise me you'll never go telling your stories. It's our secret. Got it?"

I wholeheartedly agreed. If he had said I had to rip my leg off with my own bare teeth, I would have done it.

Stanley said, "Off to bed and no messin' about."

I was up the stairs and in bed before he finished his sentence. I did the horrible as best I could that night and Stanley left my room pleased with me. As I drifted off to sleep, I was smiling and dreaming of my new life with my real family. For the first time since leaving Pately Bridge, more than a year before, I felt happy. What happened next was the cruellest twist I could ever have imagined. Mum and Stanley were, as always, one step ahead.

My dream was shattered in the middle of the night when I was violently dragged out of bed by a load of strangers. It was dark and I couldn't see who they were. Were they the men from the shipyard? Or was it the police coming to put me in prison for being naughty, dirty, bad? I kicked and fought, but then I heard Stanley and Mum telling me to stop, so I kept still as they carried me out of the house and into a waiting van. My heart was pounding in my ears. I begged them to tell me who they were.

"What are you doing?" I cried. "Where are you taking me? What's going on?"

They wouldn't answer me.

When we were in the back of the van, I saw one of the strangers was a lady. I cried, "What's happening?"

The lady said, "Because of what you did to your sister, you are going to be taken to a secure mental ward."

"I didn't do anything!" I cried, completely bewildered. "Ask her!"

"We don't need to ask her – your parents have told us that you stabbed her. They also told me that you haven't been taking your medication."

And somehow I was asleep before I knew it.

I can't talk too much about what happened next – it's just too painful – but I stayed on the mental ward for a few weeks. Mum and Stanley had indeed managed to come up with something to get me sent back to the nuthouse, just like they'd said they would. Once again, it was clear that their word was law and no one was going to question it. No one even checked to see if anyone had been stabbed. It still staggers me to this day to think how readily the social workers, doctors and psychiatrists believed Mum and Stanley's lies without question.

No one came to visit me, and I spent the time drifting in and out of sleep and worrying about whether I was still going to live with Aunt Pat and Uncle Ken. I had no idea what was happening, and no one would answer my questions.

When I finally returned home to the Noctorum, my sister was as shocked as me to hear that she had apparently been stabbed, as she had no knowledge of it and no one had asked her anything about it.

Mum got back from 'shopping' later that day, and she and Stanley broke the news that I had been dreading: Aunt Pat and

Uncle Ken had decided not to adopt me. I listened with horror as Mum told me that they had said I was far too naughty and that they were afraid that my naughtiness might rub off on their Dona so they couldn't adopt me after all.

"But I didn't do..." I tried to protest, but Mum cut me off.

"Anyway, there's no point mithering on – you're not living with them and that's that. They don't love you anymore, and you'll just have to accept it."

I was devastated and crashed to the floor. Dear God! If they think I'm bad, then I really must be!

I just couldn't take it all in. It simply didn't make sense. I looked up at Mum and Stanley, tears welling in my eyes, and said, "They honestly don't love me anymore?"

Stanley retorted, "No they don't, so deal with it."

Then his voice took on a more sinister tone. "You'll be able to see it in their faces," he said. "So whatever you do, if you don't want to get hurt, don't look at them, don't look in their eyes. They are coming round in a bit. You can stay upstairs if you want or you can sit down here, but don't look at their faces, all right?"

I nodded as I listened with horror. I couldn't bear the idea that Aunt Pat and Uncle Ken didn't love me anymore. The idea of not seeing love in their eyes was completely devastating to me and I knew I wouldn't be able to face it. I wiped my face, trying to come to terms with what had happened. All I wanted was to be alone.

"I'll go to my room now," I said, and Stanley nodded solemnly as I carried myself off upstairs. I stayed in my room all evening, lost in my own despair.

Later on, Aunt Pat and Uncle Ken came round. They called and called me until in the end I had to come downstairs. Mum told me to sit at her feet. I could hear Aunt Pat talking to me, but I was so scared that the words she was saying were "I don't love you anymore" that I tuned her out and refused to even look at them.

Mum said triumphantly, "See, I told you, she's off her head."

I didn't care what Mum said anymore. I just couldn't bear the idea that they didn't love me. I hugged my knees to my chest and disappeared inside my own thoughts.

Aunt Pat and Uncle Ken left the house soon afterwards. Aunt Pat seemed very upset. I ran upstairs to my room, trying to stop the tears from falling. At the time, I honestly thought that they believed I was naughty, dirty, bad, and that I had stabbed my sister. It wasn't until years later that I would find out the truth about this terrible day.

I knew that this was probably the last time I was ever going to see them. I was crushed, blindsided. I watched from my bedroom window as Aunt Pat and Uncle Ken left the house all crying and hugging each other, got into their car and drove off, taking my dreams of happiness with them.

Tell and Show

Over the next few months, things at home continued to spiral. The pleas that Aunt Pat and Uncle Ken had made to my parents to stop giving me the tablets had somehow worked, but the problem was that now Stanley and Mum didn't have the tablets to control me, they couldn't control me very much at all.

Don't get me wrong – I was naughty, but not the kind of naughty they would say I was. In an attempt to reassert control, they took to phoning up Social Services and reporting all kinds of imaginary incidents – their plan was to get them to take me away to a special unit, either residential or non- residential. That way, they would still receive benefits for me, which they wouldn't have done if I'd been adopted by Pat and Ken. I would later learn that they had never had any intention of allowing Pat and Ken to adopt me.

Social Services were very much involved in my life now, and incredible as it seems now, they believed every single word Mum and Stanley said without question or investigation. From the very first meeting, back when I was nine, I had sensed that Mrs Potter, my social worker, didn't like me and clearly believed that these poor, nice parents were struggling to cope with a naughty, dirty, bad child. She knew what Stanley was doing, but she firmly believed that it was me making him do this to me. No matter how I tried, there was simply no changing her mind. She looked at me like you look at dog crap stuck on your shoe, so I tried not to look at her face too much. The view that she had formed on that first meeting never changed and it completely coloured the way I was treated by the authorities for years to come.

One incident that stands out in my mind happened when I was 12. I remember waking up in a hospital intensive-care unit. I had been gang-raped on one of the ships and had collapsed not long after, because I had contracted a sexually transmitted disease. The staff were obviously very concerned because I was just a child. Their concern turned to repulsion, however, after my social worker turned up and told them something that made them change and become horrible towards me.

Social Services simply didn't listen to what I told them. Desperation took hold of me and I became more and more argumentative and volatile. Stanley and Mum used the threat of Social Services a lot to try and keep me in line.

Social Services, on the other hand, used a different threat: some care workers told me they'd add bad entries to my file if I didn't cooperate with them. At first I was frightened by this, but as time went by, I stopped caring what they said or thought about me. I had no rights regarding what was put into my file, no representation. I wasn't allowed to see my file, or challenge it and certainly wasn't allowed to remove or correct false entries. The Social Services file was like some invisible entity to me, so the threats about it seemed empty after a while. Ultimately, it seemed to make little difference to my life or what was happening to me so I stupidly ignored it.

As Social Services' opinion of me worsened and Stanley and Mum insisted that I was out of control, I was sent to non-residential and then residential special units. Many of the people who worked in these units exercised very smacky methods of childcare and I would sometimes be physically restrained or punished.

What was worse, some of these professionals had a 'pin-down, tell and show' approach. At first, they would seem like someone you could trust, so you would tell them a little something, hoping they would change how things were at home, only to find yourself being forced into showing them what was going on at home. Before you understood what they were asking of you, you would find yourself re-enacting the abuse with the care workers.

From the start of my time in these special units, from about the age of 12, I was sexually abused by the very people who were meant to be helping me. I was sent to endless care placements and only in one or two was I not abused. Even though I know it isn't true, it did seem like all care units everywhere were run or staffed by child molesters. Understandably, I viewed grown-ups as pervy, smacky, permanent erections who lied so much you never knew where you stood. I don't know for certain why I ended up at all the horrible care units, but I do know that my social worker would write off to these units to ask them to take me in and would of course always 'warn' them about my alleged attempts to suck Stanley's penis against his will. In retrospect, I can see how I was a sitting target for a new barrage of abusers. The units run by ordinary people would often say no, but the ones run by perverts would welcome me with open trousers. I used to think that 'in care' meant being sexually abused by strangers.

For a while, this further convinced me that I must be making it happen. If not, then why did it happen everywhere I went? It wasn't until I witnessed for myself other children being abused in the units that I came to realise that this wasn't just happening to me – it was happening to lots of children. I also saw that these children didn't do anything to deserve the abuse they were handed out: they were told they were being punished, but I could see that they had done nothing wrong. So once again, I considered that maybe it wasn't me turning people into abusers. Maybe, just maybe, I didn't deserve this treatment either. As this dawned on me, my feeling of injustice began to escalate. Why were people allowed to get away with this?

Life was changing so fast it was hard to form and hold an opinion on anything for very long. I had come to realise that the voice inside my head was in fact just me trying to calm me down, which was a relief, as I had honestly believed I had been going mad for a while there.

In between stays in special units, I would go back home. Sometimes Roma would be staying at home again – if Mum had claimed she'd had another heart attack and needed special looking after.

Denise and I got along as best we could, but with an added unspoken element that we could talk about without ever saying a word. It was all looks, gestures, grunts and slang, but we always knew what each other meant.

For us, Stanley was someone to be endured. He was a violent, whiney man who complained all the time about everything. He taught us to both love and hate the sports reader Dicky Davis, weekend wrestling and the poxy horseracing results. Love, because when Stanley was watching wrestling or checking his score draws, he was leaving us alone. Hate, because we bloody well loathed watching the wrestling and horseracing results, which would go on for what seemed like hours. It's nothing personal, but poor old Dicky Davis just ended up reminding us of Stanley.

I remember another time I lashed out at Stanley. Once, when I was about 13, I actually started a fight with Stanley for walking in on my sister when she was in the bath. I knew what he was up to and she knew it too, so I came out of my room, punched Stanley hard in the shoulder and ran like the wind down the stairs and out of the front door. He came after me as fast as his fat old legs would carry him, but was gasping for air by the time he got to Billy Rainbows. If he couldn't catch me at the time of the crime, he would never smack me for it later, so learning to run fast was a good thing. Thank you, Dona!

As the baby of the family Denise could wrap Mum round her little finger, and she knew that, too. Mum kept Denise little – she would dress her younger, treat her like a baby and tell her the most stupid things you could imagine, like how bingo was a profession, not a pastime. She adored Mum; she was her world, and whatever Mum said was what Denise believed, except for when it came to me. She would pretend to believe the grown-ups, but the moment we were alone, she would say sorry and that she knew it wasn't true.

Denise was also doing well at school. She was doing cycling proficiency and lifesaving at swimming. She had some friends and loved Donny Osmond. She was a sweet, tiny little thing who trusted people way too much, and I always felt the most intense sense of protectiveness towards her.

One day, when Denise was about 12 and I was 13, I was walking back from the swimming pool on the Woody estate. I had been swimming with Denise and her friend Carol, but they'd set off home before me. To get to our estate, you had to walk under a motorway, over two bridges that crossed the sewer and a railway line and across a busy road. I had just gone through the tunnel under the motorway and was about to walk over the bridge when I saw two grown lads holding a girl on the ground by her hair and pounding her head off the floor, while a third lad was throwing stones at her and a fourth was kicking her. I looked at the girl and saw my baby sister's face scrunched in pain. Her eyes were starting to roll back. I can't explain what happened in my head or what I thought I was going to do with these four big lads, but I just flipped.

I ran screaming, "Get off of my fucking sister!" and suddenly became the ninja sister, scream champion of the world. I don't know where my courage, strength or amazing fighting abilities came from, but before I knew it, I'd punched two of them off their feet, one of them was clinging to his crotch, on his knees with a bleeding nose, and the other one had a smashed lip and I had him by his hair, inches from the sewer water and was demanding, "How do you like it now?"

My sister's friend Carol, who had up to then been held back by one of the boys, helped Denise to her feet to get out of there, but my sister said she didn't want to go without me. I just yelled, "Don't worry, sis. I'm all right. Run!"

But she wouldn't, so I told the lad to say sorry to my sister or he would drink sewer water. He said sorry and I pushed him into the sewer headfirst, grabbed my sister and Carol, and legged it to a friend's house close by, where our Denise collapsed.

When they got her to hospital, they said she was concussed and badly bruised. The doctors, police, Stanley and even Mum said they were all very pleased with me for protecting my sister, and even the newspapers reported it, because it wasn't the first time it had happened at that place and because of the seriousness of my sister's injuries. Even so, they decided not to mention my part, because they said they wanted to send out an anti-violent message and that I sounded quite violent. To be honest, I was a little bit violent. The frustration and powerlessness that had been building up inside me for so long just needed an outlet, and I found that violence was a good way of getting bad people to stop doing bad things. But even that didn't always work.

I had recently beaten up Reg from the market. He was one of Stanley's pervy mates who had been abusing me for years. Stanley used to send us all down to the market to 'help out' on Reg's ladies' underwear stall. One time when Reg had dropped me at home, I told Stanley that Reg was getting at me. Reg told Stanley that I was just pissed off at him for telling me off for stealing from him. Now, don't get me wrong, I did steal from him a lot, and he knew it, but he never told me off for it and I hadn't stolen from him that day. But Stanley believed him and that was the end of that.

A few weeks later, I was told that Reg was trying to get at my little sister, so I went down to the market and asked him what he was playing at. It wasn't really a question, though, just a distraction while I picked up things from his stall and thrashed him with them. Far from defending himself, Reg lay on the floor and whimpered, so I stopped smacking him and told him to leave my sister alone. He promised, then got up and ran off. He did leave me alone after that, but sadly he carried on abusing children, including my little sister.

Stanley didn't just send me to his mates, like Reg and Dave, though. He sold me to countless men all over Birkenhead. It wasn't ever as obvious as "Here's my child – £15 a go!" It was more like, "Yes, complete stranger, you can take her out."

Then, later, Stanley would ask these people to 'lend' him money, cigarettes, alcohol and stuff, which they would always give him without argument and he never had to give it back.

I often wondered why he asked people for booze, as nobody in our house ever drank, but after a while, once Stanley had started to befriend some of the neighbours' children, the reasons became horribly clear. Stanley would give the alcohol to the children as a way of encouraging them to come to the rule-free house. He let children drink, smoke and generally do whatever they wanted at our house. It was an effective way of getting children to come over, and lose their inhibitions. Their parents wouldn't know exactly where their children were as they would often go out playing around on the estate all day. I tried to tell some of the parents about coming to the house, but Stanley found out and got me sent back to the special units.

After a few weeks the unit had a family meeting with Mum and Stanley to explain that they thought my behaviour was fine and that they thought something else might be behind these strange episodes.

They asked Stanley if he knew why I was so unhappy. He said I was a little tart and then he tried to tell them that he thought I was epileptic again.

All I could think of was, you're not giving me those fucking tablets again! In my desperation, I flew across the room at him, punched and scratched his face, then screamed at him to tell the truth.

"Tell them what you really do!" I screamed.

Right then I felt Mum's hand on my shoulder.

"Come on now, Karen," she said, her voice kind and soft. Then she turned to the care workers and said, "I think that's quite enough. Karen is clearly very upset and all this is making her worse. You're distressing her, anyone can see that."

I looked up at Mum in disbelief. I wanted to explain that it was Stanley who was upsetting me, not the care workers, but before I knew what was happening Mum was ushering me out of the room. She signed me out of the unit that day, explaining that they were upsetting me too much, that we were all moving to Runcorn anyway and she would take me to hospital there. Telling the authorities that we were moving was still her standard excuse to get people to leave us alone.

The moment we were out of the hospital, Mum became her old, hard self again. I had clearly got a little too close to convincing the officials that I really was being abused and to exposing them. Since that time when Mum had seen Stanley making me suck his penis, I had been sure that Mum knew I was being abused. She simply didn't care.

When we got home, I said nothing while Stanley beat me senseless for nearly "spilling my guts" to the unit.

"You're getting me into trouble."

I didn't have the energy to fight back so I just lay there. I spent weeks in my room, but at least I wasn't on those bloody tablets anymore.

The Runaway

If things got too bad, I did have a safe place to run and hide, a place where nobody could find me, Biddy Hill. Bidston Hill is a wooded hill surrounded by fields next to our estate. It has an old observatory at the top and stunning views as far as the eye can see. I buried lots of secret scribble notes on Biddy Hill (they're probably still there) and spent many a safe hour watching the wildlife and playing in the beautiful woodlands, but it was not and never could be my Pately Bridge. Oh, dear God, how I missed that place.

Biddy Hill was not my only safe hideaway; I also loved the Moreton and Leasowe shores. We had family all over the area and would frequently visit the seaside near them. I liked it best when I went on my own. I would wander up and down the water's edge, exploring and listening to the sea lap against the shore. It wasn't my stream, but it helped.

I would sometimes come here to hide after doing the horrible, like with Steve. I put more horrible thoughts into the sea than in my stream, because it was so big, but I was still careful because fish lived in there and I didn't want it to get on them.

These days, though, washing the bad thoughts away didn't work anymore, so I would just sit and stare out to sea and think, watching the ships that passed against the beautiful sky and wondering which poor soul the ship workers were doing the horrible to now.

Now that I had entered my teens, the grown-ups' behaviour was getting harder and harder to understand or manage. I had always felt that I was naughty, dirty, bad, but the horrible was such an everyday part of my life that I was starting to feel like a 'pervert-maker'. One look at me and everyone from policemen to priests just lost their minds.

I had long realised that there was no point telling anyone because everyone thought it was me who was dirty and if I wasn't now I would be. The stigma at the time was such that that's what everyone thought: victims of child abuse became abusers. Telling, therefore, wasn't an option.

For a few brief months in my life, I played a part in some of the horrible things that were happening to me. I had figured out how to get food and clothes without having sex with Stanley: I would secretly approach some of the men Stanley had sold me to, let them have sex and keep the money for myself. The problem with this was it made me feel disgusting, because I chose to go there. What was worse still, was that not every horrible was horrible. This confused me out of my mind and, as you can imagine, messed up my attitude about sex even more.

I can remember the very first time I actually consented to sex. It was in my early teens and I had been dropped off at a house in New Brighton for the night. The man – he must have been about twenty-something – started doing the horrible to me, and I braced myself for the pain as always, but it never came.

The Runaway

I let the man do it because I liked him, he was gentle, he never did anything I didn't want to do, and he never made me feel frightened. He made it nice. I even snuck away from our house to do it with him all on my own. After the first time, I didn't take any money from him. Then I would make my way to the beach and stare out to sea.

I had just left his home one day and was walking along the New Brighton shore when I had a terrible moment of realisation. I was thinking about why it was not so bad with this particular man, when that voice I sometimes heard in my head said:

Having sex with children is bad, isn't it?

Yes, I thought.

You are a child, aren't you?

Yes.

You like what he does to you, though, don't you?

Yes.

So you like bad sex!

What? No!

Stanley sells you to bad people for bad sex, doesn't he?

Yes.

Well, now you're selling yourself.

What? No I'm not!

You're becoming what Stanley says you are.

I don't want to be anything he wants me to be!

So don't do it again!

OK, I won't, I won't. But what about that nice man?

He is a bad man, doing bad things in a nice way, to a child.

Yes.

And you like it?

Yes. No. I don't know. Oh, shit! What do I do?

Easy: don't like it anymore and don't go back there ever again.

I never sold myself to anyone after that, and I made sure that any sex people did have with me was like doing it to concrete.

By now, I was nearly 14, had a smart mouth on me and could physically stand up for myself, but I never fought unless it was to protect myself or my sister. I also never spoke unless I had to. I was in and out of various secure units and care homes, never staying anywhere more than a few months, as Social Services or Mum moved me on. I certainly wasn't kept anywhere long enough to get an education of any description. I didn't like liars and could spot one a mile off, but in my own way I knew I was a liar too: being in my family made you one, because the first thing you had to do was not tell people anything about any part of your life as a family, as all roads would lead to the horrible. Consequently, all I could do was make stuff up. I would tell people ridiculous things – like, I'm the 18-year-old only child of English parents who died years back.

I couldn't bear cruelty and, to be honest, I didn't even like stealing: I liked the excitement but not the consequences. I didn't like people who took drugs or drank too much, and I simply couldn't get my head round the sheer level of racism I lived in and around every day. Thinking about it, it seemed that the people around me just weren't happy unless they had something to hate.

In Stanley and Mum's eyes, any goodness or kindness in anyone was seen as a weakness and therefore something to be ridiculed and exploited. I hated this side of them. In fact, I didn't like anything about them or my life and had started to realise that I was pretending my life away. I was pretending to be part of this family; I was pretending I was like them; I was pretending to be Karen.

To everyone else I knew, I was Shy. Shy was the person everyone else met when I was away from my family. The 'everyone' I'm talking about here, were all those people I met when I was either on my own or on the run; they were my secret friends and they called me Shy. As a child, my real father, my Aunt Pat and Uncle Ken and even my little sister sometimes called me Shy, so I didn't mind my secret friends calling me it as well.

One of my secret friends was a transvestite who ran the 24-hour cafe near Number 10 Downing Street in London, which was where I'd started to run when things got really unbearable. I knew that the boss of the world worked at No 10. I often walked past wondering what he would do if he knew what Stanley and others did and wished I could go in and tell him, but all that was a world a million worlds away from mine and not a door that would ever be open to me. My secret friend would take me in and let me stay the night when things got too bad on the streets. She was always kind to me and provided a safe haven when I needed it most. I suppose she was an outsider just as much as I was.

My secret friends would never meet my family. What I liked about this was that when I was with them, which was only ever for a short time, now and then, I could relax and be myself. This was a relief because at home, as time went by, I had to pretend to be Karen and hide being Shy.

When I was on the run there was no horrible, no need to protect anyone, I could be as kind and as helpful as I wanted without feeling stupid.

Social Services and education authorities continued to send me to very abusive special units. I was sent to one after another. In desperation, I had started to run away from them. I would run to London or to my other hiding places close to home. Whenever I ran away, the police would find me and take me back or send me to a different place. It wasn't always because I was being abused by care staff that I ran away; sometimes it was because my sister was calling for help. I'd often get a call from Denise and would rush home to try to take Stanley's attention away from her.

Stanley was at home a lot more, apparently disabled with a back injury and now living on disability benefits, but still working as a painter and decorator, and this, plus the fact that he didn't have me to focus his unwanted attentions on, meant things at home were more horrible for my sister and her friends. Stanley would share his victims with others – even I knew that – but he seemed to be getting much worse. I couldn't understand how everyone was letting him get away with it. These children had parents – what were they doing? Everyone seemed completely taken in by his persona as a caring father. Why couldn't they see through it?

Mum, meanwhile, was out most of the time and went away on her own for weeks to go and visit Uncle Ken in Hong Kong, and Roma and her family in Germany, where they had been posted with the army, which meant that Stanley could do whatever he wanted whenever he wanted.

I kept running away from the special units and doing everything I could to help my sister; however, this wasn't going down well with Social Services, who were sending me to more and more secure residential units. The truth was, nothing short of prison could ever keep me anywhere for very long if I didn't want to be there. I loved being on the run: I was free and an almost electric excitement would course through my veins. Planning the escape, the moment of escape and the 'running like a cat with its arse on fire' part were thrilling and just pure fun.

I drove the special units crazy with my escapology antics and would do everything, even hiding in a drawer and letting everyone think I had already escaped, then actually escaping once they had all run off to look for me. One time, I hid in a coat on a coat rack for hours, waiting for a sodding one-way door to open, and I once even climbed into the loft, moved the roof tiles, pulled myself up on to the roof and shimmied down the drain. On this occasion, I didn't have any shoes on, so I drew some on with a felt-tip pen and the bus driver let me ride for free because he thought I was special needs.

The social workers rarely called me Karen. They labelled me as a criminal, manipulative, promiscuous, wayward, attention-seeking lying fantasist. Despite them noting that I had never behaved in any sexual way towards any of them, I was only ever driven by female taxi drivers, just in case I pounced on a male driver!? They essentially covered every possible way of saying I was an absconding, thieving, lying, slut who sucks old men's willies against their wills, and I was still barely 14 years old. The more negative comments that were written about me on my files, the more impossible it was for anyone new to believe that I was anything other than the lying delinquent they said I was.

In some ways, what the care workers and Social Services said about me was kind of true. I was a liar, but not the one they thought I was. I was manipulative, but, dear God, if you weren't, you would be everyone's smack 'n' fuck mit. I did steal, but not because I wanted to. I did fantasise about a different life, but they would too if they had my life to live.

If I was at the special units for a long time, they would let Stanley write to me. Stanley was never careful about what he wrote in his letters. I don't know if the care staff read them or not, but it didn't seem to make a difference to what he wrote, and I never showed them to anyone as I had long given up trying to get the adults to back me up. His letters would start off "Hello, Karen, how are you?" and would in no time at all end up talking about the sex I had with him, should have with him and how I could do it better and said things like: "Look, Karen, when you're suckin' fings, it's no good usin' ya teef, you wanna start finkin' about what ya doin' like otherwise it's no good. Your sister does it proper now, so it's time ya started finkin' on." I hated these letters. They made my flesh crawl, but I had to read them to see what was happening at home. Managing the adults around me was mentally and emotionally exhausting; protecting the innocents and the ignorants was killing me; and keeping up the pretence was slowly drowning me in my own despair. All that was interrupted, though, when upon Mum's return from Hong Kong, she fainted and fell ill. We all thought it was just another one of Mum's fainting spells, but she had developed what we all now know to be deep-vein thrombosis. Her fainting spell turned into a full-on stroke, making half her body go limp.

After the stroke, she dribbled all over the place and couldn't talk or move her left side for a while. I came back home from the residential unit I had been in. The stroke turned things round for a bit between us, because she needed me to help her with things and therefore had to talk. When I say talk, I mean grunt to me, which I know annoyed her, but she got used to it. I say 'talking', but I really mean her telling me to do stuff for her.

After the stroke, Mum became a completely different person. She was vulnerable, frightened and disorientated. Gone was the grasping, manipulative Mum I'd always known, and she was replaced with someone helpless, someone who really needed me. Seeing her so dependent on me brought out all my nurturing instincts. I just wanted to protect her and help her. We moved her bed downstairs, ran around for her and responded round the clock to her every sigh or grunt. For the first time I could remember, Mum didn't cringe or complain when I was near here. I started to feel that maybe there was hope for us. I wanted to help Mum. Despite everything, she was a human being and I hated to see anyone suffer.

Unfortunately, as Mum recovered, she reverted to the mother I had always known. She turned from grateful and helpless into a bad-tempered, demanding, bingo-starved patient from hell. I realised that she couldn't be more pleased that she had a real, official illness that brought her tons of the kind of attention she loved, the kind she could take advantage of.

This of course meant that Stanley could continue to take full advantage of us as well, as he knew we would never say anything to Mum when she was ill.

At this time I was 14. I have a lot to thank The Real Thing, Odyssey, The Crusaders, Delegation, George Benson and The Eagles for. Their music was about to help me through some of the darkest days of my life.

"Your Mum's Dead"

What happened next is written in the best order I know. Things at home had taken yet another turn for the worse. Mum was going in and out of hospital and continued to be very poorly. So many children were now being abused by Stanley, including my baby sister, and things were just getting worse.

I had decided to do what we were all petrified of doing: I would try to tell Mum again and see if she could stop it, even for a bit.

On the day I decided to tell her, I was shaking to my bones, as all I could remember was that fateful day, all those years ago, when I had last told her, but I knew she couldn't hit me or hurt me any more than she had already. I just wanted Stanley and the others stopped, and although I was scared Mum was going to die from shock, she had recently won £100 at bingo, which was a huge sum at the time, and had coped fine with that, so I went for it.

Mum was in bed, Stanley was sitting on the couch at her feet, I walked in and bluntly said, "Mum, Stanley still makes me suck his penis, and I'm not the only one."

Stanley jumped off the couch and punched me. Then, to my utter surprise, Mum flew out of the bed and leapt on top of

Stanley's back. She started pounding him with her fists, scream-ing, "Why can't you just leave them alone?"

I was completely dumbstruck. Stanley was pleading with Mum to let him explain.

Denise came rushing in and Mum turned to her, her face white with rage, and said, "Is it true? Is he making you do this?"

We looked down at the ground and the world stopped still for a moment as I waited to hear the response; this time although she carried on looking down at the floor she nodded, yes, and Mum proceeded to punch Stanley out of the front door and slammed it closed on his pleading face.

Then she started asking us loads of rapid-fire questions. We were hugging each other in shock and amazement.

"Jennifer, love, I can explain. Just let me in, will you?" Stanley pleaded through the letterbox. "Give us five minutes. Five minutes, that's all I ask. Just to talk."

"Fuck off," Mum roared back. "You promised to lay off of them."

But Stanley persisted, coaxing her, until eventually she let him in.

"Off you go upstairs," Mum said. I tried to use my eyes to plead with her not to listen to him, but she wouldn't look at me. Upstairs, we lay on the floor to try to hear what they were saying downstairs, but we couldn't. I finally fell asleep in the small hours, with my ear still glued to the floor. The next morning, I was woken by a ring on the doorbell.

Someone opened the door and I heard an officious voice say, "Good morning, we are here to collect Karen. We are from Social Services."

My heart hit the floor. I couldn't believe it. Mum had rung Social Services again. How could she do that to me? My family's capacity to hurt me seemed to know no bounds. The next thing I knew I was being driven to Parkside Special School (for extra-bad girls) and meeting John Marshall, the scary headmaster.

As soon as I could, I called home. Stanley told me that Mum had taken a sudden turn for the worse that night, changed her mind about everything and now he was going to stay home to look after her and our Denise full-time, while I boarded at the school. I don't have the words to explain how angry and frustrated I felt. After all this time, my parents' treatment of me should have come as no surprise, but it still cut me to the bone.

Life at Parkside School was grim. John Marshall, the head, was a cruel and perverted man, and I quickly learnt that he was physically and sexually abusing many of the children at both of the schools he ran in the county. Initially, I simply heard about the abuse from the other kids, but it wasn't long before I started to witness children being abused for myself. One of those children, whom I will never forget, was poor Jane. We were in the dining room and Jane was talking when she wasn't supposed to. John Marshall stormed in, screamed at her and threw cutlery at her. Then he punched her hard in the stomach. Jane was doubled over in pain, clutching her belly and wheezing. Marshall showed no mercy. He dragged her into an airing cupboard. I still shudder when I recall poor Jane's tear-stained face and dishevelled clothes. That was just her 'punishment' for talking in the dining room.

It wasn't long before, like Jane, I was one of those who was being abused by John Marshall. He had intercepted some of Stanley's letters to me and, like some of the other abusive care workers at the special units, had been making me 'tell and show'. He had been abusing me for a while now, but I was so used to being abused that nothing surprised me anymore and it was pointless fighting it.

One day, a couple of months into my time at Parkside School, John Marshall called me into his office. I followed him in warily, expecting yet another 'tell and show'. I stood on the far side of his desk as he made himself comfortable in his chair and shuffled some papers. From his silence, I began to suspect that something might be amiss, but his expression was completely unreadable. After a few moments, he glanced up and said matter of factly...

"I don't want you making a big fuss over this, but your mum's dead."

The words could not have come as more of a shock to me. I hadn't seen Mum since she had called the social worker to send me to Parkside, after I'd tried to tell her yet again about Stanley.

I searched his face, but he remained impassive. What if he was lying? I fell to my knees and screamed, "No! You liar!"

He continued in the same no-nonsense tone, "I regret to inform you that I am not lying, young lady. She died yesterday of a stroke. Now go and gather yourself."

The room seemed to be closing in around me, and I heard a rushing sound in my ears. I simply couldn't believe it. I felt like my life was out of control and I was just reeling from one trauma to the next. John Marshall stared at me across the desk as I struggled to my feet and walked, dazed, from his office. I stood in the corridor outside for a moment, trying to compose myself, but I felt trapped.

I did the only thing I knew how to do: I ran. I took off into the countryside and ran like the wind for what seemed like miles.

My brain had gone mental, as I was trying to escape the pictures and thoughts in my head. I hurt so much inside I couldn't cry inside or out. I couldn't even feel the thorns and bushes that were scratching me to bits as I ran through them. My chest and throat felt like they were on fire, and my ears burned in the cold wind, but I kept running.

When I finally stopped, it had grown dark and I was miles away from school. For some reason that I still don't understand, I climbed to the top of this almighty tree and just sat there staring at the stars. Thoughts of my mum were flashing in and out of my mind. She'd been ill, but I'd told her anyway.

It must have been my fault that she was dead… wasn't it? I simply couldn't catch a thought and stay with it.

Eventually, as the night grew cold and still around me, my brain started to become blank. I felt as if something had just switched me off. I was physically and mentally numb. In the early hours, I walked back to the school and tried to sleep, but the blankness didn't leave me.

Through the hazy blur of the following days and weeks, I remember being put on a train on my own to go back to the Noctorum for three days for the funeral. Denise couldn't breathe for crying. She was inconsolable and terrified. I couldn't bear to look at her, because by now I was convinced it was my fault that Mum was dead: me and my fuckin' big mouth.

I recall very little of the funeral service. I was just walking around in a daze. According to my sister, I was unnervingly silent and calm throughout. The one thing I do recall is being in the chapel of rest and bending over Mum's coffin to say goodbye. Even then, seeing her body lying in the coffin, her death felt unreal. I was repulsed to see a small wad of cotton wool peeping out from under her eyelids. Stanley gestured for me to kiss my mother goodbye. I bent over, hesitating at being so close to her, but when I kissed her gently on the cheek, I knew for certain she was dead: it was the first time ever that I had kissed her without her flinching.

After the funeral, there was a wake back at the house. We ate stale ham sandwiches and drank lukewarm lemonade. I felt numb but recall promising my sister that I would always be there for her.

Later that evening, I went and hid myself away in my room. My head still felt fuzzy. Suddenly, the door opened and I saw Stanley and one of his friends, Frank, standing there. I noticed that Frank had a beer bottle in his hand. Oh shit, I thought, I know him, he is a hurter, why won't they just leave me alone. It was the day of my mother's funeral and they'd come in for a quickie.

I hated Frank because he liked sticking things up your bum and I would normally resist but I had nothing to say about anything anymore. I felt numb and empty. I didn't care what anyone did or said to me. When they started, I just lay down and took it.

My lack of any reaction started pissing Frank off and he deliberately forced the bottle really hard into my bum. A searing pain tore through me. I started fighting back, but he wouldn't stop. So, with all my might I intentionally slammed my backside against the wall really hard and the bottle broke off. Frank stared at the other half of the bottle, still in his hand, panicked and legged it.

Stanley's eyes were bulging with rage. He screamed at me, "Why have you gotta be like that? Go sort yourself out, you mad bitch."

My eyes still glued to Stanley's, I stood up, the rest of the broken-off bottle neck fell out of me and I re-dressed myself. Blood was dripping down my legs and staining the carpet.

Now Stanley was looking at me all funny, like he was scared of me. He said, "What's the matter wiv you, then? What you looking at me like that for?"

I felt oddly calm and determined, more composed than I had been in a long time. I looked him straight in the eye and quietly said, "If you ever touch me or my sister again, I will kill you."

"What you being like that for?" he repeated. "Go sort yourself out – put a pad on it or somefink – you're getting yourself in a right mess."

Still holding his gaze, I repeated calmly, "That is the last time you touch us or I will kill you. Do you understand?" Stanley seemed genuinely scared of me: "You're off your fuckin' head, you are. Why don't you fuck off back to school?"

I said: "That's the last time you touch us, or I will kill you in your sleep."

He sounded frightened now: "OK, OK just calm down. You didn't seem that upset, I thought it would be alright. OK, I was wrong, I won't do it again, just calm down."

I walked out past him and he flinched as I walked past him. I cleaned myself up in the bathroom, collected my bag and walked out of the house without saying another word. I managed to make it to the train station and boarded a train. The next thing I remember is waking up in a hospital. Some passengers had reported me and assumed I'd been attacked on the train by a stranger. I just let them think what they wanted. By this point, I knew better than to tell the truth.

The doctors tried to get me to talk to them, but I kept quiet. They told me that I had to have internal stitches and was badly cut. I was put on a liquid diet and sedated heavily. I didn't feel anything. Mentally and physically, I had completely removed myself from what was going on and drifted in and out of consciousness for the next few days.

At some point I was taken back to Parkside School, though I don't remember when or by whom. In the weeks that followed, I was like the walking dead. I was blank inside and was barely managing to puppeteer the carcass that was my body around. I wasn't sure if I was alive or dead, and I didn't care. I had become a loner, completely isolated and removed from those around me, and would spend hours in my room rocking to comfort myself. I blamed myself for my mother's death, and I suppose on some level was grieving her, but the tears never came. I simply walked around like a zombie and kept myself very much to myself.

I'd still make my secret scribble notes and bury them for comfort. I never saw my social worker, and no one ever came near me or spoke to me about anything, or even asked me how I was, and I was just fine with that.

Throughout this time, I found an enormous amount of comfort from a mixed tape that I had made up of all my favourite songs. I had a small tape recorder and would carry this everywhere I went. It was constantly glued to my ear, playing the songs that helped me stay alive during this period.

After a week, John Marshall told me he needed to check my stitches to see how I was healing. He then tried to sexually assault me during the check-up. I had had enough of John Marshall, and everyone for that matter. So I kicked him in the head and legged it. I didn't care about getting into trouble myself now that Mum was dead. I really didn't have anything left to lose.

I got to the police station as fast as I could, and told them, "I need to report a crime!" I must have looked like a madwoman, but the policeman asked me to sit down and tell him all about it. We sat in a small room with an open door as I told him what Marshall was doing to me and the others. He was taking notes and we had talked for a while when I saw Marshall suddenly step into the room outside the place we were sitting and gesture the police officer I was talking to, over to him. My heart skipped a beat.

I couldn't hear what they were saying, but the police officer kept nodding and looking my way as they went through some paperwork. The next thing I know, the policeman called me over to them and Marshall said, "Come on then, Karen. Let's get you back to school."

What? I was completely bewildered. What could Marshall possibly have said to the policeman?

I struggled as Marshall took my arm and led me out of the police station. Once we were outside, he roughly threw me in his car and drove off at breakneck speed.

When we'd gone a little way, he pulled over and turned to face me, a look of utter venom on his face. I sat mute as he leant over towards me and whispered at me, "You can say whatever you like, you know. You can tell people whatever you want – it won't make any difference. The fact is, nobody will ever believe the likes of you over the likes of me, not with your record."

I could feel his hot breath on my cheek, his breath rancid. I tried to pull away but he held me hard by the jaw, laughing at me as I struggled to get away.

He said he could make sure that nobody ever believed me for the rest of my life and that I should just shut up and do as I was told if I knew what was good for me. I decided after the second punch in the face to do as he said and spent another half an hour doing exactly what he said before he started up the car and took me back to the school.

A few days later, while playing in the school swimming pool, I was approached by three men and a woman. They walked up to me very briskly, announced that they were from the police and then, after a few bland questions, one of the men asked, very matter-of-factly, "Have you been having sex with your father, Stanley Claridge?"

I was completely taken aback by his approach. Why weren't they asking whether Stanley had been abusing me, not whether or not I had had sex with him? Nothing made sense to me, and their confrontational demeanour immediately put me on my guard. Experience had taught me that telling the truth didn't help. I thought, every time I open my mouth, things just get 10 times worse, so I didn't respond.

The man asked me again. I stared at him for ages, then said in a flat voice, "That's for me to know and you to find out."

He looked put out and said, "Look, sweetheart, we know you're upset because your mum's just died, but your father has already told us everything and we just want a chat with you."

I looked straight in his eyes and said, "I'm not your sweetheart, he's not my father, and if he's already told you, then you don't need me to tell you. Now leave me alone."

They walked away. The blankness that had haunted me since Mum's death washed over me. Little did I know, after all my years of trying to make myself heard, this was the closest I'd ever been to getting Stanley stopped.

"Calling Stanley Sidney Claridge"

A short while later, in April 1977, I was woken early by one of the members of staff at Parkside and told to dress and go downstairs. Two people, a man and a woman, in crisp, dark suits were standing in the school entrance hall. They looked stern and I wondered if I was being taken back to the mental hospital. One of the men told me to get in the taxi that was waiting outside.

"Where are we going?" I asked, panic seizing me.

"To see a very important man," one of them answered, without looking at me.

I tried to ask more questions, but they wouldn't tell me anything else. We drove for miles, and I got more and more nervous at the thought that I might be being taken somewhere even worse than John Marshall's school. When the taxi pulled up outside the building, I peered out of the window and saw that we were at a Magistrates Court. I was completely baffled.

I stepped out of the taxi and the people gestured for me to go inside. They took me to the very end of a long, narrow corridor and asked me to wait on a wooden bench while they found someone. I sat down, staring at the polished floor and wondered what on earth was going to happen next. Was I in trouble? Was it because I'd tried to report John Marshall? Just then, I looked up and was startled to see a familiar figure at the other end of the corridor: it was Roma. She was glaring at me intensely. It shocked me to see her and I suddenly snapped out of my blankness and realised where I was and why.

I looked past Roma and saw Stanley. He was sitting holding his head in his hands, and there was a group of people trying to comfort him.

Someone must have told on Stanley! The police are doing him for the horrible! Oh, my God, can this be true? At last, they will get us away from him. I wonder who told?

I looked back to Roma. She was staring at me, her face full of fury. Then she started shouting, "This is all your fault! Why can't you leave him alone? Why can't you leave us all alone?"

I was dumbfounded. I had absolutely no idea what I was doing there. I had never made a statement about Stanley to the police, so why was this my fault? In fact, the only person I had made a complaint about was Marshall! I was more confused than ever, and the thought that this was somehow my fault absolutely horrified me. As much as I hated Stanley, the last thing I wanted was for my sister to be put in care – I knew from my own experiences that 'care' was a sex hell in itself.

If only I had understood at the time what I learnt many years later – my headmaster, John Marshall, had told the police that I was being abused, but not by him. That this was a classic case of transference and that he had the letters from Stanley to prove it. The police had accepted John Marshall's word and arrested Stanley, who immediately confessed when confronted with his dirty letters – case closed.

Right now, though, I was as confused as ever about what was happening.

"Hello, are you Karen?"

I looked up and saw a middle-aged woman in a smart suit standing in front of me. I nodded. "Yes," I said simply. My voice came out a little croaky and I cleared my throat.

"Follow me."

"Can someone tell me what's going on?"

"Sorry – I'm not allowed to discuss any court cases. I'm just the usher."

She sat me in a tiny room on my own until I was called into a courtroom full of strangers, asked to sit in the witness box and made to promise to tell the truth so help me God!

I was just 14 years old at the time of Stanley's court case, and it seems remarkable to me now that I was told literally nothing about the case or what would be expected of me, but I was left completely in the dark. Still reeling from Mum's death, I felt as if I was hurtling from one crisis to the next, unable to take anything in. Consequently, I can't remember all of what happened during the trial, but I can remember seeing Stanley standing in the dock with his head bowed, looking his most pathetic, crying like he does when you won't let him do everything he wants to.

A barrister said to me that Stanley had committed some terrible crimes against me and that he had already admitted to them. He asked if I understood. I nodded.

"Stanley tells the court that he has been abusing you in a sexual way for some years now. Do you understand?"

I nodded.

He said, "Do you agree with this?" I didn't respond.

The barrister cleared his throat.

"Social Services have been keeping a file on you since you have been in their care, and the courts have asked your social workers to write a report from this file to tell us more about you, which you are not permitted to see because of your age and sensitivity. Do you understand?"

Again, I nodded.

The barrister kept saying that what Stanley had done was a terrible crime. I didn't know what to say, so I kept quiet. The barrister seemed frustrated with me, but I really didn't understand what I was supposed to answer.

Then another barrister stood up and said, "Yes, it is a terrible crime and my client, Mr Claridge, admits it, but there were mitigating circumstances. Karen is a tease who sexually forced herself on to Mr Claridge. He has repeatedly tried to stop her, but has been unable to. The problem, I'm afraid, is Karen. When Karen isn't at home, Stanley, despite having a bad back, is a loving, devoted father to his daughters and committed himself to caring full-time for a sick wife, whom he recently lost."

I listened impassively to everything that was said. I was like a statue, completely locked in my own world. Then I heard something that shook me to my core: "Karen's sister says that she has never been abused by him and agrees that whatever is happening is Karen's fault, as do Social Services, whose report fully supports Mr Claridge's statement of mitigation."

I simply couldn't believe what I was hearing. Hearing that took me right back to that terrible day all those years ago, when I'd told Mum for the first time what Stanley had been doing and my sister had denied it all. In spite of everything, I was no further on. I sat in the witness box in complete silence as the barrister continued to present Stanley's case. I could feel everyone's eyes on me, labelling me as the problem, as if it was me who was on trial.

Stanley was found guilty of indecently assaulting me (in the form of oral sex) over three years. He was given just three years' probation and sent back home to live alone and unsupervised with my little sister, and I was sent back to John Marshall. Stanley may have been convicted, but I felt as if I was the one who had been branded the pervert. I felt like a criminal.

Back at the school, I tried to call home to find out what the hell was going on, but nobody would talk to me. I could only imagine that my sister had lied out of fear and although I understood it, I felt devastated. I often wondered why all those professionals couldn't see how scared of Stanley my sister really was. I wanted desperately to get our Denise away from Stanley. I was an absolute emotional wreck, completely confused. When I tried to warn friends and family members what Stanley had been convicted for, he just told them he had been to court for fiddling his electricity. He argued that if he had been done for kiddie fiddling, the Social Services would not have allowed him home with more children, would they? So it must be Karen just lying, again. They all seemed to believe him and there was nothing I could do.

Just a few weeks later, we were in court again. This time, it was so that another judge could decide whether or not Stanley should be allowed to keep us.

"This is a custody child-protection hearing before the courts because of the child abuser Stanley Claridge's recent conviction and the issues arising from the fact that he is currently these children's only primary caregiver."

After reading the Social Services report on me and after my social worker stood as a character witness on Stanley's behalf, the judge ordered that I be placed in official care of the Social Services and placed back with abusive John Marshall and my little sister Denise was placed on a supervision order "for being in danger of being morally corrupt" and sent back home to live alone with the self-confessed convicted child abuser Stanley. I felt as if the world had gone mad and I could no longer bear to think about any of it anymore.

Tilt

Please forgive the next few paragraphs. Even now, I can't bear how much it hurts to remember this. It makes my whole being ache to tears. I still struggle to understand all of it myself, but here is what I can tell you.

I had felt loneliness in my life – I knew it well – but this was a different kind of loneliness. It was a hopeless, lost, infinite internal groan. I felt as if I was one of those dirty, horrible pictures of me being squashed into a tiny dead ball. I felt as if my whole world had tilted on its axis.

My brain screamed, *what do I do?* They say that I'm going to grow up to be a monster! How do I not be a monster? I don't want to hurt anyone, so maybe it's best to kill myself. I can't fix myself anymore, so maybe I should just put an end to it. I'm already dead to my sister. I can't take the pain. I'm falling and I can't catch myself.

I was in such a state I knew I had to get away, but I had nowhere and no one to turn to. I knew there was only one place that was a safe haven to me, one place where I felt at home: Pately Bridge.

Nanny and Grandpa weren't at Pately Bridge at that moment, but I knew that I had to go. I couldn't see or talk to them anyway, because I was too ashamed. Early one morning, I slipped out of Parkside School and hitchhiked to Yorkshire. The journey is a watery blur, and I had to walk a long way. Eventually, a lorry driver who had given me a lift dropped me off a few miles from the old train. It was late evening by the time I got there, but there was just enough light to see the tiny pottery shop at the end of the lane. As soon as I saw the old mill, right then and for the first time in far too long, I started to cry, really cry.

I was hungry and exhausted, but I was so desperate to see my stream that I just started running like a nutter. I was crying so much it was hard to see, but I could have run that road with my eyes closed and not stumbled once.

Then I heard it, my stream, like an old friend calling to me. It made me cry even harder. Then a thought stopped me dead in my tracks: What if it's changed? It's been nearly five years! What if, like everything else in this world, it just can't be there for me?

I loved and adored my memories of this place – they had kept me alive at times when I had wanted to die – and I couldn't bear the thought that my safe, happy place might have changed, but at the same time, I could hear it, I could smell it and I took off again.

As I turned the final bend, I stopped, wiped my eyes, took a big breath and looked up... and there it was. Not a single blade of grass was out of place. I felt an unfathomable relief, fell to my knees and wept.

After a while, I picked myself up, went to my secret place at the water's edge, sat down and washed my face. There I stayed long into the night. The moon was so bright it was like someone had turned a light on for me. I sat there crying a lifetime of tears into my stream and watching it carry them away.

I was exactly where I wanted to be, by my stream. Its constant, soothing sounds lulled me to sleep and I had the first good night's rest since I'd left Pately Bridge all those years before.

As the wildlife stirred, it woke me up. At first I was startled, thinking I was in a bad place, but as I opened my eyes and saw the old tree root and clay cave, my heart skipped into life and I was awake and smiling. I scanned the whole area and hardly anything had changed – grown, yes, but still the same. I couldn't get enough of it. I just sat there and let my happy memories of this place wash over me as I wrapped myself in its comfort.

I went straight over to where I had remembered hiding some of my scribble notes in the old tea tin. They were still there, only very faded. Something on them prompted me and I was reminded of the mountain of pain I was running away from and before I knew what I was doing, I was in the stream, trying to wash it all off me.

Then it started to rain, lightly at first, then harder, until it was torrential. I sat there in the stream and started laughing. I loved the rain. I loved how it always felt like a fresh new start, so I just lay back in the water and enjoyed it.

Later, after I'd dried off and eaten some food I had with me while sitting next to my stream, I started to relax. As the night drew in, I wrapped myself up in my clothes, sat outside one of the holiday log cabins, full belly, all warm, clean and dry, and watched the stream go by. Then, at long last, I let myself think about all that had happened.

Throughout my life I had mentally stored things away in my 'wait till I get older' files, and now and then I would pull them out to see if I was big enough to understand them yet. More often than not, I wasn't, so I would put them back and wait till I got older to have another look. I had locked so much away in this way that my brain was starting to look like that man's house who lived on the Woody, the one all of us kids called Bin Bag Barry. I have no idea what his real name was, but he was a poor, harmless, sweet old man. He had kept every single thing he had ever owned or found and had stacked it all from floor to ceiling in every room, in every space, in every possible place. You couldn't move for rubbish and bric-a-brac. Eventually, the council had forced their way in and cleared everything out. My brain felt like Bin Bag Barry's house and I needed a council clear-out!

I spent several days sitting by the stream, sifting through some of that mental rubbish. At night, I would stay in one of the log cabins. I knew where the owners kept the keys because I used to air out the cabins for them when I'd lived here with Grandpa and Nanny Wallbridge.

What I loved about this place was how it stopped the world for me and gave me a chance to take a thought and work it through. It also gave me comforting sights and sounds to help me through the process. The fog in my head, which had made everything so difficult to understand for so long, lifted and, for the first time in ages, I could see the terrible, awful truth that was my sad little life. I also knew that however bad it was, I wanted to live, not die. So something had to change.

I knew I didn't want to be in care, and I didn't want to be with Stanley and all his friends. They could bend any truth, poison any mind and break every living soul they touched, then blame you for it. I realised that they had all the power and that I was completely on my own. They had already written me off. I didn't want to be the dirty girl they wanted me to be, and I certainly wasn't going to let myself become a monster. I resolved that because I couldn't manage the harm they did to me or my life, I would never leave any part of myself open to any of them ever again.

There was still so much that had happened in my short, terrifying life that I couldn't understand. I was old beyond my years, but I also had huge gaps in my understanding. I couldn't deal with my dad or mum's deaths, nor could I comprehend the scale of what Stanley had done to me or my sister. I just knew I didn't belong anywhere near it all.

Thanks to the Wallbridges, I knew I could be whatever I wanted to be. Unfortunately, thanks to all the other grown-ups in my life, I had no clue how I was meant to go from wanting it to getting it.

At that point in my life, I basically worked on pure instinct. I was so tuned into those around me, so alert, that I could practically *hear* a lie when people spoke to me. I didn't even need to look at their faces, I could just hear the rhythm of how they spoke and the words in between and would just know whether or not what they were saying was true. I didn't always need to rely on sound; I was able to read lips and tell almost exactly what was about to happen, purely by body language alone. Because I had been partially deaf and blind, I had clearly developed my own way of reading people, because I couldn't hear them and, because of the other persistent traumas, I had heightened this ability to unusual levels. Essentially, I had some very strong instincts; back then, I didn't know how to turn it on or off and in those days I just knew it as the voice inside my head.

Sitting by the stream, the voice inside my head told me that I had to get away, I had to make a change. I listened to my instinct and reached a very important decision: I was not going to go back to the Noctorum estate. Painful as it was to admit it to myself, I had come to realise that my sister didn't love me anymore. There was no point in keeping on trying to force my way into her life. My whole family had branded me the problem. Social Services had written me off long ago. I was too ashamed to turn to Aunt Pat and Uncle Ken. I would simply have to get on with my own life as best I could.

I was fairly streetwise, but I was only 14 and had no clue what I was going to do and no money to do it with. I had lived in London as a young child and while on the run for short periods and it seemed far enough away from my birth family for me to make a go of things. By the time I had left Pately Bridge, I had resolved to change my life, I just wasn't sure how.

Goodbye, Karen

It was summer 1977. Berni the bloody bolt, Wonder Woman and The Krypton Factor were on the TV, the Atari 2600 (with tennis and Space Wars) was all the rage. Superman and Grease were playing at the cinema, music was going from seven inches to twelve, and I had added Gerry Rafferty's *Baker Street*, Chaka Khan's *I'm Every Woman* and Bill Withers' *Lovely Day* to my secret life album. Music was a big part of my life, and I had songs for feeling happy, sad, good and bad. I had comfort songs, dancing songs, stealing songs, driving songs, running away and fleeing songs.

I was 14, wild and free in an exciting new city. I was also penniless, an emotional wreck and had found myself living rough on the streets of London, but I was getting by. No one knew my name or where I'd come from, but everyone on the streets had secrets of their own, and were only ever passing through, so telling and accepting lies about each other was easy. So easy, that for a while I completely lost myself. Really, I was a child on the run from authority care, hiding a world of pain and in a very dangerous place, but I pretended to be Kelly, a wild rebel orphan, aged 18 to 21, depending on who was asking, and if you didn't like talking about your past and didn't want sex, I was your girl.

When I first ran away to London, I started out sleeping on the streets with all the other less fortunates, but quickly realised that some of those less fortunates were pervy, twisted little shitheads who would try and 'have a go' even while you were sleeping, and so I found that it was much safer making a nest on my own in the bushes in the local royal parks and gardens. Failing that, I slept on rooftops, in sheds or in supposedly locked cars.

My area of choice was the West End. 'Pic-a-willy' Circus was alive with every kind of predator, fruit cake, player and runaway there ever was. If you were into drugs, which I wasn't, you could buy anything from the bizarre array of night people who frequented the heart of London's West End streets – from bum to chum, blow to snow, smack to crack and everything in between. There was every kind of pub, club, restaurant, hotel and shop that you could imagine, with every entertainment catered for. Many places stayed open late or all night, and I looked old enough to get into anywhere I wanted. From the city slickers to the window lickers, the West End had a beat for everyone's drum.

Soon after moving to London, I found that the safest place at night for a runaway female child was the Regency, a late-night gay club just off Leicester Square. Not only was I completely safe from any sexual predators (or ordinary hopefuls) but I was among kind, friendly, funny and wildly flamboyant human beings who, back in 1977, were forced to live a life in hiding. They befriended me and gave me a safe place to be. Whenever I was asked if I was, "Gay, bi or straight?" I would always reply that I was FROW (Fuck Right Off, Wanker) in a nice way. I quickly learnt to revise this response to ensure I got no sexual attention from anyone: if I was talking to a gay person, I was straight; if I was talking to a straight person, I was gay and so it went.

In no time at all I had all kinds of different friends – club friends, pretend friends, street friends, all sorts. I would meet up with my street friends at the Circus, the Square or at the few all-night cinemas and cafe's dotted around that area, then go off and find something to do, eat or steal.

My childhood had made me fearless. My instinctive reaction whenever I saw something I wanted to do or be was very simple: how do I do that? Social position, education, class, culture or religious divides were never a consideration. Fearless is all well and good if it knows its limitations, but the problem with being fearless is that you have to learn to be sensible the hard way. Consequently, there were a lot of sad, bad and dangerous times during this period of my life.

Everyone, including me, was into some kind of crime or another. I had no money whatsoever and needed it, and as I would never and could never sell myself sexually, stealing things became my criminal element. I was really very good at it.

I had rules, though: I was a sort of vegetarian criminal in as much as I couldn't touch 'red meat', so my crimes could never physically harm anyone, nor would I ever steal from children, old people, the disabled or the mentally ill. In real terms, if I wanted something, I could pretty much get it. For the time being, though, I was only interested in stealing enough to survive.

At first, it was things like 'fake shopping' in the food halls – I would eat as much as I could as I went around filling my trolley. Then I'd leave the trolley of food at the checkout, claiming to need more money, saying, "Gosh, don't you always pick up more than you mean to?" before fleeing.

Another trick was to return to a shop saying that the hamburger, sandwich or pie I had bought earlier had been off, horrible or cold and that I had had to sling it in the bin. "I'm so sorry, madam. Would you like a refund or replacement?" Or indeed the old "I was in here earlier during the breakfast rush. I ordered and paid for four, but when I got to work, I only had three." The response? "Sorry, madam, here you go."

After breakfast, it was off to wash and change clothes. As you could never appear to look homeless, you couldn't carry a bag or case of clothes around, and keeping a railway-station locker was a pain in the arse, so you always travelled light. So 'change clothes' really meant pick the next few days' fashion statement from whatever shop, go in, put it on, then return your old clothes to the rack.

To begin with, my stealing was a way of surviving, but it quickly progressed into something else. I would often sit outside the posh hotels on Park Lane, like the Dorchester, and see these incredible-looking cars swooping up to the hotel entrance and watch as the drivers opened the car doors to let these amazingly dressed people, dripping in glitter, waft by the polite and attentive uniformed staff without so much as an acknowledgement. I think this was the first time I started to notice the gaps between us all and I really didn't like what I was seeing, but at the same time, my brain started thinking, *how do I do that? How do I get some of what they have?*

I was getting bored with pretending to have found dead insects in my food and never having one place to go every night, so I decided to raise my expectations, and of course my criminal activities.

A few months after I'd arrived in London, I was introduced to a guy who became my criminal mentor. He had a suitcase full of stolen chequebooks and he wanted me to forge signatures for him. He gave me a magic wand – a pen for signing stolen chequebooks, which I had to keep on me at all times so the police couldn't find it left at the scene and fingerprint it. I was a dab hand at forging ladies' signatures. With this magic wand – the 'kiter's pen' – I could magic up almost anything I wanted, and now I wanted everything.

I knew what I was doing was wrong, but to my mind, my crimes were victimless, happy crimes. Everyone in them was happy and smiling. The man who wanted me to sign the cheque-books he had acquired from the happy victims was always happy with me. The bankteller was always pleased to serve me. The shop assistants would be smiling their heads off when I paid them at the till, and I would be grinning from ear to ear as I sashayed out of the shop with a whole lot of goods bought with stolen money.

Now that I had money, a whole new world opened up to me. Now people opened doors for me. In no time at all I had everything I could want: a flat in Kensington, a motorbike, flash cars, a wardrobe full of high-end clothing, more glitter than anyone needs, the entire range of any costly cosmetics and some very expensive handbags full of cash. Everything I owned was either stolen by me or bought with money I had stolen.

My wealth also bought me a whole new group of wealthy friends. I had nothing in common with any of them, but I was a social chameleon. I was an expert at the art of bullshit and could fit in with whoever I was around. I slipped into my new role as friend to the uber-rich. I hung out in all the super-cool spots with my new super-cool friends, who did lunch and thought everything was super cool. And to be fair, everything is super cool when super cool daddy is paying for it. It was a superficial world and I didn't belong, so I didn't stay. To be honest, I didn't belong anywhere, and I never stayed around long.

My mentor, who had introduced me to kiting chequebooks, taught me all sorts of tricks of the trade. I learnt quickly and had no sense of limitations and had lost all sense that what I was doing was wrong. Growing up as Jennifer's daughter had taught me that stealing was simply a way of getting something you wanted but couldn't afford. She almost always got away with it, so I blindly assumed that I would, too.

Over the next few months I had some wild and wonderful days. I tried most drinks and didn't like them. I tried most drugs and didn't like them, either. I tried pretending to be someone else for a while and that was fun, like the time I booked into a suite at the Hilton as Lady Ponsonby-Wootton and had more fun than you can imagine, working out how much blind faith people will place in you when you have a double-barrelled name and a chequebook.

I had kited many chequebooks by this time. I understood how to look and behave. I knew that as well as the chequebook, you needed the card and some ID, so I'd make sure I had it all. Then I came across a chequebook that was different to all the others. This one was pure magic all on its own. If you produced it at any of the top places in London, you could get anything you wanted, at any price, without question and would always be served in the most impeccable and professional manner. All I needed was a chequebook from Coutts, and it didn't take me long to acquire one. It turns out that Coutts was a super-rich bank, and you had to be a squillionaire to even hold an account with them.

Though I looked older than my 14 years and people would assume I was in my early twenties, most shops would ring the bank to ensure that larger cheques would clear. If you had a Coutts' chequebook, however, it would be beyond thinking and all rudeness, indeed an unforgivable insult, to even consider checking by phone. When I discovered this, I felt a rush, *like a rolling ball of thunder spinning my head around. Oh, what a night…*

Every time I hear the song *Lovely Day*, I see me in a stolen open-top Porsche roaring through the countryside without a care in the world. I was young, independent and wealthy – I didn't need anyone around me, and for some months I continued to lead this high life. I revelled in the freedom and the anonymity. No one knew my real name or where I was from; I had, effectively, completely reinvented myself.

I have heard it said that power corrupts and absolute power corrupts absolutely and I was about to learn this for myself. No matter how strong you are or what your personal rules are, you always end up breaking them. I had started out as a vegetarian criminal, but then I unwittingly stole from a carnivorous criminal, and had to turn carnivore myself to get out of the situation. After bitch slapping an over-zealous bag thief, things were starting to get out of control for me.

I was no longer stealing to survive. This kind of life finds and brings out the worst in most people, and I was long past greedy and well into arrogance and total denial. After many wild months in London, I was about to get my comeuppance.

Following a glorious day of designer shopping, I was relaxing in my Kensington flat when the doorbell rang. I opened it and was confronted with the fatal words, "Hello. You're nicked!"

"What's your name?" Lie.

"How old are you?" Lie.

I thought, I could do this all day, you know. And I did – all day and all night.

The next morning, after a night of questioning, the police finally worked out who I was. Unsurprisingly, they came down hard on me. I was taken back to Liverpool and put in a padded cell in a children's detention centre called Derwent House. After months of living the high life, this came as a real shock to me. Sadly, though, it came as no surprise when the Derwent House staff started abusing me.

My social workers didn't mind showing me and everyone else their contempt and obvious dislike for me and I ran away at the first opportunity.

I planned to return to London, but decided to try and see our Denise first. I had tried on several occasions to contact her, but Roma always told me that Denise hated me. Still, I wanted to hear it from our Denise.

Now, me and my little sister had many secret pacts and one was that if I was on the run and needed to contact her, I would stack three stones just inside the garden gate to let her know I was close by. I didn't know if she remembered or even checked anymore, but I snuck up in the very early morning, put the stones there, hid up on Bidston Hill and waited. I was cold, hungry and starting to feel a bit worried. Only she knew where to meet me if she wanted to, but after all that had happened, I wasn't sure if I would see our Denise – or the police – come up the path, if anyone at all.

I needn't have worried. After a few hours I heard this demented half-crying, half-happy voice yelling, "Kaz? Are you there, Kaz? It's me. It's only me, sis. I know you're there – you made the stones!"

Overjoyed, I quietly stepped out of the bushes as she came running past me, and said, "Here I am."

She fell into my arms and cried her eyes out. She tried telling me things while she was sobbing, but she couldn't say the words properly, so I let her cry it all out of her first. She was 13 now, and her pain wasn't as easy to comfort as when she had been a child, but after she had got over the shock of seeing me, she calmed down and stopped crying. I got her smiling and we started to talk like never before. She told me things that plunged me into a brand-new world of pain, guilt and shame.

"Kaz, it's all got worse. There are other children now, lots of them. Everyone's kids are being got at. There's kids all over the house. I've tried to stop him, but I can't, and…" She broke down in tears again, and I held her close to me.

A cold wave of horror crept over me. As I pictured all these poor new children, their lives ruined, the mental fog started to descend once again.

Denise and I sat in silence for a few moments, oblivious to the drizzle that had started to fall. Then, through her tears, Denise stammered, "He told me to tell you I hated you. He told me to say that I never wanted to hear from you again, he told us to say it was your fault and he said that if I ever spoke to you again, I'd be killed and buried on Biddy Hill with the others."

She was shivering and looking at me with imploring eyes.

I shook my head. "He's making it up, Denise. He wouldn't have the guts to do it."

This was one of Stanley's favourite threats and something he always tried to implant in our brains. For some reason, Stanley always wanted us to believe that there were mysterious dead bodies buried under the floorboards at 29 Stratford Way or on Biddy Hill. This was just the sort of rubbish he would say to make us think he was even scarier than he already was, but there was more to it than that. Many years later it would all fall into place.

The problem then was that Denise believed it might be true and was very frightened.

Denise put her hand on mine and gripped it tightly.

"He made me say nothing had ever happened. I never hated you, Kaz. You know that, don't you?"

I squeezed her hand back, not knowing what to say. It felt so good to hear those words.

"I missed you. I thought you were dead for ages."

She shivered again, and explained that Stanley had been telling everyone that I was an international, junkie drug mule who had just murdered a police officer in an undercover prostitution sting gone bad. He claimed I was on the FBI's most wanted list and the whole country was looking for me. The stories were so ridiculous that I couldn't help but laugh.

I heard that Denise had spent most nights sleeping on Mum's grave, though she had later found out that Stanley had even lied about where Jennifer had been buried and she'd been lying on someone else's grave, telling them all her sad secrets. Stanley's horrible abuse of her had got so much worse and he was now full on battering her.

"He's out of control, Kaz. I've tried everything I can to make him stop, but now Mum's gone and you went…" She didn't finish the sentence. She didn't have to.

I couldn't hide my emotions any more when Denise told me that she'd tried to kill herself. As the whole nightmare unfolded, I cried silent tears.

Denise said, "I've told my teachers and the social worker, like you told me to, but they won't do anything about it. It's like they don't believe me or they do but they think it's my fault."

This was so sickeningly familiar that I was lost for words. It wasn't until years later, when I read the Social Services files, that I discovered that Social Services had put Denise's bruises down to her 'bad behaviour'. Somehow, they seemed to believe that she was to blame even though Stanley had admitted to it when confronted. According to the records they appeared to believe that she was battered by Stanley because she was that naughty.

This from the people who were supposed to be protecting our Denise under her supervision order, and despite the fact that Stanley was a recently-convicted sex offender.

When I heard that Social Services had ignored Denise's pleas for help, white-hot anger rose inside me. I took a few deep breaths, willing myself not to explode.

Then our Denise said, "Did I tell you Stanley's told our Roma that you're a high-class prostitute?"

I couldn't believe my ears. Poor Denise was just the messenger of all this terrible news, but I knew some things that she didn't. I had called Roma a few months earlier to try and find out how everyone was. They were fine but still didn't want to speak to me. Roma then explained that she and her family were about to be made homeless because they were in such crippling debt. My stomach lurched when I heard this. I knew that if they were homeless, they would have to depend on Stanley, which would put them all at risk. I felt it was my responsibility to protect them if I could. In a bid to try to ensure that they didn't have to rely on Stanley, I helped them out.

I sent a limo to Roma's house in Merseyside, to collect her and her children, and bring them to London. I then booked them into Park Lane's Intercontinental Hotel, took them to Oxford Street, bought the kids all the latest toys and brand-new wardrobes for the next two seasons. Gave them a five-star tour of London tourist spots and four days of fun outings. I finally sent them back home in the limo, with pockets full of cash, all the bills paid in full and well into the future. I even organised a legitimate high-paid job offer abroad, but they couldn't take this up because of ill health. This wasn't how any of us really lived and Roma had no idea that I had paid for the lot – with money previously made from fraud – and I just couldn't tell her that, so I had to let them believe what they wanted. I just shrugged it off.

Denise said, "Stanley's told everyone on the estate that his conviction was for fiddling the electric. As you're never here, people only get to hear what he tells them about you. He says that if we say anything, we'll end up on Biddy Hill or, worse still, in care getting raped in a padded cell like you."

I asked Denise, "What about school?"

Denise said, "There's no school anymore and no matter what I do, he won't stop. I think he's even into little boys now."

My brain couldn't take any more. Nothing's what it is supposed to be, everything is broken and nothing makes any fucking sense! I couldn't stand to hear another word and something just took over me. A burning fury gripped hold of me. He may not be a murderer but he was killing everyone he touched, and absolutely nobody was going to stop him. That was it – the final straw that broke the final hair on the back of this totally fucked-off camel.

I left Denise at Biddy Hill, ran to the house and virtually smashed my way through the front door and was up the stairs like a rocket. I barged into Stanley's room and a frightened, half-naked lad scampered out. Stanley was lying in bed, red-faced and startled and I just lost all control.

My mind went blank as I proceeded to kick the unholy living shit out of Stanley Sidney Claridge. I had such a rage within that I smacked that whimpering lump of lard around his bedroom like a deflating, whining beach ball. He tried to hit me back, but he was about 30 years too old, 10 years too late and about 15 stone too fat. When I'd finished, and he was black and blue all over, I calmly said, "I told you what would happen if you touched them again."

"I know, I know, Kaz. Look, I'm sorry. Calm down – I can explain," he pleaded. "I've missed your mum since she died, you know what the others are like – they just won't leave me alone – and you know our Denise – she lies about everything and she only does it with me when she wants somefink."

I let him think his words had placated me and then roared, "Would you like some Vaseline with that bullshit, you lying slippery piece of shit! You couldn't even let me say goodbye to Mum without turning it into another horror-fest."

"Listen, Karen, you didn't even like 'er, and she fuckin' hated you. Who do you fink got me making all those calls to Social Services?"

I tried not to let Stanley see that I was taken aback. I composed my voice and said, "Go on…"

"Well, it was 'er, wasn't it. She wanted shot of you, but I was getting sick of 'er interfering, like."

My breath caught. So, Mum really had wanted rid of me. I wanted to know more, so I played along, pretending to Stanley that I was calm and taking on board his explanation.

Stanley's voice changed. "Look, Karen, it wasn't always me, was it? Be fair. What about the times you used to do it without me even asking? It wasn't just me – all the fellas liked you – but not your mum. You would have been sent away long ago if it weren't for me fighting to let you stay."

"Really, Dad?" I asked, making my voice sound as soft as I could. "Why?"

Stanley took the bait and proceeded to tell me all that our Denise had told me and more besides. He also told me that Mum was to blame for everything that had happened. She hated me and there was nothing he could do to change her mind.

"I fink she got a bit jealous of me and you, like, but what could I do? We had what we had together, what am I gonna do? I couldn't leave your mum. She was ill, like, and she needed me. I loved you all equally, but she was getting' on my nerves – she couldn't do anything anymore. I wasn't getting any more benefits to look after 'er full time, and I was having to feed 'er out of my money, clean her shitty arse and carry 'er to the bathroom all the fuckin' time, like, and me with my bad back. It was doin' my head in. She was a pain in the fuckin' arse, wasn't she, Kaz?"

I nodded, still playing along. "That's why I did it."

I held my breath. "Why? What did you do?"

"It was kinder in the long run. She had no life. They said she would be dead in a month anyway, and she was like a fuckin' vegetable, so I just popped over Billy Rainbows, then came back and called the doctors... She was peaceful like... she didn't feel no pain."

I didn't know what I thought about what he had said. I think he was trying to show me he was a humanitarian or something but he just came off as a lying, slimy arschead and the fury inside returned with new venom. I lunged at Stanley and punched and screamed at him like a madwoman, my arms flailing. Confused by my sudden change of mood, Stanley was completely unprepared and fell to the floor like a stone. I felt repulsed by his bruised, half-naked, flabby body and somehow unsatisfied by hitting something that wouldn't fight back. I had to get out of there.

I ran to the hills, sat down and started rocking, as the terrible mental fog engulfed me. All the noises, the pictures and the voice – everything I'd managed to forget when I'd been living in London – were back in my head on full blast and nothing, not my music, not my Pately Bridge, not anything was going to help me now.

Even now I can't tap into the pain around that night, but as I sat and watched the sun rise on Biddy Hill, shivering my teeth out of my head, something dawned on me. I realised that most of what Stanley did, he did in secret. I didn't want to keep his secrets any more. I decided there and then that I would tell everyone Stanley's secrets and not just some of them, all of them. So that is what I did.

I started by telling our immediate family and some of our extended family. I also met and listened to some of Stanley's non-related victims, male and female, who all pleaded with me to help them stop him. I promised I would try. Then I met with some other families on the estate – parents of the children who were being abused.

One or two of the parents acted as if they didn't believe me, but had the good sense never to test my honesty and simply never allowed their children near Stanley again. Unfortunately, the way of life on the Noctorum being what it was, it was just far too late to get some of the parents to take more than a passing interest in their children or in anything they did. Not one of them was pleased to see me, let alone hear what I had to tell them, but I made sure they heard it anyway.

Then I called the police and told them. I made a statement that said Stanley sexually abused me, my little sister and all those others and that it had been going on for years. The police took my statement seriously and promised to arrest Stanley and investigate my allegations. I was so relieved. This was the very first time that the police had allowed me to make a statement. They were genuinely horrified for me.

My relief was short-lived. Very soon, I was dealt yet another blow, when social workers had a 'meeting' with the police. The next thing I knew, I was told that my allegations were not going to be pursued and that I would have to return to Derwent House. Once again, Social Services' poor opinion of me and what had been written about me in my files had thwarted my attempts to stop Stanley. I couldn't believe it. What did I have to do to make people believe me? I could have screamed with frustration. I probably did.

Even on my return to Derwent House, I didn't give up. I knew I shouldn't trust the social workers, but I opened up and told them, as well as the Derwent House staff and anyone else I could find, about everything – all the stealing and all the horrible. I even told them about John Marshall.

Then, after the other victims I had told them about denied the allegations, Social Services were completely dismissive of anything I had to say about anything ever again.

I wept silent tears of frustration at every hurdle, but I was still utterly determined. I told Social Services anything I could to make them investigate. They just called me an attention-seeking liar and reported me to the police for prosecution on all of the crimes I'd admitted to committing in London. The police were now talking about criminally prosecuting me for being every kind of thief (rightfully so, might I add) from deception and burglary to car theft, kiting, bilking and shoplifting.

What was more, now that the authorities had aligned themselves again with Stanley, his other victims were even more determined never to go up against him and end up like me.

As for me, I had just been sexually abused by a Derwent House carer in the children's padded cell and was using a plastic knife and fork to ease the putty out of the window frame around the unbreakable security glass. I managed to escape. I was in a right state and needed to clean myself up. I ran straight to a family member's house, knocked on the door and pleaded with them to use their bathroom. They refused to let me in. I begged, but they turned me away. They said, "You're nothing but trouble you, causing bother wherever you go. Go on, piss off." The door slammed.

Afterwards, I stood in the street outside, oblivious to the rain that was falling all around me. I had run out of options, used everything I had, and still got nowhere. It was growing dark and I had nowhere to go and no one to turn to. In desperation, I found myself on top of a 15-storey block of flats, ready to put an end to it all. I just knew it was time.

I stood on top of the flats and gazed at Birkenhead, which was spread out before me. No matter where I looked I was reminded of one horrible memory or another. Parks, housing estates, docks, streets – everywhere made me cringe and recoil. I felt the world was slowing down. The voice inside my head was saying, *When you jump, you mustn't look – it'll make it worse. Don't do it while things are slowed down or it will seem like forever.*

For an instant, I thought about whether it was the right thing to do, but the voice said, *Oh, yes – there's no way back from here.* I knew no one would mourn my death. I was more alone now than I'd ever been, and I'd run out of fight.

I was oblivious to the cold, wintry night air or the wind that was cutting through me, and though there was still plenty of traffic making its noise, I couldn't hear a sound outside of what was going on in my own head. I had told everyone everything and nothing had changed. Somehow, I had always believed that the victims would all come together and help each other stop Stanley and his friends, and the police would do the rest.

But then, nothing was ever like I thought it would be. I think I watched too much TV.

Why should I be made to stay trapped inside this hell, forced to watch these monsters destroy every single child whom fate had brought their way? Stanley had us all by the throats. There wasn't anything any of us could do individually and we somehow couldn't do it together. There was nothing to do but jump –

"Hello? Hello... Please, for God's sake, please, don't move. My name is Glyn. Can we talk? Can we just talk?"

A voice startled me. I thought, No, we can't fucking talk! Can't you see I'm busy? But I said nothing.

I turned slightly to my left to see a young, anxious-looking policeman standing on the next ledge over to me. To me, the police were just uniformed people who would force me back to hell by car, but as I looked up at this poor, young, freezing policeman, teetering on the ledge near me, I could hear in his voice that he just wanted to help me. Unfortunately, he didn't know he was already talking to a corpse – I just hadn't been buried yet.

I turned my head away from him and looked back down at Birkenhead. Through tear-blurred eyes, I suddenly became aware of all the fire trucks, ambulance, police and reporters gathering at the foot of the flats.

Oh, shit! This is not what I wanted!

I was disorientated and frightened by all the different lights flashing on and off. I started to take in just how far down it was from here, and how very near the edge I was!

I didn't want people to watch me die. I wanted to be alone. I wanted to think. I took a big breath and sat down quickly, making everyone, particularly Glyn, gasp.

Glyn was talking to me, reassuring me. I couldn't take in his words, but as I looked into his eyes and saw the desperation there, I suddenly felt very sorry for him. He looked worried and confused; everything seemed very clear to me. I hated Karen's past life and was deeply afraid of what fate had in store for her future. I hated her present life and thought it was unbearable, so killing Karen was the only answer I could see. Right then that voice I hear said: *You don't have to kill yourself to say goodbye to Karen.*

I took a moment to think about this and in what seemed like an eternity I made my choice. I stayed sitting down on the ledge but, mentally, I stood up and leapt off the building with my eyes tight closed.

As I did so, I said farewell to Karen forever. There was no pain, no sudden impact, just total blankness. Karen was dead and whoever lived here now was currently out. Goodbye, Karen. RIP.

Much to Glyn's relief, I didn't cause a fuss as he led me away. I did exactly as I was told, even when I was taken back to Derwent House. I felt completely detached. I didn't care what happened to me. Shortly afterwards, I was charged for all the stealing offences I had committed in London. I had already been charged with some of them, but now they threw the book at me. I was guilty and they knew it, so I broke down and confessed to everything. I was remanded to Risley Prison in Liverpool, then on to Holloway in London. As an added treat, my social workers were asked to prepare a court report from my files for my upcoming criminal trial.

My court-appointed lawyer was hopeful that given my guilty plea, along with the fact that my mother had recently died, my father ("He's not my father") had just been convicted for sexually abusing me and the length of time I had already been in prison waiting to come to court, I would receive a non-custodial sentence. Indeed, he pointed out, 'recent bereavement' had been a successful mitigation in Stanley's case.

My lawyer was trying to help, but I was too busy coping with the brand-new hell that was life in remand to absorb what he was saying. The screws had taken away all of my survival mechanisms, including any access to music, so I didn't cope and I just didn't care. I was now on very strong tranquillisers and most of the world blurred its way past me.

Just before my court date, my lawyer broke the news to me that he had seen my Social Services report.

"These people hate you," he said in disbelief. "I have never seen a report like it."

He shook his head.

"I'm not so sure we're going to be able to keep you out of prison," he said. "In fact, I don't think there's a chance. Not in light of this report."

I wasn't surprised. Nothing surprised me anymore.

When my case came to trial, the judge said that he was very sorry for me and didn't think I was a criminal, just a very misguided 15-year-old girl, but, after reading the Social Services report, he was sending me to prison to calm me down. I was numb as the sentence was read out: six months to two years at Bullwood Hall Prison in Essex. I didn't care.

Life in remand had been easygoing compared with life in prison. All of a sudden, I woke up and realised that I cared. God, I cared.

I immediately regretted my decision not to stand up for myself. For the first time in my life, I wasn't being sexually abused, but the inmates were violent and threatening, and the staff really didn't care what happened to you. In my hazy state, I was subjected to a lot of 'new girl' beatings by the wing bullies.

A few weeks into my time in prison, I received a letter from home telling me that Denise was pregnant to Reg. This news snapped me out of my apathy. I realised that I had to wake up and learn how to survive. Talking things over nicely was not going to work with these hardened cows, so I dragged the three main wing bullies into my cell and pushed my bed against the door, which completely freaked them out. What bitch in her right mind would trap herself in her cell with three psychopaths? And there you have it. No bitch in her right mind would. I'm not proud of it, but I had to stand up for myself.

It took seven screws and an injection to drag me down to solitary confinement. The screws told me: "You behave and stay out of trouble and you could be out in just six months, or be here as long as two years: the choice is yours."

There wasn't really any choice. Prison was a hell all of its own. I had been locked up before, but never anywhere like this noisy, chaotic hell-hole. I had no space to think and I could feel myself sliding into the darkness. I wanted out so I quickly resolved to be good.

Although it was a terrible, soul-destroying period of my life, the rest of my stay was fairly uneventful and I was a model prisoner. Unfortunately, just weeks before my six months were up, the prison officers broke the news to me that although I had been good, I couldn't leave because I was around 16 and would be on probation and the probation had nowhere for someone my age to stay, so I would have to stay!

Unless I agreed to go back and live with Stanley. I couldn't believe it – what kind of system gives you a choice between returning to live with a man who has been convicted of abusing you or remaining in prison?

I wasn't going to stay in that place a second longer than I needed to – I had already resolved that I wouldn't ever do anything again that would bring me back there – but I also really didn't want to go back to the Noctorum. In desperation, I made a plan to use Stanley to get out of jail and then find a way to get away from him and the authorities once I was free.

When I got home to the Noctorum, I discovered that things for everyone were just as bad, if not worse. Stanley hadn't laid a finger on me since his conviction – and wouldn't again. Denise, meanwhile, had given birth to her baby. Everyone thought she had been pregnant to Reg, but the baby was blond, and Reg was black, so it was quickly ascertained that he couldn't have been the father.

There were so many children at risk from Stanley at this time and it seemed there was nothing anyone would or could do to stop him, so I did what I thought I could do and what I thought was best at the time. I told everyone again what a giant pervert Stanley and his friends were. Once again, of course, no one listened.

I no longer knew what to do for the best. So, when a man I'd met in London asked me to marry him, I didn't hesitate. I hardly knew him, but he'd written to me in prison and we'd stayed in touch. He proposed when I was 17 and, seeing my escape route,

I accepted without hesitation. We moved to Germany but, inevitably, after just a year of marriage, I was back in London on my own. I was just 18 and I felt like my life was already over.

End Movie

As I emerged into my late teens and finally resolved never to return to Birkenhead, I felt as if I had been plunged in and out of one confusing hell after another. Now back in London, I found myself alone in the big wide world, with a truckload of everyone else's secrets and an empty pain.

I went into the world only knowing what didn't work and had to learn everything the hard way. I didn't have a family or a place I belonged, and I didn't have a clue who I was. All I knew was who I didn't want to be.

I was determined never to find myself back in prison and to leave Stanley and everything else that had happened to me well and truly behind, so I did my best to stay out of trouble and work for a living. I had a passion for motorbikes and so I got myself a job as a motorbike courier, found a flat and tried as best I could to make a fresh start.

When you've been through as much as I had, though, starting over isn't as easy as it sounds. With no anchor, I couldn't see myself in my past, my present or my future. I was like another person, trapped inside the shattered remains of an old human being, trying to make all the broken parts work and survive day to day.

Broken

I was like a human ghost ship drifting on a wild and treacherous sea, with the hull ripped away and nothing left inside of it.

For so long I had lived in a world where people had been unable to believe what Stanley really was. Even those people who said that they believed me, still blamed me, and accused me of being the cause. It was as though when they looked at me, they saw Stanley for what he really was and hated me for it. Some social workers had said they were sure I was going to be a monster, and so I would spend endless unhappy years waiting for that sodding monster to appear in me. When it never materialised, I hated them for putting that stupid idea inside my young head. I wasted a few more years resenting the time I had lost waiting for it, until I learnt to stop doing that as well. They had found it so easy to see some imaginary monster inside me, but could not see Stanley for the monster he was. It would take me many years to come to terms with this. And a lot longer to let it go.

Society hated and feared Stanley's crimes, but because they did, they discriminated against me. I wasn't just a child victim of mental, physical and sexual abuse, I was also poor, an orphan, had been in care, was a former mental-hospital patient and an ex-convict. I didn't fit in anywhere, but I didn't feel as if I fitted into any of those social black holes either. Once an authority found out about my background and read my Social Services file, I was immediately in very real danger from all kinds of system abuse, exploitation and discrimination, so I was forced to hide my past and my identity. I didn't register for anything in case the authorities found out who I was. If I had to, I'd use false names. Essentially, I lived a law-abiding life but in complete hiding from the authorities.

I would speak to Denise and the others on the phone occasionally. They'd tell me how things were at home, and I'd help out financially if they needed it. I never went back to Birkenhead to live, but did return a few times. Once, after speaking with some of Stanley's younger victims who were telling us again that they wanted help to stop him, I had again tried to step in. I went to the parents and to the police, but the children denied anything was happening once the authorities were involved and yet again it all came to nothing.

Mostly, I avoided contact with anything to do with my old life and tried to make a go of my new one. Despite everything I had been through, I was still drawn to the good in people. I liked people to be kind and I liked to be kind to them. I immersed myself in music and motorbikes, and tried to surround myself with good, grounded, real people. I made some good friends through motorbiking. I didn't, as a habit, drink or take drugs, but I did smoke pot to Olympic gold-medal standards. However, partying and riding didn't go well together, so we always did one or the other. I made the same kind of mistakes most people make when evolving from childhood to adulthood, but I always tried to be a better version of the previous me.

By day I was a courier, and by night I was that little brown-eyed, leather-clad woman who rode around the streets of London on her big motorbike, with her music playing loudly inside her blacked-out crash helmet. I once heard a motorbike lad describe me to his mates, without realising that I was standing right behind him in the queue for the burger van on Blackheath, as "that motorbike bird with the long, brown hair, big tits and nice arse. Never speaks much, but I wouldn't mind a piece." As the other lads wondered whether I would keep my handmade thigh-length motorbike boots on during the 'wild sex' we were all apparently going to have, I coughed and made my presence known. We all laughed and I made some good, forever platonic, friends.

My motorbike gave me a freedom I could never have expressed in words back then, but these days I can see that inside my crash helmet, on my fast, powerful bike, I could ride around safely and anonymously, and see how the rest of the world lived. On my bike, I always had enough power and skill to escape fast, if I felt I needed to.

My bike friends and I would roar around the streets of London, screaming off from the traffic lights on our back wheels and racing to the next set of lights. This was well before the days of speed cameras or police cars that had a hope in hell of catching us, so we'd be a blur racing round the North Circular, only stopping to eat a 'mystery illness in a bun' from the many burger vans dotted around London. We would stop at Notting Hill to pick up the gear, then off to Box Hill in Surrey, or Blackheath to warm the bikes up, then back home to get stoned, listen to music, cheat at cards or laugh at the telly. There were also many excellent biker pubs that our crowd could always get into without any bother, mainly because they had a biker bird with big tits in their gang, so we had a lot of fun finding out which scary pubs we should never go back to ever again.

I wasn't the violent sort, but I could certainly stand up for myself if I had to, and I seldom had to. Once, after getting a bit proactive with someone I caught hurting their pet dog, I got the nickname Peta. It stuck and it ended up being my name to all those who didn't call me Karen or Shy.

As for relationships, I steered well clear. If a man asked me out, I would always say no. I would occasionally sleep with men if I fancied them, but it was never anything more and I never let them get close to me emotionally. I couldn't mix sex and love.

Learning to trust people was hard enough, but learning who to trust came at a very painful price for me, as I quickly realised that being good or kind 'out loud' makes you a target for every dirt bag in the world. One night, when I was 19, something happened that changed my life forever. I went to a party with a group of bike friends, but I didn't remember what happened there or how I got home. I thought it was strange that I couldn't remember anything, but wasn't unduly concerned. Shortly afterwards, though, I started to feel unwell and went to hospital. They examined me and apparently, though I had no memory of that night, I had been drugged and sexually attacked. When I heard this, heard that I had been abused all over again, it made me feel so vulnerable, so weak. The pain and consequences of this attack finally broke my spirit; something snapped inside of me and I started to sink into a deep depression. I had an emotional breakdown from which it would take me years to recover.

I was still so young, but felt utterly world-weary and exhausted. My early twenties were nothing but a black, soul-less agonising despair. I drifted through life, desperately trying to find ways to put a stop to the pain. It was as if I was watching myself from above, watching my body going into self-destruct while my mind wandered elsewhere.

In the depths of my breakdown, I rarely went out at all. I was broken and I lived in fear that the authorities would discover who I was. I managed to haul myself back to Birkenhead once, for the last time, to help get our Denise and her family out. She found the courage to tell the police what Stanley had been doing over the years and they arrested him. Denise was now 22 and after threats to kill her and her young family if she proceeded, she fled into hiding in Europe with her family. Last I heard, Stanley had been jailed for what he did to Denise and that was the last I saw or heard of any of them for the next couple of decades.

In the late 1980s, as I entered my late-twenties, I was still very confused and empty. Not good at relationships, I wasn't able to connect or communicate properly with anyone. I couldn't trust at all and I had lied so much about me, my life and my pain that I didn't even know how old I really was. I had completely lost my way.

It was during some of those dark days, at my lowest, that I had started watching some tapes from the US of Oprah. As I watched some of her shows, I began to cry. She did shows that spoke a language I understood. She stopped me from feeling so desperately alone and helped bring me back from the brink. Because of her, after years of never going out, I was suddenly overwhelmed by this urge to suit up and sling my leg over my motorbike and take a wild night ride up to Box Hill. This triggered an even wilder ride, back to my beloved Pately Bridge.

Working its unique magic and after some of the most incredibly emotionally intense weeks of my life, I re-emerged from Pately Bridge ready to try again, but I had some new rules.

It had always been my fear that I would turn into a monster, so I made a pact with myself that I must never have children. I also promised myself that I would always, no matter what the cost, trust my instinct. I would always live a good life and live it my way. I would be helpful and polite, but never take any shit, ever. I would learn to accept the bits of me that were never going to work and try to focus on what did or might. I would try to let someone close enough to be a real friend and learn to stop trusting the wrong people. I resolved to address my problems with relationships. And finally, I would just enjoy the things that made me happy – I'd listen to my music, ride my bike and take life one tiny step at a time.

As I moved through my late-twenties and early thirties, I found that there was plenty in life for me to enjoy and plenty that fulfilled me. I loved to ride my motorbike and go horse riding through the countryside. I loved music and even sang in a band. I loved calm and tranquillity, narrowboat rides and 'no fish' fishing (I became known as the Essex Maggot-drowner). I made some real friends and really started to trust my instincts. Despite the fears of becoming a monster that had always haunted me, I had overcome my fear of having children and had decided that I would like to be a mother one day. As for my attitude to sex, I was a fun-loving, straight-lines kind of woman. Unfortunately, I still found it hard to let boyfriends get emotionally close and was, unintentionally, something of a heartbreaker. Although it's a cliché, in this case it really wasn't them, it was me, and as far as this part of my life is concerned, it was always going to be me.

I felt like I had come back into the world as the real me. Music and my passion for motorbikes had given me a way of expressing myself, something I had never had before. I still lived in fear of the authorities ever finding out that I was Karen Claridge. Although I lived a happy enough life, there was always this element of fear about my identity that strangled a lot of the fun out of living.

Because I had lived in hiding from the system, by my early thirties I had still not received any kind of help or treatment (other than my own herbal medication) for all that had happened to me. I had put most of it to the very back of my mind and was doing OK, until a late miscarriage. I sank into a depression and was put on prescribed medication. Finally, after too many months, I realised that I needed some real help and so I turned to the mental health charity MIND, who were brilliant to me, always there when I needed to talk and, as it turns out, along with my friends and my music, were all I needed to start to recover my life again. As part of my recovery, one of my very dear friends suggested that I take some of my old scribble notes and poems and try to turn them into recorded songs.

I was negative at first, as I couldn't read music, play an instrument and had no way of recording such a thing, but after being firmly told off for my 'can't do' attitude, I was given a PC (which I also couldn't sodding work!) and microphone and was told to get on with it.

I learn fast and by the tried-and-tested 'press it and see what happens' method, I taught myself all I needed to know to record my own songs. I was able to write, produce, arrange and record a whole album of songs on my own. Thanks to my friend's encouragement, Bill Gates and his idiot-proof software and my beloved Cubase, I was able to express myself in a way that actually helped me. The whole process felt very much like washing in my stream at Pately Bridge.

I hadn't created that album to sell – it was for me to have and to share (if I wanted) – but this thinking changed after some music friends heard it and thought it showed some real talent. I decided that I wanted to sell the album. The problem with this dream was that if I wanted a successful career in music, I would have to keep my childhood a secret. I was advised that because of all the stigma, if I came out and told the truth, nobody would want to buy my music, and as rotten as that is to hear, it is sadly true. I decided to start selling the album, but keep my childhood experiences to myself. I didn't feel as if I had a choice.

I had always been a motivated person, but as I grew older, I became more and more aware of all the things I couldn't do because of the stigma and prejudice towards people like me. As an adult – with official 'victim of child sexual abuse' status – people seemed to assume the worst of Stanley was somehow within me. As if paedophilia were some kind of sexually transmitted disease or, worse still, some highly contagious mental illness. I used to wonder why, if this were true, the women these child molesters marry and have sexual relations with don't catch paedophilia as well? How come all the policemen, probation officers or court staff don't catch it?

People would never dream of suggesting that burglary victims are likely to turn into burglars or rape victims are likely to become rapists, but they could quite coldly look at me and ask me if 'all victims' turn into monsters. Practically asking me if I was a pervert yet. Apparently, people can't be talented, honest, sincere, respected, successful, famous or empowered and be a known victim of these crimes. It's either one or the other.

With a lot of time and effort, I managed to come out the other side and emerged into my mid-thirties a happier, more grounded person. I felt as if I had finally moved on with my new life and become my own person. Then I met an incredible man, whom I married and made a family with. I had a wonderful family of my own, good friends and my songwriting had come on in leaps and bounds. I now had a chance at a recording contract and was starting to make a living from music. Things were really taking off for me. I was now a completely different person from the blind, emotionally shattered, misguided fool the paedophiles and authorities used to abuse and exploit with impunity.

I was a charitable soul and helped those who asked me for advice on how to help children they suspected were being sexually abused. Over time, I gained a lot of experience advocating on the victims' behalf and, at long last, I had a life that, for me, was well worth living.

As 1999 drew to a close, I got to thinking about my sister and wondered how things had turned out for them. I was a much stronger person these days and I had decided that it was time to find them and see for myself. Which is why, on Millennium Eve, I phoned Denise in Europe and, for the first time in decades, was talking to my sobbing and excited baby sister.

Choices

After talking with Denise for the first time in all these years, I was numb. For all my growing up, moving on and surviving, the moment I heard her voice I was emotionally right back there, but when I tried to go back mentally, to look for the memory files that go with those emotions, it was like walking into Bin Bag Barry's house, only Bin Bag Barry had essentially moved into a whole block of flats and was using every bloody room.

I was thrilled to speak to Denise and frightened stupid at the same time. All the old feelings of wanting to protect her washed over me as I sat and listened to her talk about her life in Europe. She still had her 90 miles an hour Merseyside accent (that we all used to have), only now she had this European twang too. It was so funny we spent the first two hours just trying to understand each other. We took a moment to forgive each other for any pain we may have caused each other ever and moved on from it.

Denise started to cry when she tried to talk about Mum, and as though only a single moment had passed between us, I told her that Mum had probably been booted out of heaven for feeling up St Peter and stealing baby Jesus' bingo card. When she heard this, Denise went from crying to laughing in horror. Denise was now a deeply religious person and, between uncontrollable fits of hysterical but frightened laughter, she spent the next hour apologising to God on my behalf, praying for my blasphemous soul and for the spirit of our dead mother. I won't tell you what I said back, but our Denise spent much of our time laugh-praying. I knew then that we were still connected. Then she told me some things that were no laughing matter at all.

To my shock, I learned that Stanley hadn't gone to jail at all and had continued to abuse countless children over the 25 years that I had spent away from Birkenhead. To my horror, Stanley was now working on even younger child victim boys and girls.

When I finally got off the phone to Denise, I fell into an absolute panic. I knew there was still plenty to be said, but I had spent so many years blocking painful memories that I simply couldn't remember much of my past. It seemed an impossible task to retrieve it all. It also felt impossibly painful. I was a very different person these days. I had a wonderful family of my own, incredible friends and a potential career in music. I had confidence and a good instinct, and now I felt as though I was about to be plunged back into that old hopeless hell. I didn't know if I could rake up all those old emotions and survive.

In spite of my fears, though, I knew that I had to protect my own family from the nightmare that is my birth family, and in order to protect them I would have to remember... no matter how much it hurt.

I recalled that I had attached many of my life memories to certain songs. Before I knew what I was doing, I had dragged out all my old secret life albums and was sitting in front of the tape machine, waiting to push play.

Choices

Rocking back and forth, I thought, OK, pushing 'play' may well open all those locked doors. Is that what I want? No, I would rather be skinned and pickled, but if I can't remember, I'm in big trouble. I have to protect my family, so let's just go.

Nothing was happening at first until it came to the golden-oldies tape and Jimmy started up – *boom, dat, boom, boom, dat* – and, as if by magic, some of the locked doors to my memories burst open. Far from upsetting me, Jimmy's song was now an incredible comfort. Through this song, I was able to see my past from the safety of the present and could press 'stop' the moment I wanted to.

I rang Denise back and we spoke in more detail. Both she and I were extremely concerned for the safety of any child that came into contact with Stanley. Now that I knew that children were potentially in very real danger, I knew I had to act. I knew what was going to happen, but I knew I had to act.

I called Roma. She hadn't changed much, and she told me that she couldn't remember anything about her childhood or my childhood, except that I was a little bastard and she hated me then, but not now. She also told me how none of her kids or family wanted to talk to me on account of all the pain and suffering I had caused their grandfather over the years.

We talked for hours more and as I listened to her, I began to feel deeply sad for her. Roma's childhood had been a nightmare of its own. When we came along, her own father completely rejected her and she had never really recovered herself. She was now 50 years old and he had poisoned her entire life. I began to see that Roma was just another victim of Stanley's; none of us were in a good place back then and it was time to put all that behind us. As with Denise, we forgave each other for any hurt we might have caused each other back then and left it where it belongs.

After I had spoken to Roma, I rang Aunt Pat and Uncle Ken. It was so wonderful to hear their voices and they seemed delighted to hear from me. A short while later, we arranged to meet up. In the past, I had always been too frightened to tell them the reality of what Stanley had done to me, too ashamed and fearful of driving them away, but now that I was an adult, I finally felt ready to tell them the truth.

On the day we met up, after hugging them for hours, we talked and talked and I learnt much more about my birth family during this short period than I had ever learnt in all the years before. Uncle Ken hadn't changed a single, wonderful bit. I smiled wryly when Aunt Pat told me she now worked for Social Services, helping broken families communicate, and our Dona was busy working and bringing up a family of her own.

I was thrilled to see them, but what I learnt that day shook me to the core. I had never forgotten their plans to adopt me and their apparent change of heart.

"I was so upset when you decided not to adopt me," I said, looking down at my feet.

There was the briefest of pauses as Aunt Pat looked at Uncle Ken.

"But we did want to adopt you, love," she said. "You know we did. We even came to collect you. Don't you remember?"

I thought back and remembered that Stanley had told me not to look at Aunt Pat when she came round. I remembered that he had told me that I mustn't look in their eyes or I'd see that they didn't love me anymore. A cold, sick feeling swept over me as I realised with a lurch that Aunt Pat and Uncle Ken had come over to collect me after all. Stanley and Jenifer had lied yet again. I listened in horror as Aunt Pat explained that she and Uncle Ken had been trying to adopt me for years. Stanley and Mum had blocked them all the way, until in the end they told Aunt Pat that I didn't love her or Uncle Ken anymore.

"He told us that you wouldn't look at us or speak to us because you didn't want to live with us, love," Aunt Pat said, shaking her head. "He said we were to come round and see for ourselves that you weren't interested. So we did and when you wouldn't look at us or speak to us, we were broken-hearted."

It seems I had been just inches away from escape and all I had to do was look into their eyes. All I had to do was trust in real love and I could have escaped and maybe even got the others out sooner. How I wish I could go back and choose again.

That evening, Aunt Pat and Uncle Ken asked me to stay the night. As I lay in the safe, warm bed that should have been mine, in a home that should have been mine, with the family I should have grown up with, I cried like a baby.

Of everything I had learnt over recent months, this single revelation had more of an impact on me than almost anything else. Stanley had stolen my happiness in the cruellest of ways. It made me challenge things I had long believed without question. My brain was re-evaluating everything I had ever known against this one particular revelation and suddenly so many things started making sense to me.

I now had very real concerns for the very little children being identified as at risk from Stanley. I had been away for years and nothing had changed. All of a sudden, I realised that if I didn't stop Stanley, nobody else would, indeed, nobody else could.

I was so completely sick to death of watching this creature ravage my birth family and all those others, totally unchallenged. I had simply had enough of having my life choices dictated to by a cruel and unjust fate. At the same time, though, I wanted to protect my own family. If I stood up to Stanley now, there would surely be a backlash against me. I didn't even know many of the children now involved, but I knew my help would not be welcome and I was afraid that they would try and take revenge on my own family, which I just couldn't allow.

I was left with a new set of awful choices to make. Do I step in and try to protect these children, or do I become one of the many people I had met in my childhood who found it easier just to turn the other cheek? Do I try and help people who hate and fear me, knowing that in doing so I could be putting my own family's future at risk, or do I simply walk away and carry on with my life?

In all honesty, the choice had been made back when I was a child; I just hadn't realised it yet.

Fighting Back

I resolved that the first thing I had to do was talk to my family and friends, tell them everything and see what they thought about it all. After a long talk, they asked, "What would you do if you weren't frightened for us?"

I hesitated, even though the answer was simple.

"I would fight," I said softly, my voice catching in my throat.

They looked me in the eye and said: "Do what you have to do and trust us to protect your family."

The decision was made. We worked together to put a plan in place to protect them from any backlash from my birth family or anyone else. At the first sign of danger, they would be taken and hidden abroad. With my own family as safe as I could make them, I got back in touch with our Denise.

Denise and I talked long into the night and by the end we were both deeply worried about what Stanley and his friends were doing. To put this into some perspective, Stanley was now about 70 years old, living alone and on state benefits in pensioner housing. He was an active, mentally alert man who drove a car, worked and visited his family most weeks. We knew we had to call the police.

Our aim was not to lodge a formal police complaint against Stanley for what he had done to us as children. Stanley had already been convicted of sexually abusing me as a child, Denise's attempts to have him convicted (back before she fled to Europe) had failed and would now be viewed as double jeopardy. Instead, we wanted to tell the police about what Stanley had done to us, in order to help them properly identify the risk he really posed – so that they would take action to protect the children whom he currently had access to.

It was January 2000 and, even in this more enlightened climate, I took my heart in my petrified hands when I picked up the phone and called the police.

After being advised that there was no police unit for historical child sexual abuse, I was finally put through to a police officer whom I told about our history and current concerns. These were principally that Stanley had unaccompanied access to two very small children, a boy and a girl. Stanley was already talking about these little children in an inappropriately sexualised manner, calling the little girl "a tart" and claiming to have had her running around his home naked. He was also, for some reason, lying about the frequency of his visits to the other child, not yet out of nappies.

I had thought that because we had told the police together, they would act to protect those children currently at risk. I expected action, sirens, police statements, child protection and victim support. I should have known better. I was essentially told that they had a lot of current cases to deal with and didn't have the resources to deal with historical cases. I argued that we had only raised past evidence about Stanley to help protect those little children at risk now. I emphasised that Stanley was a convicted sex offender and that the current victims couldn't even talk yet, but the police were unhelpful to say the least.

I realised that we needed to go back to the drawing board. Hearing evidence from adult victims wasn't good enough, and the children couldn't speak for themselves. What was left? A good friend of mine suggested that the only way to remove all doubt that the victims were telling the truth, would be for the police to hear the words out of the offender's own mouth. My friend suggested that we record Stanley and see if he incriminated himself.

We thought there was a better chance of Stanley talking to Denise than to me and so, despite the fact that she was still scared of him, Denise agreed to call him.

We hatched a plan to get him to talk about our childhoods and, with a frightened determination, Denise set up a three-way telephone conversation between herself in Europe, Stanley in Merseyside and me, secretly listening in on a muted third-party line and recording everything back in Essex.

Hearing Stanley's voice for the first time in decades was utterly chilling. I shuddered and had to steady myself. He talked about nothing much for ages and I was ready to signal to Denise that she should end the conversation when out of the blue, Stanley admitted that he had sexually abused me (although that was not how he put it). Our Denise was struggling to know what to say back. I could hear the shock in her voice and that she was trying not to cry. I knew this could be it, but Denise wasn't coping, so I signalled to her to end the call. She said she would ring him back and hung up. I called her immediately. She was sobbing incoherently. We had, of course, hoped that Stanley would confess, but had never dreamt he would do so without a fight and with such cold graphic cruelty. I don't think we had thought about how it would make us feel to hear him talk about us as though we were all baby sluts.

My baby sister was crying, so I did what I always did and tried to make her laugh. I asked her how many Stanleys does it take to wallpaper a living room? She sobbed, how many? I replied, it depends how thinly you slice him. It was a crap joke, but she stopped crying and started laughing. Jokes aside, I knew this wasn't easy for her. This monster had destroyed her and so many others. Neither of us thought it was funny; this was just the way we coped. If we hadn't learnt to laugh, I don't think we would have ever stopped crying.

When we stopped laughing, we considered whether or not we were wrong about this, but we both knew without question that if Stanley had access to children, he was hurting them and no doubt blaming them for it.

Denise agreed and we set about arranging to call him back. Denise would tell him that their conversation had triggered some memories that had really upset her. She would say that she needed to talk to him about them or she would have to go and see a therapist, and she didn't want to do this, as over in Europe telling your therapist such a thing would trigger an automatic police investigation. None of these statements was true. Not the needing to talk to someone urgently in order to keep the authorities out of it – nor the "talking to him" part.

Stanley would never admit to your face that he abused you; however, when pushed, he would admit it to others. So if Denise challenged him, he would admit he had abused me, but not that he had abused her. Likewise, if I challenged him, he would admit to abusing her but not me. I told Denise to agree with everything he said even when she knew it wasn't true. Even if he said he never touched her, Denise would have to agree. This was like asking the rain not to be wet or the fire not to be hot, but Denise agreed to it.

Stanley told us more than we had ever hoped. He told us things we didn't know and confirmed things we did. He admitted to abusing us all and to sharing us with others. He even grassed his old friends up, like Reg whom he said was still at it. As always, he slipped as many lies as he could in between all the truths, but these days they were so obvious, they were laughable.

Over the next few days, we gathered a few hours of conversations and I edited the tapes down to the soundbites that I thought were relevant and important to prove we were telling the truth about Stanley and anything that supported our concerns about the risks he currently posed.

It was the end of January 2000, I had typed up the transcript of the secretly recorded taped confession and along with this edited tape and a covering letter explaining the issues (and letting them know how to get the full tapes) I sent the whole thing off to the police and Social Services by recorded delivery and waited for them to take action. I had waited decades for this moment, and I was certain that at long last it had come. No one could argue with the words out of his own mouth.

A Family Affair

As I waited to hear back from the police and Social Services, it really felt as if we were almost there, but then days of waiting turned into weeks. Firstly, I was given a string of excuses as to why they hadn't yet taken action – staff members were on leave, then they told me they were waiting for someone else to listen to the tape, next I was told that they had a backlog of work, and finally I was informed that the tapes had been lost. I knew that they were deliberately stalling and simply wanted me to go away.

Despite their historical opinion of me, I felt it was crucial for Social Services to read my childhood files in order to properly and independently identify those currently at risk. So I applied for them. This was, however, a problem, as the Social Services had sworn for decades that my childhood files had been lost or destroyed, which is what they said when they replied to my application.

They further explained that even if they did exist, I couldn't see them all anyway because of the millions of pounds Social Services were losing in civil cases of child abuse and neglect up and down the UK. The insurance companies had apparently long instructed all Social Services not to disclose self-incriminating evidence to those who had formerly been in their care, citing third-party privacy at first, then about a dozen other excuses like it, until they put you off. I was not after their money, though, and I told them so.

Not to be deterred, I wrote to every establishment I had ever been sent to as a child, to the bodies that governed them, to all the medical authorities – hospitals, doctors and dentists – the police and the education authorities. Not one of them was able to help: most of the places I had gone to no longer existed, and I discovered that I didn't appear anywhere, on any file, in any name. They had practically erased all evidence of my childhood and, along with it, any hope of protecting those children.

When many weeks had passed and nothing had been achieved, I wrote to the police and Social Services bosses. When that didn't work, I enclosed the tape, along with a brief outline of the issues and concerns, and sent it to both MPs and members of the House of Lords, as well as to child protection agencies and charities, and even some of their esteemed patrons, only to be completely blanked across the board.

To be clear here, I was no learner: I had advocated for years on behalf of victims of sexual abuse; I knew how to present an issue in the appropriate manner and how to keep to clear, concise points, backed up with strong evidence. Even so, nobody wanted to know. All my efforts were met with a deafening wall of silence.

I tried contacting some friends in the victim advocacy world, but this wasn't moving things on. I was in total despair. No one seemed able to help. In utter frustration, I toyed with the idea of turning to criminal measures. I even posted parts of what Stanley said on the internet to try and muster some support for action, all to no avail.

So there I was, with the worst-case scenario possible: everybody knows everything and yet nobody is going to stop Stanley. The children currently at risk will be lost and I will be forced to watch it happen. I had reached a brick wall. I couldn't sleep, and I couldn't think of anything else.

Once again, my internal dialogue returned. I asked myself, why didn't anybody help me when I was a child?

They couldn't.

Why couldn't they?

Things were in the way.

What 'things' could possibly be in the way of protecting an innocent child?

I don't know. What's stopping you from going down there now and putting a stop to Stanley yourself?

I can't just walk into people's lives and start removing children and jailing suspected child molesters.

So you already know the reasons why.

That's just not good enough. What can I do?

You could kill him.

Then I'd go to jail and he would not only have hurt my childhood, but all of my adulthood and my own family as well. Why would I give him that?

You're not giving him anything. He's giving you no choice: he won't stop.

I do have choices: I could go to the media.

So what's stopping you?

If I come out in public now, I will have to say goodbye to my music career forever. No one will want to buy my album if they know about my past. I'm so close to my chance, and I've worked so hard and invested everything to do it. I can't see me doing anything else. Besides, how will I support my family? At that moment, the internal dialogue stopped and I knew that, come what may, I would love and protect my family, rich or poor. I didn't know how, but I knew I would find a different future for us, because I would never know a moment's happiness or peace if I walked away from those children. I decided to close the door on my music, and I haven't opened it since.

I now knew that I didn't need the police, the authorities or a legal team behind me to achieve what I wanted to achieve. I didn't need to turn to crime either. In March 2000, as a desperate and absolute last resort, I turned to Colm O'Gorman from the victim support charity One in Four and asked him to help me approach the media.

He looked carefully at the evidence, made some enquiries of his own and upon our second meeting, to my complete and utter amazement, he said that he had rarely seen a case, so well supported and with such strong evidence, go so completely ignored. I was overwhelmed with gratitude and relief. Colm said that he was 100 per cent with me and would do whatever he could to help protect those children. Then he told me what had happened to him and right then I knew that I had found a truly incredible kindred spirit and a new forever friend.

Together, we approached the BBC with the tape and before we knew it, we were at our first meeting with the team behind their award-winning flagship news programme Newsnight. I couldn't believe it!

I was a little nervous about meeting the team, but they were extremely friendly and put us immediately at our ease. My heart sank a little when they explained that they didn't normally do this kind of journalism and so I wasn't to hold out much hope, but they said they were intrigued to hear the details. Colm and I began to tell them all about Stanley and his friends. By the time they had heard and seen the evidence, they had gone a strange grey colour and their voices were choked. They asked me to leave it with them and they would get straight back to me.

I was crushed: I knew that fear-stricken look. These were good, decent people who cared and showed it, and they were used to dealing with difficult stories, but Stanley's voice seems to frighten everyone but me.

When the call came, I was shaking like a leaf. They said the team were moved to tears by the case, but emotions aside they wanted to get the authorities to take action and were calling in special top producers to film an unprecedented 60-minute special about the whole story. They wanted me to come in and talk to them about my part in it.

I was alone in the house when I got the call and as I put the phone down, I felt a world of painful responsibility lift from my shoulders, just enough for me to cry a bit. Hang in there, little ones, help is coming.

We met and talked about what would be needed from me and I agreed to everything they asked. Then they asked me what I needed. I said that I needed to protect my own family throughout. They also agreed. They brought Colm in for full- time support for me. Then we met Sarah MacDonald, a stunningly beautiful and highly respected film producer, born in New Zealand and known for her courageous direct approach to very complicated, controversial issues. Again, I met another forever friend.

When Sarah contacted Social Services to ask about my files, they magically reappeared, but only a very brief synopsis of the files was eventually released – on the strictest instructions of their insurance company.

Filming for the Newsnight special started in April 2000. After secretly going back and forth to Merseyside to uncover evidence and film it, my whole life picture started to unfold and the risks that Stanley, Reg and the others currently posed became more worryingly clear.

During the undercover filming in 2000, eight-year-old Sarah Payne was abducted and murdered by a known paedophile. I was deeply affected by this crime and was moved to my core by the way in which Sarah's mother, Sara, dealt with the whole ordeal. I privately vowed my support for Sarah's Law and knew that I would one day do so publicly – when all this was behind me.

Returning to the places of my childhood brought back all sorts of memories. I remember on one occasion, not too long into filming, when I went on my own down to the old castle and gazed across the Moreton and Leasowe Bay. It was a beautiful and familiar scene. The sound and sight of the sea lapping against the shore has always had a very calming effect on me. When the sun sets on the water, the sky sometimes explodes in a burst of colours. It never fails to still me, and it always feels like the first time I've ever seen it. Gazing out to sea that day was, however, a bizarre and uneasy contrast of beauty and the beast. Ahead was this awe-inspiring view of natural beauty and tranquillity; behind me were Leasowe and Moreton.

In my mind's eye, I could see exactly where I had hidden and played as a child. Everything seemed a little different and, as always, much smaller. As the childhood memories started to flood back, the tears came.

I cried for the sad, deluded child that I could see scurrying off to one of her safe places along the seafront. I felt sorry for her, sitting there thinking herself lucky because she got to choose what kind of sex she would have today or how she didn't have to go the whole way to get the cash. Oh, dear child, was that really your idea of lucky? Was that really your idea of a choice? More shameful tears started to flow.

As always, though, the sound of the sea against the shore was immediately calming and eventually soothed me right back to just thinking. Thinking how much I fecking hate Leasowe! Everything I remembered was either closed down or derelict, and the only local shops that seemed to have survived (in abundance) were the laundries, the off-licences and the chippies. All were fully equipped with the latest anti-theft technology, placed behind a Plexiglas shield so you could put your money through a tiny hole and get out.

As filming continued, the Newsnight team and I always passed on any new information regarding our case to the authorities as we found it. They had basically told me that if I wanted them to take any action, I would have to find the evidence myself and bring it to them, gift-wrapped in certain conviction. After Sarah MacDonald contacted them, they sent a social worker to the parents of the child we thought was at risk. Apparently, they basically told them that 'mental Karen' was at it again, but did nothing else to assess who else might be at risk from Stanley.

I had been secretly filming at various locations for several weeks when the call came in from the police that after looking at everything we had collectively told them and shown them, they had decided that they would simply pop round to tell Stanley to stay away from children.

It was decided that we needed more evidence against Stanley and his friends. So now you know why, a little while later, I was sitting in a hotel room with the Newsnight undercover recording equipment, waiting to meet Stanley for the first time in all these years and freaking right out. I had remembered everything from my nightmare of a childhood, but it didn't change what I was about to do; it just made it more scary.

I tossed and turned 'till morning and pondered how this genius puppeteer had got away with abusing children for so long and asked myself how he would react to seeing me in a few short hours. When my sleepless night finally came to an end, we went over the remit with the team. I re-agreed no violence, no matter what, I then put on the hidden cameras and left to drive to Stanley's house for my surprise 'cigarette- giving' visit.

It was a cool, clear day. Lene Marlin's *Flown Away* was playing in the car, and my heart was pounding out of my chest as I pulled up near to Stanley's house. I asked myself, how will I fake a smile for the Beast of Birkenhead? What if he won't talk to me because of the recent police visit? Then I reassured myself that I had our Denise's permission to lie through my teeth and say it was all her. What if – *no more questions girl, just get out of the car.*

Stanley now lived in a small row of bland, identikit council bungalows. As I walked towards his door, I became very calm and focused. Everything slowed down as I took full control of my senses. I took a few deep breaths and started posting the cigarette packets through his letterbox. I could hear him moving about inside and before long could see his shadow through the glass in the front door. He was hovering behind the door, watching the packets fall on to the mat. For a moment, I thought he wasn't going to open the door. Then, just as I had hoped, the door swung open. He greeted me as though not a single moment had passed between us, as though nothing bad had ever happened, as though he was actually pleased to see me.

He no longer looked like the giant Beast of Birkenhead to me – he was just some short, fat, bald, pathetic old pervert. I smiled and said 'hello' as he welcomed me into his home. He put his arm round me in greeting and beckoned me in. Feeling his hands on me made my flesh crawl. Then I remembered the cameras concealed in my clothes and fear shot through me. What if he'd felt them? I searched his face anxiously, but he seemed none the wiser, so I stepped inside and willed myself to stay calm.

As I followed him down the hall and into the dingy sitting room, I noted a few old tatty things that he had kept from our past – like some furniture and ornaments. The wood-panelled walls were littered with pictures of three generations of his victims, all taken when they were children. Their blank eyes stared out hopelessly, belying their forced smiles. It was like walking into a memorial crypt for lost souls. I felt a stab of remorse that I had left it so long to bring help.

I took a seat on a faded floral sofa and listened to my abuser drivel on in his usual manner. He didn't seem reluctant to talk about the past. I was honestly shocked. For the first time I realised that this man, this pervert who had smashed up so many lives, was not a criminal genius at all. A liar, yes. Manipulative, yes.

But also completely transparent. For the first time ever, I saw Stanley and Mum in a whole new light. He was just a sad, twisted pervert and she was just his needy wife, hand-picked for her weaknesses – her selfishness, her disregard for her children and her greed. Stanley wasn't that clever – it was just that Mum was that stupid and the authorities always had too much to lose by exposing Stanley, because it would have meant exposing what they had failed to do and so, as they protected themselves, they had by proxy protected him.

In a strange way, seeing Stanley in his old age, seeing his complete inability to comprehend the devastation he had had on so many lives, actually helped me to understand that he wasn't the Beast of Birkenhead at all, he wasn't a genius or a puppeteer extraordinaire – he was a dirty old man who would do whatever it took to satisfy his own perverted cravings.

As I returned to my car after that first meeting with Stanley, I breathed a sigh of relief. Adrenaline was still coursing through my body, but I knew now that I could get him to face justice. His complete inability to understand his own perversion had ruined countless lives, but it would also be his downfall. It had made him careless and loose-tongued. Facing him had been the hardest thing I'd ever done, but I knew for certain that it would be worthwhile.

We filmed Stanley a few times. Each time, I refused his offers of drink, food and cigarettes and got straight down to it. He grassed himself and some of the others up, he identified some of the victims, and he confirmed our concerns for the children he currently had access to. He seemed unable to keep himself from bragging about his exploits. Each revelation repulsed me, but I also smiled inwardly as he implicated himself and dug himself deeper.

On my last meeting with Stanley, he told me about the recent police visit and their recommendation that he stay away from children. He laughed at their pathetic attempt to stop him, mocking them for even trying. He got up to make a cup of tea for himself and I followed him into the dreary kitchen at the back of the bungalow. He was talking about the family and looking me straight in the eye. Suddenly, out of nowhere, he lunged towards me, grabbed me between the legs and squeezed my crotch through my clothes. I froze.

Time stood still for a moment. I couldn't believe he had touched me. For a split second, I seriously considered killing him. He had done that right in front of the hidden camera. I knew that no jury in the land would blame me if I attacked him now. I felt a rage surge, but just as quickly, it calmed. I realised that I wasn't in danger. I could kill him on the spot, just like I had considered in the hotel room, but I was here because I wanted to choose my own fate and that was to stop him and help the others.

I realised at that moment that at long last, where he was concerned, I got to choose. I chose my family. I chose those children. I chose to stay calm and walk away with the taped evidence.

When I got back to the car, the rage returned. The voice in my head screamed, *the son of a bitch touched me!* I turned the key in the ignition and pulled away out of the estate as quickly as I could. The undercover surveillance team followed. They had heard that something was wrong over the microphone, but hadn't yet seen the film, so they weren't sure what had happened. They looked extremely worried for me, but I signalled to them that I was all right. Robotically, I started driving to our pre-agreed safe place, but I didn't make it.

Never drive and cry – it's too bloody dangerous. I was doing my best, but the harder I held down my emotions, the harder it was not to cry. I tried not to think about him touching me, but it was impossible and I started to feel sick. I tried crying out loud, just to ease the pressure, but in the end I had to pull over on to the hard shoulder, throw up over the guard rail and have a good cry. Then I climbed back in the car and continued on to the safe place. When I got there, everyone was so kind and looked so concerned for me. Colm was instantly by my side, as always.

I smiled and said, "I told you I was me."

They looked puzzled. Then we replayed the tape and they saw with horror what they had just been listening to. It was then that they realised that Stanley had molested me and I had not retaliated. We all had a bit of a wet-eye moment. This was a very big moment for me in so many ways.

Filming had started back in April and it was now November. While waiting for the police to tell us they were going to do nothing, Sarah had been both secretly and openly filming with and without me all over Merseyside, gathering the evidence. When we secretly filmed Reg admitting to sexually abusing us, I was much calmer and more able to focus, but it was during these meetings that we found out that one of Reg's current victims was a wonderful little eight-year-old girl who lived close by and whose parents presumably had no idea that this seemingly harmless old man was in fact an active, predatory, lifelong paedophile.

Nobody, not even Reg, had referred to her by name, so we had no idea who she was or where she lived; we just knew without a shadow of a doubt that she needed help and fast.

In order to help her and the other children, we needed to get the Newsnight documentary finished. Sarah set to work doing what she does best and soon I was sitting in the control room in the Newsnight office about to watch the live screening.

I hadn't seen much of the footage that Sarah had done without me. I was petrified. When I get this scared, I emotionally lock down. When I do this, I look completely unmoved by what is happening around me, even though nothing could be further from the truth. The alternative would be to sound and look as scared as I am, and I can't do that, so I sat like a statue looking at the rows of TVs that were lining up shots of Sarah's documentary and freezing them ready to play them in turn. I started shaking as I saw my whole life in freeze frame on the wall of screens.

As I was sitting waiting for the documentary to start, I couldn't stop thinking about what would happen next. Would the police make those little children safe? What would my birth family do? What would Social Services do to me and my own family for doing this? What would I do once everyone knew me as 'that abused girl'? What about my dreams of becoming a stand-up comedian? See how I joke when I'm scared? Really, though, what were people going to think of me now..? Then I realised – I didn't care. Everyone just needed this to end now. I was trying to stay calm when Sarah called from the editing suite to tell me that she had door-stepped Stanley and Reg with her camera crew. Reg hadn't let her in, though he did make a brief response. Stanley, on the other hand, had warmly invited her and the crew in to talk about everything. I was astonished, but also curious to see what he would say when he was told what had really been going on all this time.

Denise had wanted to come over to share the broadcasting of the Newsnight documentary, but was having to undergo a serious spinal operation back in Europe. I was sad that she couldn't be there, but I was keeping her updated, and like me, she was scared.

With the help of Colm's team at One in Four, the BBC Newsnight team had set up help, support and information lines for those affected by the documentary, and everyone who needed to know it was airing had been told. My own family was safely hidden away and I was as ready as I could ever be. The whole team gathered to watch the programme. As I sat and watched them stare at the wall of TVs, I knew that this had been no ordinary job for them – they had changed over the months. I had taken them back to my childhood, they had seen for themselves what I had been fighting all of my life, and they were different now, we all were. I felt as though we had made it out of a dark, hostile war zone, had somehow escaped with our enemy's secrets and were about to report them. We had bonded as friends during the making of this documentary, and although we made it back alive, one way or another we were all emotionally scarred by the experience.

The team had shown me kindness, support and faith throughout, and I knew that what they were doing was very brave. In an unprecedented move, the BBC had reduced the news to a brief synopsis and extended the airtime for that night and the following night to allow for a discussion with MPs and authority chiefs. You could feel the tension emanating from the building from two streets away.

This documentary was going to be disturbing and distressing. It was going to upset people, and it was going to have an impact. I just didn't know what form that impact would take. I hoped it would protect the children at risk, but in truth, no matter what happened next, I fully expected to be crushed into tiny pieces...

Strange Calm

What happened next was very much like trying to keep hold of a live electric wire with wet hands: hold on tight and hope it doesn't kill you. As the Newsnight theme tune began to play, the documentary unfolded and I saw things I didn't know Sarah had filmed, I felt as if I had gone from completely invisible to entirely transparent in an hour flat. I felt emotionally stripped bare, as if people could see my very DNA. I would normally struggle to stay in a crowded room and would need to find a space alone somewhere to settle down, but I was suddenly gripped by a strange calm. My phobia of crowds, something I had suffered with for years, suddenly upped its level of tolerance, and I felt in control. Instead of feeling overwhelmed by the noise and movement of others, everything slowed down.

Something was happening to me. I didn't know what it was or even why; I just know that whatever it was, it started right then. The only way that I can describe it is that before this moment, I think I was living my life like an untuned radio: I was unable to tune into most channels and couldn't understand the different sounds anyway. Now, I could tune into all the channels and understand everything that was being said. What was more,

I now had the mental time to comprehend the information. I felt as though I had just been electrocuted. I felt alive, alert and incredibly calm.

On the screen, I saw Denise, me, Roma and other victims.

Then Stanley and Reg. Then Aunt Pat, an old neighbour, old care workers, family friends, old pictures of the family flashing up before me like some surreal near-death experience. There is something wholly captivating about watching your life play out on film. You feel removed but still very much connected. It was invasive and yet agonisingly cathartic.

They played part of a song I had written over the scene where I'm on top of the flats in Birkenhead, about to commit suicide. I suddenly felt really sorry for the Karen in this story. Then twenty Stanleys appeared across the TV wall, grabbing at my vagina and I remember thinking, Tell Sarah how I asked for that, you bastard!

I was doing all right until I saw Stanley sitting in his living room talking to Sarah and essentially saying that he didn't abuse me, except for when he did, which wasn't all his fault as there were others and how you really had to know what I was like back then to understand why people kept having sex with me so much.

Then, before I knew it, the documentary had finished and the discussion was under way. Soon even that was over, the end credits were rolling, and we were all hugging each other in tearful relief.

So there you have it: a family torn apart by unchallenged child abuse; the little children currently identified as potentially at risk from Stanley and Reg; and their anti-victim facilitators from the authorities, who now have the filmed confessions of those accused and can no longer claim that the only thing stopping them from acting is whether or not they can believe the victims.

As far as I was concerned, the authorities had known months earlier that those little children were at risk and could have stepped in to help them when the issue was first flagged. I believed that if anything had happened to them during this period, then it would be their fault and they should be made to answer for it.

It was now midnight and we all felt drained. We went and had a drink and a quick debrief, then I excused myself to go and talk with my family. Once I was sure they were OK, I went to my room and collapsed on the bed. I was woken early the next morning. The TV was still on and I was confronted by my own face, which is as weird as hell. I shot up like a bolt and started shaking uncontrollably as the memory of the night before flooded back. Oh, dear God! What have I done?

I called my family, who were still OK, and then I picked up a voicemail message to come to the team office immediately as something big was happening. I tried calling back, but all lines were engaged, so I was up and out like a shot. By the time I was at the entrance to One in Four's offices, I was quite terrified. What was I going to walk into? What if nobody had seen it? What if they had seen and just didn't care? What if nobody believed me?

I quietened my thoughts and pushed open the door to the office. A tremendous noise greeted me. The office, normally tranquil and orderly, was packed solid with people trying to answer the phones, which were now ringing off the hook. It was mayhem, but when I walked in, everyone started to congratulate me. I, of course, got teary and had started backing out of the room when Colm appeared out of the crowd and took me to a quiet office, where we could talk.

Colm was exhausted but elated. He quickly brought me up to speed with the incredible things that had happened. Following the broadcast of the documentary, the BBC had been so overwhelmed by the sheer volume of calls that the phone system had temporarily crashed. Colm and his team had worked long into the night and had not slept yet. A jubilant Colm then told me that Newsnight had its highest viewing figures ever, and there were literally hundreds and hundreds of enquiries, emails, phone messages and faxes coming in from all over.

Then I found out that Stanley had been arrested for his own safety, while some members of my birth family were going mental and calling me all kinds of lying everything. Other victims were now contacting the police; one of them, who had twice disclosed to me in the past but denied it when the authorities got involved, had gone to the police station to defend Stanley's innocence and to demand his immediate release. I felt sad for him, but I knew this was the only way. Barely able to contain his excitement, Colm said, "We've had a mountain of messages for you. If you want, I can read them with you."

"Yes, please," I said, gratefully.

I appreciated the moral support. I knew I was bound to get some negative comments. Colm handed me a pile of printouts. I frowned. I really hadn't expected there to be quite so much criticism. I braced myself, but as I looked through the first few, I was completely taken aback – they weren't hate-filled, angry messages telling me to shut up; they were all messages of support and kindness.

They really moved my heart.

I was bewildered: the things people were saying were touching and some were so very sad, but as I looked through them, I started to feel a lot less alone and a little less afraid. Reading them, I had to swallow back my tears. Over the following months, I was to be contacted by many people from across the country who helped to reaffirm my faith in humankind. I don't even know where to begin thanking you all, but I do and I want you to know that I will never forget.

As the day wore on, my new calm was doing a brilliant job at keeping me steady and I was taking in news moment by moment. By this time, the world's media were calling, everyone was supporting the call for action, and things were moving at an incredible pace. The team were still working flat out on the phones, dealing with enquiries from connected and unconnected disclosing victims, messages of support, media enquiries and official calls. Suddenly, everything went quiet as Colm hushed the office and took a call from Merseyside Police.

I had already been asked to make a statement and was about to write up my request for an independent police investigation into the concerns raised in the documentary, when I got the news that the police wanted to talk to me. I thought, I bet you bloody do! The Merseyside Police Force was, in my opinion, inept and too easily corruptible and I was solidly determined that this time it would be me that would not be talking to them. The policeman told Colm that he understood my unwillingness to talk with him, but he'd be very grateful if I could just give him a moment of my time. I told Colm to tell the policeman that I had no confidence in Merseyside Police and had been down this dead-end road one time too many. I added that I would like to respectfully ask if their Chief Constable could request another force to investigate this as soon as possible so that we could proceed.

Colm raised an eyebrow at my terse response and relayed back to me the policeman's response.

"Shy, they say they accept that, but they still want to talk with you for just a moment."

After a moment's thought, I realised they weren't going to give up easily and I needed to think things over, so I said, "Ask them to call back in 10 minutes."

Now that I had 10 minutes' grace, I sat and thought. OK, what do they want to talk to me about? They are just trying to get themselves out of trouble. They will threaten me with criminal charges or set Social Services on me to silence me and nothing will change for those children. I bet they're shredding documents right now! I don't want to waste any time listening to how it wasn't their fault, nor do I care how sorry they are now. I just want those kids away from Stanley and Reg.

Then a familiar voice inside me asked, *are you all done now? Did you get your certificate for strongest and best argument ever?*

What? No. Why?

So you can send it to those kids when they ask you why you wouldn't talk to the police.

I told Colm that when they called back, I would speak to them, but I wasn't going to take any of their crap. I flipped on *Firestarter* by the Prodigy, played it loud on my headphones and sulked at myself until the call came in.

Twenty-five years of anger and frustration at their failure to act bubbled up to the surface, as I waited for them to call back.

I was going to tell them exactly what I thought of them, and I was not going to put up with their denials, as I had the evidence down in writing and on hours of secret recordings. I was ready for them!

Colm handed me the phone. I looked at him questioningly and he nodded to indicate that it was the same policeman who had rung earlier.

"Hello, is that you, Karen?"

"Yes," I replied, making my defiance clear.

He gave his name and senior rank. Then, in a gentle but serious manner, he said, "I understand that we have seriously let you down in the past, and I speak for us all when I say that we are very sorry for that. We are a better police force than this, and although I can make no promises about any outcomes, if I promise that we will listen to you, would you at least agree to talk to us?"

The police officer's apology and courteous manner completely took the wind out of my sails. I had been ready to fight – I had my winning arguments and killer knockdowns all ready. If he was going to be completely rational, appropriate and open, then I had no choice but to meet him halfway. Swallowing hard and trying to keep the tears from falling, I simply said, "Yes."

We arranged to speak to each other properly later that day and hung up.

In just a few words that policeman had mended some badly burnt bridges and given us all a way forward. It took my breath away to hear an apology after all these years. I felt utter relief. I smiled at Colm, and this time, rather than holding back, I let the tears flow.

Surfacing

The Newsnight documentary was the breakthrough I had waited my whole life for. I felt as if I'd been trapped underwater and had finally broken through the surface. I soon heard that the victim who had protested at the police station had returned the next day, only this time to tell the police the truth about the abuse he had endured.

I had lived a good part of my life without the odious influence of Stanley Claridge and knew that beyond all that secret-keeping was a much better and emotionally healthier life. I wanted this life for all those who had suffered at the hands of Stanley and his friends, but was fully aware that in order to achieve this, they would have to want it for themselves. I hadn't seen or spoken to most of the other victims in years, but I didn't have to know this one, to know how much courage it had taken for him to walk into that station after years of denial and tell the truth. My heart ached for him. I knew his pain, and was both sad and pleased that he had finally found his way to tell.

Then the floodgates really opened and many of the victims started to come forward. This produced some mixed feelings for me. I had suffered unspeakable pain throughout my life because the other victims wouldn't back me up. Not only had they not told, but they had denied it, said I was lying, then cut me out of their lives in favour of Stanley. This painful betrayal had never left my heart, but I couldn't feel any anger towards them now, because I understood how hard it was to tell and I could only guess at how much harder it must have been after so many more years of keeping Stanley's horrible secrets. I was also very glad for them: if they let it, this would start their healing process.

The police advised me that they had received so many complaints about Stanley and his friends that they were setting up a multi-agency joint criminal investigation called Operation Phoenix. It would have a 40-plus-strong team of investigators, and they had already arrested Stanley, Reg and some of the others, and had moved to protect the children who were currently identified as at risk. The operation's name was picked at random, but it was certainly meant for us. I felt like I'd finally risen from the ashes of the old fated silence.

What 'multi-agency' meant to me was that Social Services would be working with the police to investigate crimes that they had helped to perpetuate. Despite all that had happened, Social Services were still refusing to give me full access to my file.

Some time after I made my statement to the more helpful police, and to my gobsmacked astonishment, I was informed that the conviction Stanley had received back in 1977 had only been for oral sex crimes against me, and that after looking at all of the evidence, it was now clear that there were more charges pending. They also advised me that they had now seen my childhood

Social Services file in full and because they needed to use some of it in the case, they would have to disclose it to me.

When I saw my Social Services file, it was as though the jigsaw puzzle that was my crappy childhood finally came together as one big picture.

For the first time in my life I saw a straight line from there to here, and it was a very unpleasant experience to see in writing all that you had suspected... your whole sorry life and much, much worse besides.

I saw the file in full, but it angered me that it had important chunks missing. It had been made up to look like one complete Social Services record, when in fact the file was loosely made up of various reports, letters and documents from everyone from Nanny Wallbridge, the police, education departments, Social Services, the medical profession, Stanley and Mum, abusive and non-abusive care staff and even Stanley's probation officer. However, as misleading and incomplete as the file was, what was in it was shocking beyond words and totally damning.

The file clearly showed Social Services' support of the child abusers and that many innocent children had called out for help and been failed and ignored for years. It also showed an astoundingly obvious dislike for me, an unyielding judgemental coldness that simply beggars belief. I was described as 'promiscuous' and 'wayward'. One probation officer noted, on the day of Stanley's conviction for sexually abusing me, that I (referring to me as Sharon) was a "rather promiscuous young lady" and "seemed to have little remorse for her behaviour and almost enjoyed witnessing the sufferings of her stepfather". Even after Stanley's conviction, apparently I was the one who should have showed remorse. There seemed to be no acknowledgement of me as a victim. I was always and forever portrayed as the cause of the problem.

Once you read between the lies and prejudices, you are left with nothing more than a desperate child screaming for help. Not only had Social Services known about many of the abusers, but they had lied to me and everyone about exactly what they knew. For example, over the years they had sworn to me and the police that they had no evidence that I had ever made any complaints about Parkside School's headmaster, John Marshall; yet there, in black and white, was the whole sorry story.

My social worker had told Marshall that I had tried to suck Stanley's penis against his will, so unsurprisingly he had agreed to take me. John Marshall had indeed intercepted my mail from Stanley and had used it to abuse me. Months after I had left, some of the other children at the school had independently come forward and made similar allegations about Marshall to the police, and when the police had contacted my social workers – to ask if they could speak to me – they basically told them they didn't know where I was, even though I was at that time being held at Derwent House. The police failed to prosecute Marshall, but at least they closed down his child-victim factory once and for all.

For years the Social Services had told me and everyone else that they had no record of a 'John Marshall' on my files; strangely, this particular lie only ever served to undermine me at times in my life when I really needed my credibility.

In the course of their investigation, the Operation Phoenix team found and identified many of the abusers that I could remember, which was no easy thing, as there were so many that some of their faces would just blend into one; others were more easy to remember, as they were connected to some other event or memorable experience outside of the horrible. For some, there simply wasn't enough evidence to proceed; some were charged; some were too old, untraceable, already serving time for a similar crime or dead.

Over the two-year-long Operation Phoenix investigation, I discovered that most of the staff who had abused me at the various schools, care homes and secure units I had been sent to had gone on to be prosecuted for sexual offences against other children before, during and after I had been there. Many of them were already in prison for these offences. This was why more people were not prosecuted for sexual offences against me. Because they were already serving time it was deemed not in the public purse's best interests to prosecute them for further similar offences. Over the next few years. I would have to learn to accept this kind of 'justice by proxy' many times over.

There were so many offenders and victims spread over so many years that the CPS decided that they would split the trials down 'generationally' into three different trials, with the oldest going first, working their way through to the youngest, most current victims. I wanted to ask why Social Services was not in the dock with the paedophiles, but I bit my tongue.

The CPS decided that there were so many charges and so much evidence to back them up, that it would overwhelm the jury, so they slashed the numbers down to 20 or so charges against Stanley, Reg and Dave King, to which the defendants all pleaded not guilty. In early 2002, over two years after the Newsnight documentary had been aired, I found myself at Liverpool Crown Court, waiting to give my evidence along with many of the other victims, including my baby sister.

Why Me?

As I stood in the long court corridor waiting to go in, my mind was consumed with worries for my sister. She, like me, had never coped well outside of her safe place, and this was far, far away from that. We were about to be questioned by complete strangers on something deeply painful, and all under the glare of the world media. I could so easily remember the last time Stanley and I were in a court together, back when we were children, and this made me more frightened still. Because we were not permitted to talk about our evidence with each other before our court appearances, it had been very difficult for us to talk at all for a long time. Hopefully that would be over soon.

Neither the Newsnight documentary nor the secretly recorded confessions could be included, so, aside from my own police statements, I had no idea what the Crown Prosecution Service's case was like – of course, I knew what the strength of the evidence could potentially be, but the CPS's overall strategy in court was a mystery to us all.

From the court corridor, I stood and looked out of the window over the River Mersey and pondered how many times I had sent my sad thoughts away upon it, how I had always come to the riverbank throughout my life and how each time I had been a totally different person.

This time, I was the strongest 'me' I had ever been. I had changed so much in just the past few years that, to be honest, I had kind of lost myself a little, but the justice process has a way of helping you define who and what you really are, and I was starting to see exactly how this horrible childhood had come to be mine. I had often wondered, 'why me?' and because I had never really found the answer, I had always been left feeling a bit lost. But just then, looking out over the Mersey, I asked myself the same question and the voice in my head suddenly answered: *because you were born into a bunch of perverted nutters who sexually abused you because they wanted to and because they could.*

Because my childhood had been so painful, I felt there ought to be a bigger, more complicated, scientific explanation, but the hard truth is that perverts abuse children because they want to and because they can. They will lie to, separate, divide and conquer everyone they touch, smashing human beings into broken, frightened fragments, leaving them isolated and alone. Some victims will always remain sad shadows of the people they really wanted to be, while others stand and try to fight back.

I knew it was time to move on. There had never been an option to 'go back and fix it' on this journey, and if I spent too much time counting the scars, I would run out of time before –

"Karen, I'm sorry to bother you, but your father…"

"He's not my father."

Realising her mistake, the court employee standing next to me apologised, "I'm so sorry. Mr Claridge has complained that seeing you in the corridor is distressing to him, so could you please come and stay in this room?"

She pointed across the corridor.

I agreed immediately, and followed her into the side room, but couldn't help observing the irony that my presence in the corridor was upsetting to him.

I had seen Stanley and some of the others as they had entered the courts. They had looked unaffected and almost oblivious to the seriousness of what they were facing. You might think it would anger me that they still didn't seem to acknowledge the gravity of what they had done, but I had long since come to accept that I wasn't going to get an apology. The most I could hope for was that the world would recognise that what they had done was wrong. And that was what today was about.

Entering the courtroom, they had looked like a group of disabled octogenarians. Stanley hobbled in on a suddenly necessary walking stick. Dave King, who was only 57 and had been found up a tree taking down his Christmas lights when the police had arrested him just days before, had turned up to court in a wheelchair. Reg was doing his best to feign a heart attack, and they all looked as old and dithery as they possibly could.

A few moments later, my years of waiting were over. We filed into the courtroom and took our seats. The court was packed full of people and you could feel the tension rise as the trial began in earnest. While the atmosphere was tense, Reg, Dave and Stanley still seemed unconcerned, and at one point, quite ridiculously, the judge was forced to intervene when Reg's supporter suddenly stepped up to the dock (during a witness's testimony) and handed him a box of homemade sandwiches and a flask of tea, which he promptly started to eat, until the judge put a stop to it.

That said, the attitude of the accused changed quite a bit as the evidence rolled out. Then it was my turn.

I approached the witness box nervously. The courtroom suddenly seemed huge, and I didn't recognise many of the faces sitting watching me. Despite being clothed from head to toe, I felt completely naked. How on earth was I going to talk about such deeply personal things in front of all these complete strangers?

I anxiously smoothed my trousers and straightened my suit collar. I took a deep breath and composed myself. I knew exactly who I was: I was the part-broken remains of what those animals in the dock and their facilitators had left behind. I was what a fear-groomed society can do to a human being. I knew this was who I was, but as I sat there in the stand, I couldn't help but worry that they wouldn't believe me. I knew that the defence team would say that I was a bad kid and had brought a lot on myself, but I just had to hope the jury would believe me when I told them the truth.

A million thoughts and fears raced through my head. What about the times when I hadn't fought back or had gone to paedophiles' houses on my own? All I could do was tell the jury the truth and hope they understood that at the time I just didn't know that I could have made other choices. Besides, was it ever all right to rape even bad children? I willed myself to look the jurors directly in the eye, even when it hurt, and promised myself I wouldn't cry. I could cry another day; today, I must tell.

I took another deep breath, filling my lungs. I was ready.

OK, defence teams, I thought, release the hounds.

Why Me?

As the first barrister for the defence stepped forward, I looked across at Stanley and the others in the dock. You could see they weren't best pleased to see me, and as I looked Stanley straight in the eyes, he gave me that look I knew so well: "Say whatever you want, bitch, they won't believe you," it said.

I turned away from Stanley, all the more determined, and faced the barrister head on. Before I knew it, the interrogation had started. I was asked about my childhood and my allegations. It felt strange to be asked a question by someone to my left but respond to the jury on my right. It was a little surreal that there I was, under oath to tell the truth to a room full of people whose job it was to seek out the truth, yet there was also a great deal of Stanley's truth that I wasn't legally allowed to talk about, like his previous conviction or his confessions.

The defence was robust and lengthy. Although I did my best, after hours of what can only be described as soul-raping torture, my calm was tested to its limits as they attempted to question my motives and attack my credibility. I stood my ground, and when they realised that tactic hadn't worked, they took out my childhood Social Services file. I was furious that it could once again be used as evidence against me. I was so angry I turned to the judge and asked him why Social Services only ever gave up my childhood file to people who want to hurt or prejudice me. Why do they never use it to help or protect me or the others? I told him that I had tried for years to see the file in full and explained that it had been proven to be incomplete, inaccurate and that some of it had been written by now-discredited professionals and convicted sex offenders. The legal teams were instructed to move on.

Each accused had their own defence barrister and each took their turn at me. When I finally stepped away from the witness box, I felt completely drained.

Denise was sworn in and gave her deeply distressing evidence. At this time Roma still had no memory of her own childhood before we had joined the family, so was not giving evidence as a victim at this trial. Then the others followed. It was agony hearing about the others. Their stories were so horrific and they were so courageous. I couldn't bear to listen, so I sat and waited in the side room for updates. I was aware that not all of us had made it to this day, because it wasn't their time to tell or, worse still, they were no longer with us, but there were so many others who were here that it was just too much to hear how yet another life had been shattered in exactly the same terrible way as ours.

Our Denise couldn't stay to the end, as she had to fly back to Europe after her evidence, but not before we got to meet up to hug, cry and talk. I told her that according to the defence, I was born sucking dicks and telling lies. She started laughing, all embarrassed, mainly because the Newsnight team were filming our reunion, but also because she needed help to stop crying. After the film crew had gone, we talked properly. To my horror, I learnt that many of the victims had been falling to pieces since they had told the police. Because of the way the judicial system works, nobody could get any help without it prejudicing the court case and none of them trusted the Social Services, which at the time was the only help available. So there was simply nothing and nobody to help them.

This was not what was supposed to happen! Where was all the help and victim support? When I raised this with the

Operation Phoenix team, I was told that the case would be over in a few days and all the help would come then. I remember thinking, 'Please, please let it come'.

It had been good to see Denise. I was sad to wave goodbye so soon, but she was still recovering from surgery and needed to be close to her doctors.

So, I would be on my own when the moment of truth arrived. As I waited for the court to hear the last of the evidence, I was starting to feel as though we could tell the truth till the cows came home but they were never going to understand and they were never going to stop those bastards. I was just allowing my mind to dwell on the possibility that Stanley, Reg and Dave could walk out of here with nothing more than a slap on the wrist when this tiny-framed woman who looked as though she had been crying her whole life walked up to me and said, "You're Karen, aren't you?"

I had been lost in thought and replied without checking who she was, "Yes, I am."

She started to cry and I thought for a terrible moment that it was one of the accused's relatives about to shoot me dead! Instead, she thanked me for saving her eight-year-old child from Reg who, unknown to her until the Newsnight documentary, had been being sexually abused by him for many months. Following the airing of the documentary, the police had taken action and Reg had been charged for abusing this child. They were preparing to go to trial along with the other victims involved, who were awaiting the result of this trial before they proceeded to theirs.

"Thank you so much," she sobbed, grasping my hand.

"You are more than welcome," I said, swallowing hard to stop my own tears from flowing. "If there is anything I can do to help, I will."

The lady nodded gratefully and, after many kind words, left. Once she had gone, I was overwhelmed with a strange mixture of sadness and happiness that only our kind can truly understand. I collapsed and sobbed for ages.

I had to hand it to the Operation Phoenix team. They had kept their word – they had listened to the victims, looked past all of the bullshit and had acted to protect. More than this, they had pulled together a formidable case for the CPS to try. Come what may, they had done their job. Just then, someone from the Operation Phoenix team popped his head round the door.

"The jury are back to deliver their verdicts," he said, smiling grimly.

This was it. I composed myself and followed him towards the courtroom.

Stanley and the others stood accused of indecently assaulting, raping, sodomising, buying and selling many innocent boys and girls for decades. I thought, "This was it, complete strangers of the jury, our whole lives are in your hands."

Members of the Operation Phoenix team flanked me as we walked into the courtroom. As we found our seats, a member of the team gave me strict instructions not to "overly react" to the judge or the jury.

Not overly react? I had witnessed these creatures slither their way through life, poisoning everyone in their path, blissfully unchallenged and avoiding all consequence. I had been forced to surrender my entire childhood to their vile, selfish perversions and had had to fight every step of the way to prevent them from consuming my entire adulthood. If the verdict was not guilty, I would be forced to pay like never before – I feared for my own family and for my own sanity, but I was also worried about how all the other victims would cope. Besides me, my sister and the others involved in our case, there were many others waiting for their justice. This trial had only addressed offences that had occurred in the 1970s. As for me personally, I had lost everything fighting this battle – my home, my music career, my life as I knew it and even my future as I had wanted it to be. I had spent the last two years working towards this day, and I had waited my whole life for this one single moment in time. Overly react indeed.

As I looked into the jury's eyes, they gazed straight back at me with a look I have never seen before. I didn't know what that look meant, but I didn't have long to wait to find out.

Amid quiet mumbling, the judge asked the foreman to stand up. The packed-solid courtroom hushed as the clerk asked for their verdicts and the first reply came back.

Guilty.

My head was spinning and I was finding it hard to breathe. Had I heard that right? As the third, fourth and fifth guilty verdicts were announced, it was getting hard to believe that I could have misheard. Then I heard the ninth, tenth and eleventh guilty until, in the end, it was guilty on all counts and said so many times that it became impossible not to believe that this was real.

I didn't, I couldn't, make a sound, but the tears were pouring down my face. Some of the jury were crying and as I looked into their eyes, I mouthed the words "Thank you" and again I saw that look.

Stanley was found guilty of 19 charges, including rape, buggery and indecent assault and jailed for 15 years. Reg and Dave were also given lengthy prison sentences.

Through my tear-blurred eyes I looked at Stanley and the others. Reg and Dave suddenly appeared very worried indeed, and had gone a pasty-grey colour. Stanley was still claiming to want to know what all the fuss was about, even as the burly prison guards shuffled them off to the prison cells below, walking stick, wheelchair and all.

I made my way to the side room with my family liaison officer, Dave, who had been my main support throughout. We hugged and I started to cry properly. All I could say to him between sobs was, "You said you would and you did. You said you would and you did."

He must have thought I was mental. I was trying to say that he had promised to listen and he had. He promised to look past all the lies and he had. He promised to bring it all before a judge and he had. I wanted to say, "I thank you more than you could ever know," but I just couldn't get the words out. I felt elated, relieved and, for the first time in my life, I felt believed.

I looked at Dave, who was clearly moved by the whole thing, and I said in a childish Merseyside accent, "Seeee, I told you so, eyewipe." ('Eyewipe' is a local saying meaning 'so there'.) We both laughed, which helped me to stop crying, and then he said something that made me start crying all over again.

He simply said, "I always believed you," and then he looked at me with that same look I had just seen a moment ago from the jury. So that's what believed looks like. Then off I went again, crying like a baby.

Why Me?

Most people never really know when things changed in their lives, or when they suddenly took another path, but I do: it was this very moment. As I calmed down, I realised I felt different and that something very big had changed, right there and then. The verdict was a cathartic closure on that whole part of my life, but it was also so much more. At that point, I couldn't measure or explain it, I just knew it was happening.

The judge, who had been brilliant throughout, had said that he hoped I would see this moment as a fresh start in life. I was touched by his words and his kindness. I didn't know how I was ever going to thank the jury, but I was determined to find a way.

There was a great deal of fuss going on inside the public area of the court and I could already see that there was a media frenzy outside the courts as well. As soon as I could, I called my sister, who sobbed uncontrollably. We were in a happy-sad place: happy because we had won our fight for justice; sad because so many lives had been lost or destroyed during the battle. There was no triumphant celebration, just relief that we no longer needed to live in fear.

After briefly phoning my family, who were thrilled for me and after exchanging hugs and saying thanks to all those who had helped bring about this verdict, I braced myself to face the rest of the world.

When I stepped out of that court, I knew I was already a very different person and that my old life was behind me. I was about to step into a completely unknown future. I was worried, not because I wasn't ready for the world, it was more that I didn't think the world was ready for me.

Broken

Outside the court, I read out our press release to the waiting media with trembling hands, and after they had gone off to air it, I found myself standing on the court steps completely alone. Night was closing in around me, and I was mentally trying to take in all that had just happened, when my mind started repeating the judge's words over and over: Fresh start in life. You can put all this behind you. Your life begins today.

I was indeed gifted with a 'fresh start', and I planned to embrace it. Despite my happiness, I couldn't help but wonder why, if my life starts today, I get to be born a poor, 39-year-old, toothless, morbidly obese, uneducated orphan, with more baggage than Heathrow's lost and found?

What is more, the system abuse and social prejudice that I had endured had been bad enough before, when only a few people knew about my life; but now everyone knew, sordid details and all, and when the newspapers came out, they would be left in no doubt about the whole terrible truth of my childhood. If my life was going to start today, why didn't I get a really clean slate? Still, at least I have a life.

Over the previous two years, I had dropped everything to

fight this battle. It had taken virtually every ounce of my focus and emotional strength, and while I had been away fighting it, I had let my own work and domestic responsibilities slide and was facing a mountain of bills and problems at home. As I walked away from the court, I felt as if I was doing and thinking everything for the first time, like some recently freed prisoner trying to get used to life on the outside. I took a deep breath. It was time to go home.

I had worked so hard to break the vile chain of abuse that had plagued my family for decades. I had put everything into raising my children and as I travelled back home to see them, I ached to be with them again. My family were my secret strength and my greatest achievement. Their unconditional faith in me kept me steady. If I had anything – courage, strength, spirit – it was because of them. It was, and is, my most precious joy to know and love them, and to be loved by them.

I was coming home to my family a very different person, and we had a whole new life to rebuild around us. We had each other and, save for my music, that was all that mattered to me. The very idea of living a life without my music made me feel empty and sad to my bones. I had always wanted to be a professional songwriter and it had been so hard to let go of this dream. Now that I had come out in public as a victim of sexual abuse, I knew that my ship had sailed. It was time to move on.

I returned home to a warm and wonderful welcome. It was like walking into a completely different world. An open fire, a soft couch, a home-cooked meal and precious time with my family and friends. We sat and watched the Newsnight updates and all the other news on the convictions, and we talked late into the night. By bedtime, I was exhausted, but I just couldn't quite shut out a nagging fear at the back of my head that kept saying, *all this is well and good, but brace yourself for the inevitable backlash — you must know it is coming.*

I knew only too well, from bitter past experience, that this wasn't the kind of truth people wanted to hear and that perverts don't like it when you expose their secrets or empower their victims.

Despite trying to stay awake to worry myself stupid, I was out like a light the moment my head touched the pillow. I was awoken the next day to continuous loud knocks on the front door, a non-stop ringing phone and endless faxes, emails and texts. This sent me into a bit of a panic. We never had visitors or many phone calls at our home. Up until now, I had kept all of this stuff away from my own family and done it all through the One in Four team in London, but I was now too scared to read, open or answer anything, as I was worried that this was the dreaded backlash.

Throughout that day, our story was plastered across the news. I hid at home, just trying to savour the moment. Stanley and the others were in jail. I now knew, without any shadow of a doubt, that the most effective weapon against them was, and always had been, the truth.

The next day was the same, only then I received bags of mail for my attention and I started to really panic. It is hard to explain, but if I looked at any of these letters and they were negative, it would have spoilt a very big moment in my life. This was something I desperately wanted to feel, before it all got changed into something else. Of course, I realised it could be a bag full of support but, knowing my luck, I just didn't want to risk it. I let the letters and messages pile up in my study and closed the door.

Realising that I needed help in dealing with the media, I reached out to a publicist to manage all the media interest. With the One in Four team working on all the other enquiries pouring in, I now had the time I needed, in my own safe place, to properly reflect.

When I finally stopped and stood still, something amazing had happened. For the first time ever, my life made complete sense to me. I didn't like it or think it was fair or right, but it did, at long last, make sense.

For all these years, I could never really understand why my sad, lonely childhood had been so bloody awful, but I could now clearly see that despite all my bravado, I had lived my life in fear of them and of myself. I had lived in fear of them and what they had taught me, and in fear of myself in case I ended up anything like them. I was so scared of turning into them that I had lived a half-life with the brakes on. What is more, I had spent my whole life asking, "Why?" when in truth, what I really meant was, "How could they?"

The "Why?" was easy – they did it because they wanted to and they could. I just couldn't reconcile myself with the "How?" And that's when it finally dawned on me. The reason I couldn't understand how they could have done these things to me was because *I wasn't anything like them.*

When human beings look at each other, by instinct we seek something we recognise. When we look at each other, we are essentially looking to recognise something of ourselves, and when we can't see ourselves reflected, it can be very frightening. In my case, it turned out to be a complete and utter blessing. The fact is that when I looked at any of my abusive family, I could never see myself reflected back.

This was an explosive, profound revelation to me that suddenly turned on the lights in every dark corner of my soul. No wonder I had felt so alone – I was. No wonder I never felt like I belonged – I didn't. No wonder I couldn't understand them and never would be able to – I simply wasn't anything like them.

After all these years of living in fear, living in the shadows of what always looked like a much better life, all these years of standing up to these monsters and suffering the consequences, all these years of wishing I was someone else, now all their poxy secrets were melting away before my eyes. Suddenly I was looking at a very different me, living a very different life. I had, to a large degree, blamed society for its unjust fear, prejudice and discrimination. I had felt as though all of my life choices had been severely limited by the terrible truth of my childhood, and although this was to some extent true, I could now see that I was just as bloody guilty as society. I had not always believed in myself and had perhaps been too ready to see what I couldn't do because of my childhood, rather than what I could do, despite it.

I know that there is no way that anyone could live through what I had and come out the other side unaffected. I do accept, and always have, that because of it, I am broken, with bits of me that work and bits that don't. However, for the first time ever, I could clearly see how all of the broken and working bits could function together to make a 'me' I could truly believe in.

The day I realised all this proved to be a massive turning

point in my life. The children involved were now safe, some justice had prevailed, and the many wrongs had indeed been righted. Being believed had healed some very deep wounds, and I had been released from my partially self-imposed jail to start my life all over again.

I wasn't sure exactly what kind of person I was going to be or what path my life was going to take from here, but I did know that it started with going into my study and facing all those messages. Little did I know what was waiting in there for me.

Phoenix Rising

I took myself downstairs, got a strong coffee, walked into the study and locked the door. OK, world, I have been invisible to you for so many years, fighting this battle on my own and against all the odds. I know that I represent a terrible truth to you, but I really don't want to go back into the shadows. I did realise that my fate was, in part, in others' hands and I still didn't know what my future had in store for me at this point, but I was just about to find out.

As I started to open the mail, I was shaking and silent crying because each and every message was full of support and kindness. I was just blown away. This wonderful, incredible moment in time, was like nothing I had ever felt before. I had felt lost, alone and isolated in my life, but this feeling kicked all those feelings' butts. As I opened each and every message, I felt a world of pain lift from my bones and just float away. OK, world, not only do I forgive you, but now I'm starting to like you.

There were thousands of letters and messages from all over the UK and from across the world. Some were from people who had walked in similar shoes, others were trying to find the courage to, while others offered me their heartfelt support. My faith in good people had finally come full circle. I already knew what a little bit of good could do, now I was about to find out what a mountain of it could achieve.

I had not realised just how many of us there were, but as I did, I also started to realise that I was… and always had been… part of a tremendous community full of our wonderful, courageous, inspirational kind. A vibrant intelligent community that supported each other in standing up to a common enemy. People I could really look up to and aspire to be like. There were also those who had not survived or recovered themselves and those still trapped and looking for their way out, who needed help and support that I knew just wasn't out there for them. I felt for them all and as I did, I realised what I should be doing with my future.

As for the present, the police and Social Services did a massive internal investigation (past and present) and found that they had completely failed us. They apologised and they agreed to change the way they deal with historical case disclosures in the future. The Social Services agreed to add a factual amendment report to my childhood Social Services files to set the record straight.

I understand now, better than ever, why paedophiles pick on what society perceives as 'bad kids'. Bad kids already have no voice, no credibility and even less hope of any justice if they are the victims of a crime. They are hopelessly easy targets. Children have no rights unless they are 'by proxy' through an adult and once the adults have written you off as bad, you don't really stand a chance. All I ever needed as a child was for someone to help me invest in the good in me and not judge me on a childhood that would have brought out the worst in anyone.

There were never any dead bodies buried at Bidston Hill or under the floorboards at 29 Stratford Way. For a long time I didn't fully understand why Stanley told these lies, but I always knew it wasn't just to try and scare us. It did eventually become clear. If I had said, look Mr Policeman there are dead bodies under the floorboards and he sexually abused me, when they went to look and couldn't find the bodies, anything else I had said would have looked like a lie. To set such a perfect credibility trap for his victims, so far into the future, shows a devious and cunning I have learnt to respect and never underestimate.

Many people ask me how I was able to survive my childhood and my answer is always the same – good people like my Aunt Pat and Uncle Ken and my Nanny and Grandpa Wallbridge. Their tiny ray of light in my dark miserable childhood gave me hope, balance and a dream of better to cling onto. Also, my beautiful Pately Bridge and, later in life, my family, friends and various good people I have met along the way.

It was a classic case of good over bad and despite the fact that there was a great deal of bad, it amazes me even to this day, that the little bit of good I found back then, was enough to save me, but it was and it did. So, if I'm ever asked how we can help children we don't know are victims, I would always say, do your best to be someone's Aunt Pat or Uncle Ken.

Another question I am often asked is how do I feel about my abusers? I don't feel anything for them, but I do respect the danger they pose to everyone. They are inhuman, selfish cowards, hardwired to exploit every single decent human trait. They abuse children because they can and because the world they live in doesn't do enough to stop them. I wish I could undo all the lies they have told the world about us victims and show them how to really help us. I wish I could change people's minds about how they should deal with the offenders and I hate it that offenders get more help and support than all the victims they leave in their wakes.

I'm sometimes asked if I'm stronger because of what happened to me. My childhood abusers don't own any part of my survival. I'm not stronger because of them or what they did to me, I'm stronger despite them and because of me.

I had always wondered why paedophiles worked so hard to destroy the good in us, to twist every truth and destroy our ability to love, trust or communicate, but not after I finally realised that the only things that can actually put a stop to them are truth, love, trust and communication. Indeed, I honestly believe that the only way to stop abuse is to find a way to tell.

I am also asked if I could ever forgive my childhood abusers and I have to say that I have never needed to. It's not that I can't, I, like every other human being in this world, need to both give and receive forgiveness, but I also know that decent human traits like forgiveness are seen by paedophiles as a weakness to be exploited. They don't need my forgiveness quite so much as they need my courage and conviction to help them stop themselves.

As for blame, guilt and revenge, I stopped taking the blame a long time ago, and came to terms with the guilt for not stopping them sooner as best I can. And as for my revenge, to have survived and survived well is revenge enough for me.

Lastly on the questions front, I'm often asked how I feel about my birth family. There was indeed a time when I used to resent them, even blame them, back when I didn't know any better. Not every member of my birth family was a victim of the abuse, but for all those who were, my saddened heart breaks for them.

We all faced the same beast and I understand how hard it is to come to terms with the shame and pain that paedophiles inflict upon those they abuse. As bad as things were for me, with hindsight, I was in fact one of the lucky ones. I got out with enough of me to survive; many didn't, some lost everything. We all coped differently, some didn't cope at all but, at least now, how we proceed is up to us.

Talking of how we proceed, I had made my decision and before I get into it, I just want to thank the internet and all the wonderful software and information technology that comes with it. Some people say that all the internet does is facilitate paedophiles – like never before. There is no arguing that paedophiles have exploited the internet for their own perverted ends, but what is also true about the internet, is that it has helped authorities catch more paedophiles than ever before.

Another truth is that because of it, I was able to catch up on my education, develop my communication skills and find my voice. Without it I could never have launched Phoenixsurvivors.com, which I needed to do, because I had decided that I was going to take everything I had ever learnt and use it to stop paedophiles and help their victims.

I launched the two-page site to offer support and information for the victims from Operation Phoenix and in no time at all I was inundated with information and cries for help. I took everything I'd learnt and put it to good use and before long I was indeed stopping offenders and helping victims, but also advising authorities, guiding government think tanks, assisting the media and successfully campaigning for changes in anti-victim pro-offender laws.

I had struggled for so long to find a voice and now the world's media was quoting directly from my website. I had just qualified as a private investigator and was working on my studies in criminal psychology. The site was developing and getting bigger all the time and I was learning 10 new things a day. Before too long Phoenix Survivors became a team of dedicated child protection advocates with an incredible support network to back it up.

One very special day, I received an abusive email from a member of the thriving 'online sex offender community' (or OSC) talking about a piece I had written called *My child porn smile wasn't real* (written before I realised how deeply offensive and prejudicial the term 'child porn' is, to our kind) and was horrified to discover, that like so many other victims of this crime, the indecent images collected and swapped by child abusers over the years, by post, were now being scanned onto the internet and shared. Sadly, unlike most products, pictures of naked people don't really date and can therefore be exploited forever.

This vile messenger claimed my child porn smile looked real enough to him and that he was off to have a good night with it! It was then that I realised the full impact of those pictures taken of me. Once taken, it's like a crime that never stops being committed, a crime that helps another crime be committed, a crime that never lets you forget you were the victim of it. It was then that I discovered the full extent of the OSC's grasp on the internet and it was then that I became part of the frontline in the online child protection battle against them. Since then, I've gone from being one of their favourite downloads, to their most hated female.

That same day, I also received a phone call asking me to come to Number 10 Downing Street to receive a Children's Champion award from Cherie and Tony Blair, for *working tirelessly for the welfare of children*... I spat coffee out of my nose and mouth in shock, I just couldn't believe what I was hearing. Are you sure you mean me? *Yes, we mean you, Shy; you were nominated by the children's charity Barnardo's, the News of The World, a police chief and Sir Trevor McDonald, to name a few and you've won our top award!* I didn't know what to say, so I just screamed like a girl.

Which is exactly what I did when Sarah McDonald won a BAFTA award for our Newsnight documentary. And when I received an award for being one of Britain's Bravest Women, a real woman of achievement, and was celebrated at the Woman of the Year awards 2008.

Going to Number 10 was a very big day for me in so many ways. I was no longer Shy Keenan, victim of child sexual abuse, but Shy Keenan – victims' advocate.

During this next part of my life I got to rub shoulders with the great and the good, the ordinary and the extraordinary, the powerful and the rich. I even met some famous people I liked and admired, like Tina Turner, Richard and Judy, Rebecca Wade and Margaret Thatcher. Simon Cowell even sent me a very kind message of support.

I no longer felt invisible, excluded, or powerless and my insight was now a valuable tool in the fight against those who sexually abuse and exploit children.

It was during this period of my life that Sara Payne and I first made contact. We clicked immediately; we knew all about each other, so we didn't have to go there, but for those of you who don't know, Sara's eight-year-old-daughter Sarah, was abducted, abused and murdered by a recently released known paedophile who was then re-caught and sent back to jail for life. Sara launched a campaign for 'Sarah's Law' to give parents the right to know if local dangerous sex offenders posed any risk to their children.

Sara, a writer, an award-winning child protection campaigner and a staunch victims' advocate, is a true Phoenix in every sense of the word. Like me, she prefers to find and get after the solution, rather than spend too much time complaining about the problems. We had a lot in common and shared a lot of the same insights, thoughts and opinions and had very similar ideas on how to make things better for us all.

We became fast and close friends and, at first, we stayed in touch for moral support only, then worked together behind the scenes for a while. After a few years of working with the victims, alongside the authorities and against the abusers, we both came to see that the only way to make a real difference to victim support and justice, the only way we could challenge the social prejudice or the pro-offender system and its laws, was if we did it for ourselves.

So, at the beginning of 2006 Sara and I came together as the Phoenix Chief Advocates. We put together a top team of child protection experts, victims' advocates and victim recovery specialists to help develop the first ever centre of excellence in this field and launch the first ever Phoenix victim support retreat.

In our roles as Chief Advocates, we advocate for the victims of child sexual abuse and exploitation and their families and for the families of children abducted and/or murdered by child molesters. Thousands of people visit us online every week looking for help, advice or information; many come to share their stories with us and some just drop by to offer their support.

Together, we have worked on some of this country's most high profile cases and gone up against some of the UK's most infamous monsters. We have helped to bring individuals and whole networks to justice, and helped to change old laws and bring in new ones. We have worked to increase dozens of unduly lenient sentences and campaigned against victim discrimination. We've worked with the media to highlight injustice or bad practice and much, much more besides.

We have met some amazing, incredible Phoenixes along our way and some incredible child protectors proudly named on our online Phoenix heroes board, like Lord Goldsmith, CEO Jim Gamble and DC Shirley Thompson to name just a few.

In fact, Sara and I have both decided that we want to tell you a lot more about our work, our successes and our failures. We want to tell you more about the good and bad people we have met – across the board. About those we have fought for and against, about those who helped us and those who tried to stop us. About the OSC and their vile network of online supporters. We want to tell you why people like Prince Harry and Wayne Rooney are on our heroes board, so we are writing a book together that will no doubt shake things up a bit.

Having my little sister back to tease whenever I want is more fun than ever, and she is doing as well as can be expected. A great many of the other victims involved in Operation Phoenix are still coping with the aftermath of the court case. Those that came after us never got their day in court because the CPS decided that because the offenders were so old and they had already been given such stiff sentences it was not in the public purse's interest to proceed with their cases. I fought hard to get them help, support and justice, but despite my best efforts, not all of them made it to this day.

After securing a conviction, one victim, a staunch Everton fan, left a heartbreaking note describing his life-long agony at being sexually abused as a child by Stanley... which he signed moments before he dramatically took his own life. He was not the first poor soul to go this way, but we want him to be the last and although his death was a devastating blow to everyone, it inspired us all to work harder still to make the Phoenix retreat and advocacy team happen.

My own life has changed beyond words or description and I know that I have many good people to thank for that. All I can say is that I will try to make them proud. I was indeed born and then broken, but I'm living proof that broken can recover a life worth living. As for me personally, I've never been happier. My faith in good is stronger than ever. I live in a beautiful home, with a loving family, in the stunning and tranquil heart of the Essex countryside, supported by an amazing community full of good solid Essex people. I have wonderful friends, a rewarding job and a bag full of hopes and dreams for the future... Not too bad for broken.

Epilogue

Well, hello you, put the kettle on. Yeah, 'I know!', I'm back, I'm as shocked as you are! I hope you are well and winning.

I can't thank you enough for the next bit, I'm (no touch) hugging you right now. This book became a *Sunday Times* Bestseller, a giant international voice for me and my Broken kind, it has even worked to empower and inspire others to take their own brave broken journeys, I know this because they write to me and tell me so.

I always say that the only way to stop it, is to find a way to tell, and that the very best revenge, is to survive and survive well. I don't just say it, I mean it.

Thank you for all your wonderful support and messages over the years, if you don't know – I wouldn't be here without you. Forever thank you from my heart for that, you've pulled my Phoenix chin up many times, good bless you.

I wrote *Broken* after all of the convictions, to tell you what really happened during that 'horrible' childhood, how it was able to happen (Anti-Victim Prejudice or AVP) on such a massive scale, why it wasn't stopped or challenged (AVP) until BBC Newsnight shamed the authorities into stopping the abuse of a known active paedophile network and into protecting the very young children they were 'evidently' getting access to. Which, in turn, launched 'Operation Phoenix' and the giant bag of systemic, institutional 'Anti-Victim Prejudice' worms that followed!

And as for me personally, I'm 10 years older, 10 years wiser and 10 years 'more stupid' at the same time. As I write this, the last decade of my life has been some of the hardest, darkest, years of my entire life, which, as you can imagine, are big words for me, the person who lived and wrote *Broken*.

I've been beyond any broken words I can say, mixed with the unfathomable, relentless, aching 'dark hole' left behind, when you lose your (just turned) 14-year-old child, to suicide.

Phoenix down.

I used to tell you that I was "three times stronger than any household bleach", that my own inner 'Phoenix' and the love of my friends and family had helped me to manage the legacy, that *that* Broken childhood had left behind and it remains true in so many ways. But there have been times when I could have pig scratched the stupid out of my Phoenix, whilst begging it to stay down, please, please! Just, stay, down.

As you know, I did get some justice in my case though Merseyside police's 'Operation Phoenix', launched as a result of the BAFTA winning undercover documentary, where I went back to my past to secretly film their confessions. Claridge, Moreton and King were jailed, all three released early, then, some time later, separately and from various medical conditions, they each passed away.

Despite the Police needing to launch Operation Phoenix 1/2/3/4/5 and so on, not *all* of my childhood abusers faced the justice they deserved. Not because I didn't try, with every fibre in my Phoenix DNA, to lawfully do exactly this. And not just for me... please hear me out on this one.

One of my childhood abusers was allowed to abuse hundreds of children (boys and girls) over many decades, well before and long after me. He destroyed childhoods and obsessively placed files full of lies about each child victim into their files to, as it were, 'Feck It Forward' or as we call it FIF. This was done to stop future 'disclosing victims' from ever being heard or believed. Relying very much on that 'AVP' culture I keep mentioning, he was able to not only destroy already traumatised childhoods, but entire lives. It worked for many years. Despite many disclosing victims, he went mostly unchallenged for decades, until he came across this Phoenix.

This will need three books and its own documentary series! I'm just a tiny part of what that known monster was allowed to do and, despite his death at 100, I'm still hopeful that the AVP truth, in this real life horror, will still find its way to the public's ears, for the sake of future child protection as a whole and more specifically for children in care – or, as you know, we call it being in "don't care".

Standing up to paedophiles in any way comes at a price. They have, for years, socially groomed a clear and visible prejudice towards our kind for decades. We call it Anti-Victim Prejudice or AVP. In brief, this is where someone, anyone, uses the fact that your lives have been victimised by paedophile crimes to, in any way, socially disadvantage or unjustly prejudice you for the crimes of another.

Epilogue

Well, that's what it says in words, the reality of Anti-Victim Prejudice is where the social and judicial systems and the whole medical and social structures are so AVP towards me and my kind, that victims can hardly speak, let alone identify ourselves by disclosing or trying to get the help we really need. The help available, better known to us as the AVP 'Fist Of Help' which is as lovely as it sounds and always does more harm than good. In short, they've made it too hard for crime victims to tell.

We've always believed and said that Anti-Victim Prejudice is the lead cause of victim silence. I am sad to report that in 2021 the same remains true.

Suspended disbelief: One example of AVP is that, before I even start most conversations, I start with most people 'hoping' I'm not telling the truth, then go from there. I've spent years living in other people's AVP 'suspended disbelief'.

Never do people ask adult rape victims if they've become rapists yet? But we are constantly being treated with that unspoken, but clearly palpable prejudice, just for being victims of child sexual abuse and, well, I just can't do it anymore, certainly not with any good grace.

So yes, I did become very disillusioned, maybe even a little numb by their cold prejudice and indifference, their failure to act (when they knew and could) – and their social disadvantage and exclusion of me and my Broken kind, was openly crushing.

Many still wrongly treat me with the sort of prejudice they should treat our abusers with. So, I can't be 'emotionally arsed' to deal with their blindness on this anymore. Gone are the days when I would try to AVP explain. These days, I'd say, I'm a lot more get on with it you liars! Yeah, I know… sad face.

Over the years and in this update, I wanted to be able to tell you that the long awaited, hard fought for and promised (AVP free) 'Victim's Law' had finally been passed, that they've finally updated 'Sarah's Law', brought in an 'Ayden's Law' (protecting the child's right to an education without fear) a Stalkers Register and all the rest of the work that Sara and I have been doing 'for free', through our registered not for profit *The Phoenix Post* for over two decades. Collectively, we call this our 'Think Human' work.

I can speak bolitian (*sic*), it's just not my first language. We've often felt like we (Sara and I) were almost there in our fight against injustice, only to find that the moment we learn to speak their particular brand of bolitics, all the important ministers have moved jobs and or different parties had taken over and are reshuffling their fecking brains out!

Suffice to say, without complaining too, too much, it's been like trying to knit with unwilling, lying, angry live eels and added bullshit politics.

We're still fighting for justice on our 'Think Human' work and have made some great progress, that puts us 'almost there'. When Broken goes out in May 2022 I'll probably need another book deal to talk you through this one (if you want) but I can't promise I can do it without swearing a lot more! So, there you have them, my Phoenix cards on the table.

Meeting my real Dad's family through Twitter. Goodness, where do I start? Just a quick brief: my real and very troubled father and mother married, had me and split. My mother, from a big but estranged family, went on to marry the paedophile 'Beast of Birkenhead', the rest is a matter of Broken record, and my real father, Fred, went on to commit suicide when I was still a child.

Well, we confirmed his suicide, but I had also been told that my real father was an only child of only children. Turns out, after all these years, right out of the Twitter blue, that none of that part was true! That's right, after all these years alone, I have 'dad family,' I have aunties, uncles and cousins I already adore. It's been a real sad/happy time, sad because it has taken so long to find them, and happy because I love having them in my life.

The truth I had to learn. To love, no matter what! Love my children, my family, friends and my Phoenix peeps. Some profoundly smart person once said "I've seen hate do so much damage, never seen it fix a thing". I could not agree more, despite everything I'm still not tempted to join the 'haters' club.

Diabetes! For crying out loud! I nearly slow killed myself! Not because I wanted to die early (I do not) I plan to die of 'unnatural old age natural causes', but because I nearly comfort ate myself to death! It has such a pretty name doesn't it, 'comfort eating', arrrh, sounds like a friend. Yeah, it's not, they should call it 'Instant Early Death Eating', you know, just to keep it real.

Don't even lie! You know delicious food is delicious and all that, but 22 stone of delicious equals slow early death. Turns out I needed a lot of 'comfort' and yes, it was kind of comforting, but it also gave me giant portions of can't move, 'fat arse' and 'gonna kill me' diabetes!

Yeah, I was a brave, happy faced 'fat girl' and yeah, I kept my triple Phoenix chin up, but the other real was what an utterly 'miserable' existence being morbidly obese was. Yeah, you heard me, *was*. OK, go on, grab a warm beverage, turn the page and I'll tell you some more.

Carrying the weight of a 'whole other person' gave me the killer diabetes. Gob full of yucky tablets every day, pricking my fingers sore every day, eating 'the most disgusting food' ever, losing more and more of my interdependence and independent mobility than I had ever bargained for.

Oh, oh and all those lovely 'small marquees' made to look like clothes. OMG! I thought some peeps were very AVP, until I found out how bloody horrible they are (in the main) to fat people. You don't see all the life limiting stuff 'till you look back or, as in my case, are forced to.

I already have lifelong severe post-traumatic stress and some other medical challenges that are a direct legacy of that Broken childhood and the subsequent decades long battle for AVP free protection, justice, support, compensation and the right to lifelong recovery support.

It is still my firm belief that no children abused in (don't) care should ever be forced to live on benefits. To counter the social disadvantage of being in (don't) care and being a human abused in childhood whilst in (don't) care, they should be awarded enough compensation through court, placed in trust, to generate enough income for them to survive and thrive for life.

What the known abusers get away with doing to the children they abuse is an unfathomable indictment of the way an AVP groomed society treats some of our most vulnerable – and indeed, how they keep them that way.

Taking the paedophiles (and subsequent paedophile supporters) to court, being AVP abused by the judicial system, desperately needing (AVP free) help and not being able to access or afford it, meant I was forced to make do. Big mistake.

Losing my little boy to hate when he took his own life in 2013, I couldn't get the help needed before, during or after, so I had to make do again. Big mistake.

My world ultimately imploded, I lost my family, my life as I knew it and everything I had worked so hard for. Trying to 'survive and survive well' wasn't working for me, nothing was, my faith in human good was solidly shaken. I couldn't get the help I needed, plus, all those 'make do' mistakes were about to come home to roost. Life was never the same again and then again, and then again…

The thing about strokes, is they have a way of halting you and your life dead in its tracks, without fear or prejudice. It will take you down and make you re-evaluate what's important and, more importantly, 'who'.

There were no accidents or injuries, no sagging face, no nothing. I went to sleep and woke up unable to move a thing. I'd had three (bloody three!) minor ischemic brain bleeds. Cheeky bastards didn't feel very minor and I had to relearn and retrain every single part of me. I had an excellent prognosis with the right help, but then the pandemic came and all of the NHS support went away. I didn't let it stop me, though, it just slowed me down.

Getting back up, I might be an 'old one' in some people's minds, I'm only 50somethingshutup, I can still clutch me mud, remember me date of birth and who the Prime Minister is (think it's still Dominic Cummings, right?) tee hee, no, no really, as soon as some people find out I've had a stroke, I can almost hear them playing the fecking 'goodbye song' in their heads. Sod Off You Lot! I'll die when I'm dead and not before, don't treat me like that! It brings the 'fuck you' out in me and, despite everything, I'm still trying to be a good girl. I still hope to die of unnatural old age natural causes, surrounded by my own family, so I plan to keep on living 'till I die, keeping my faith in human good as strong as ever. But I do still need help and support to live anything like the 'normal life' most people can take for granted. So, it was time to find my Phoenix and get whatever my new normal is, started.

Finding my Broken voice again was just a wonderful surprise. It had been 'temp pulled', because of the stalker lies (another book) and 'not to prejudice' ongoing criminal court cases. These went on for bloody years and my book Broken was put through the most rigorous, lengthy, legal fact check ever, only to eventually confirm my Broken voice had, of course, been telling the truth, the whole truth and nothing but the horrible truth, all along.

It was wrong, unfair, unjust for the system to let the 'bad people' do that to my life, my justice, my voice, my career, for all those sodding years. All along, I was, (for some mind-messed reason) waiting for this big 'duh duh moment'. You know, the one where justice comes in and puts right all those wrongs and gives back all the stuff that had been stolen or denied, for just being 'the victim' in the criminal justice system.

That day never came. Instead, it was a slow but steady, horrifying realisation, that there is no 'moment', no rescue – save yourself or drown. Thank goodness for my Phoenix during these dark times. I was almost ready to walk away and leave you lot to it, but for some reason, you've grown on me over the years and I just can't leave you to a child protection battle you often don't know you're having, until it's too late. All I could do was wait and pray to 'human good' for some human magic.

But then, out of that dark, unfairly-silenced, miserable mist, came the amazing 'book knight' in shining armour, *Mardle* books, to put right a dreadful wrong and give Broken back the voice it always deserved. Good bless their 'truth-loving' souls.

Look, it wasn't a TV happy ending after Operation Phoenix (and all that came after it). I still remain estranged from all but a few of the old family, and now, after everything, I found I live 'a better life' with my own loving and supportive family and friends.

My book, *Broken*, has proper been through it though. Why? Well because I know what truth they're (the powers that be) still not telling you. However, for some reason I feel a certain calm that comes from knowing the truth is about to find its way. The fact is, it remains true that the very best revenge is to survive and survive well – and I'm still working to make that my real.

Surviving that AVP justice and that giant 'Fist Of Help': As a 'Broken' child, it was said of me, that I was always the first one to speak up and the last one to shut up. I don't think I've changed that much and it is still true for me that, "whatever doesn't kill me, had better start running".

Supported: I'm coming outside for the first time in 10 years (love what you've done with the place), relearning to do everything again and I'm completely obsessed with my independent mobility – it's getting there.

Health: Still losing all the unhealthy (at a healthy pace). Only now, I've got no clothes that could ever fit again (even with sewing skills). I need a whole new wardrobe, new shoes, yes, I said it, new shoes, still need help and, if everything works to my 'hopes and dreams' plan, no more wheelchair...

New chapter, my new hopes and dreams: Alongside Sara and our amazing Phoenix supporters, I will always be there to see our Phoenix 'Think Human' work through. The digital 'Phoenix Spotlight' is our lifelike avatar, doing some of our physical work for us and is our way forward but, like everything, it needs cash we don't have and haven't been able to raise during a pandemic time, so it's treading water, waiting for its time to shine.

I made this: Creative therapy has been my absolute go to Civilian Post Traumatic Stress (or CPTS) management tool. Writing, singing/songwriting, crafting, scaled models, digital art, the real CPTS friendly House & Garden and the AR/VR game. All of this has helped more than I can say here (need another book :0), I am working on it.

Special forever love and thanks to my family, friends, my care team, our wonderful Phoenix supporters, to my readers, my agent and publishers – good bless you, thanks to you, *Broken* is back.

Acknowledgements

My very special thanks go to my own precious family, my close circle of friends and to one friend especially – your collective love and friendship made my life worth living and helped me to mend my broken spirit. I love you.

To my Aunt Pat, Uncle Ken and our Dona, to Jimmy Ruffin and all my much-loved music, to Nanny and Grandpa Wallbridge (may you rest in peace) to my beloved Pately Bridge, you were all the light in my dark.

To Oprah Winfrey, Bill Gates, Cubase, AOL, the internet and to Kawasaki, for my education, my voice and my freedom.

To Colm O'Gorman, Sarah Macdonald and the BBC Newsnight team. For hearing me, for believing in me, for helping me to stop them. To all those who found the courage to speak out when it mattered.

To the jury in our case, I will never forget your faces, all I can do to thank you is try to make you proud of me.

To all those amazing, kind, wonderful, inspirational people who have supported me and my work, to Sara Payne and the whole Phoenix team, to all my work friends and colleagues, my media friends and all those I cannot name but want to thank: better in my next book about 'The Phoenix Chief Advocates'.

To David Riding from MBA. Writing this book has been sincerely healing and cathartic. I want to thank you for believing in me, for giving me this incredible opportunity and for helping me to change my life so spectacularly for the better.